Robert Dudley
EARL OF LEICESTER

By the same author

HISTORY

Medieval Pilgrims
Voyages of Discovery
Elizabeth I
Their Finest Hour

MUSIC

The World of Musical Instruments
Benjamin Britten
The Tender Tyrant — Nadia Boulanger
Vivaldi
The Life of Beethoven

ALAN KENDALL

Robert Dudley

EARL OF LEICESTER

CASSELL
LONDON

CASSELL LTD.
35 Red Lion Square, London WC1R 4SG
and at Sydney, Auckland, Toronto, Johannesburg,
an affiliate of
Macmillan Publishing Co., Inc.,
New York.

First published 1980

ISBN 0 304 30442 5

Photosetting by Inforum Ltd., Portsmouth
Printed in Hong Kong

For Andrew

CONTENTS

ILLUSTRATIONS

Following page 84

The carved inscription in the Beauchamp Tower. (*National Monuments Record, London*)

Elizabeth's coronation procession. (*College of Arms, MS M.6*)

Dudley in his early thirties, attributed to van der Muelen. (*Wallace Collection, London*)

Ambrose Dudley, Earl of Warwick. (*Marquess of Bath, Longleat House, Wiltshire*)

Dudley's signature. (*Marquess of Bath*)

Hollar's views of Kenilworth. (*Department of the Environment*)

An entertainment on the lake, Elvetham. (*Mansell Collection*)

The barn at Kenilworth. (*Department of the Environment*)

An Elizabethan deer hunt. From Turberville's *Book of Hunting*. (*Mansell Collection*)

The Garter Procession of 1576 as represented by Marcus Gheeraerts the Elder. (*British Museum, John Freeman*)

Nicholas Hilliard's miniature of Robert Dudley. (*National Portrait Gallery, London*)

March — an illustration from Spenser's *Shepheards Calender*. (*Mansell Collection*)

Following page 180

Lettice Knollys, Dudley's third wife. (*Marquess of Bath*)

Portrait of Dudley, *c.* 1575–80 (*National Portrait Gallery*)

Lady Mary Sidney. (*Petworth Collection, Courtauld Institute, London*)

Hollar's engraving of the Noble Imp's tomb. (*Chapter Library, Windsor Castle*)

Sir Philip Sidney. (*National Portrait Gallery*)

Armorial tapestry commissioned by Dudley. (*Victoria and Albert Museum, London*)

A medieval gittern bearing the arms of Dudley and of the Queen. (*British Museum*)

Elizabeth receiving Dutch ambassadors. (*Kunstsammlungen, Kassel*)

Elizabeth in Dudley's garden at Wanstead. (*Private collection*)

A suit of armour made for Robert Dudley. (*Department of the Environment*)

A painting traditionally held to depict Elizabeth dancing with Dudley. (*Viscount De L'Isle, Penshurst Place*)

A view of Rycote. (*Country Life*)

ACKNOWLEDGEMENTS

My thanks are due to many people for the very positive help and assistance they gave me with this book, but in particular I must mention at Windsor Sir Robert Mackworth-Young, the Queen's Librarian; Mrs Priscilla Manley, the Chapter Librarian; and Mrs Grace Holmes, the Chapter Archivist. In Cambridge my thanks are due to the staff of the University Library, and in particular the Rare Books Room there, as well as to the Council of King's College for permitting me to reside there during periods of research. In London I must thank Dr Roy Strong, and Mr Robin Gibson of the National Portrait Gallery, as well as Miss M. M. Condon of the Public Record Office, and the staff of the Department of Manuscripts at the British Museum. I am also grateful to Mr M. W. Farr, the Warwick County Archivist, and to many other curators and archivists of private and public collections for their time and help, and of course to the owners of items in private hands. In particular I would like to mention the Lord De L'Isle, VC, KG, and the Marquess of Bath and Lord Christopher Thynne for their generous help. As far as Longleat is concerned, however, I could not have achieved a fraction of what I did without the unceasing help and enthusiasm of Miss B. M. Austin, the then Archivist. Her attention to my wants went far beyond the realms of duty, and her love for and knowledge of Longleat and its archives was invaluable to me, and has laid the basis for a valued friendship. I would also like to thank Miss Dawn Norreys who helped me with details of Rycote and her family for the book. And on a more domestic note, I must thank the various members of the Whitehouse family for their generous hospitality on several visits to Warwickshire, and for their continuing interest and encouragement during the book's various stages. Last, but by no means least, I should like to thank Simon Scott whose enthusiasm for the project made its publication possible, and Dominique Enright who saw it safely through the various stages of production.

St Michael and All Angels, 1979

1

A Family and its Fortunes

. . . my chiefest honour is to be a Dudley . . .

Sir Philip Sidney

When Henry Tudor, Earl of Richmond, came to the throne in 1485, founding a new dynasty, one of his chief concerns was to find men to help govern the country. Talent was the criterion for selection rather than noble birth; a fact which was to create bitterness and jealousy for the next century between those called to rule and those of the old nobility who expected it as of right. Henry was not making any innovations in this respect, however, since the process had begun under his Yorkist predecessors.

When it came to rights, moreover, there were at least ten people with a better claim to the throne than Henry Tudor, so that the test of the acceptance of the Tudor dynasty proved — in the long term — to be not so much the matter of its initial legality, but of its subsequent success. When Edward VI died, and his half-sister Mary Tudor's claim to the throne was disputed by John Dudley, Duke of Northumberland, in his attempt to put Lady Jane Grey on the throne in her place, the English people rallied to Mary Tudor precisely because she was the legitimate heir, the elder daughter of Henry VIII; and this in spite of her known attachment to the Roman rite. For all her Protestant virtues, Jane Grey did not appeal to loyal English people. Indeed, Mary's tragedy lay

1

ultimately in the fact that she failed to recognise this, but rather assumed that her known affection for Rome was part and parcel of her initial popularity. This may also have been due to a certain effect of backlash because, in the opinion of some, the process of reform had gone too far too fast, but Mary even managed to kill this by her zealousness when the burnings began.

By and large, however, the Tudor dynasty established itself remarkably quickly, in a period of considerable social mobility, which the advent of the dynasty accentuated and encouraged; and many of the great aristocratic families of England, even to the present day, began from modest origins with the advent of the Tudors: Sackville, Russell, Cecil and Cavendish, to name only a few. They typified the men of ability who, through their application, rose to fame and fortune. Most typical of all, and arguably the most successful, were the Dudleys, being atypical only in that their splendour evaporated within a century because there was no direct male descendant to carry on the dynasty. In this, fate played them a cruel trick, for having come within a hand's breadth of the crown in two successive generations, it was not the headsman's axe that snatched it from them in the third, but common mortality.

The fortunes of the Tudor Dudleys were founded by Edmund, who was probably born in 1462. His detractors claimed that he was the son and grandson of carpenters, but there is little doubt that he belonged to the old baronial family of Dudley, alias Sutton, and that he was the grandson of John Sutton, Baron Dudley (1401–87), made a Knight of the Garter in 1451. Edmund's father, also called John, was Sheriff of Sussex in 1485, and his uncle William was Dean of Windsor and then Bishop of Durham.[1] The Windsor connection is of particular interest, because of the close circle of friends who worked for the accession of Henry VII, in collaboration with Margaret Beaufort and Elizabeth Woodville — namely Christopher Urswick and Reginald Bray, together with William Dudley. Although he did not live to see the accession, William Dudley was a close friend of Elizabeth Woodville, and signed — as Bishop of Durham — the deed dated 20 March 1478 of conveyance of the Manor of Wycombe and other properties from Elizabeth Woodville to the Dean and Canons of Windsor.[2] William died in 1483, but Urswick became a canon and eventually Dean of Windsor, and Reginald Bray gave the money to complete St George's Chapel, which had been begun in 1475, when William Dudley was dean.

There were several ways in which Edmund Dudley might have come to the notice of Henry VII. He was, for example, a lawyer in land matters working for Edward, Duke of Buckingham (executed in 1521), and though there is no evidence for it, it would have been strange if William Dudley had not introduced his nephew Edmund into his circle of friends, as a promising young man, and that Bray — himself a financial expert — in turn brought Edmund to the King. Certainly Edmund was a member of Bray's estate council.[3]

Edmund had probably gone up to Oxford in 1478, and then studied law at Gray's Inn. According to Polydore Vergil,[4] Edmund's legal knowledge had attracted Henry immediately on his accession in 1485, and by the age of twenty-three he had become a Privy Councillor. We find a reference to him in the Middleton papers, dated 23 June 1508, as overseer of the will of Sir Henry Willoughby, which refers to him as 'Councillor to the King'.[5] Seven years later Edmund helped to negotiate the Peace of Boulogne, and when his first wife died, some time before 1494, he married his ward, Elizabeth Grey, daughter of Viscount Lisle, and through her the first title eventually passed into this branch of the Dudley family.

Elizabeth bore Edmund Dudley three sons, and it was the firstborn, John, who was to recover the family fortunes when his father was executed. The methods Edmund Dudley used to serve Henry VII's financial and political designs created many enemies for him. An interesting document, found among the papers of the Marquess of Anglesey and published in 1972, is a confession of no less than eighty-four cases of unjust exaction, for which Edmund Dudley thought that the executors of the will of Henry VII ought to make redress.[6] Awaiting execution in the Tower, Edmund Dudley had leisure to reflect on his somewhat dubious service in the King's employ. It was a service fully endorsed by the King, however, since we still have his initials on the pages of Dudley's account book from 9 September 1504 to 28 May 1508 as evidence.[7]

It was no surprise, therefore, that when the King died and Henry VIII came to the throne, Dudley was sacrificed (along with his associate, Empson) to popular demand. It was easy for the brave new King to sweep to power on the solid financial basis created by his father and his servants, without questioning very closely how it had been achieved, and to win approval by appearing to punish the wrongdoers whilst enjoying the fruits of their crimes. Edmund Dudley's son, John, was to reflect on this rather bitterly more than forty years later as he, too, became entangled in the web he had spun.

It was interesting, however, that the indictment of Edmund Dudley made no mention of his financial dealings — possibly because the King realised that he was walking on very thin ice — but rather brought a charge of constructive treason, in that during Henry VII's illness the preceding March, he had summoned friends to attend him at his house in London, under arms, in the event of the King's death. From Edmund Dudley's standpoint this was a very natural precaution to take in view of the number of enemies he had made. It was construed, however, into a plan for an attempt on the King's life — not the last time that such a charge would be brought against the members of the Dudley family.

Whilst in the Tower, as well as musing on his career of maladministration, Edmund Dudley attempted to win the new King's pardon with the book he wrote there, *The Tree of Commonwealth*.[8] Unfortunately for him, this argument in favour of absolute monarchy never reached the hands of the King, his attempted escape failed, and he and Empson were beheaded on 18 August 1510.

Edmund's heir, John Dudley, was only eight or nine at the time of his father's execution, but was well cared for by Sir Edward Guildford, whose daughter, Jane, he subsequently married, and after whom he named his sixth son, Guildford. In a very short time — early in 1513, in fact — John Dudley was restored in blood by Act of Parliament, and his father's attainder was repealed. He became known at Court for his athletic prowess (which his fifth son, Robert, was to inherit), and his skill in military matters. In 1523 he attended Charles Brandon, Duke of Suffolk and the King's brother-in-law, when he went to Calais with an army, and John Dudley was knighted by his general in France. The next year, when the King kept his Christmas Court at Greenwich, John Dudley was one of the knights who took part in the tilting, tourneys, and assault of a castle erected in the tilt-yard.[9]

From this time John Dudley steadily began to consolidate his position of power and influence; though whatever purely personal ambitions he may have had, even at this time, his considerable talent and ability cannot be denied, especially in military matters. In 1533 — the year that Elizabeth Tudor and possibly his son Robert were born — he was made Master of the Tower Armoury, and three years later he served as Sheriff for Staffordshire. In 1537 he was in Spain on royal business, and was also Chief of the King's Henchmen that year. In 1538 he was Deputy Governor of Calais, and in 1540 Master of the Horse to Anne of Cleves — a post his son Robert was to hold under Queen Elizabeth for most of his life, and one he set great store by. With this acquisition of honours went lands and houses, too, and as early as 1540, for example, he set his heart on Kenilworth, though he did not acquire it for another twelve or thirteen years.[10]

We do not know where or when Robert Dudley was born. It may have been in the Tower, or possibly at his parents' manor of Chelsea. As to the date of his birth, William Camden was responsible for saying that it was the same as that of Elizabeth Tudor— 7 September 1533.[11] Astrologers of the day found a collusion of the planets — *synastria* — at the birth of Dudley and the Queen, which has always been taken as proof that they were born on the same day. Camden was related to Dudley by marriage: his mother-in-law was Robert Dudley's paternal grandmother, from whom Camden may have had precise information.

The other date most frequently given is that advanced by George Adlard in his *Amy Robsart and the Earl of Leicester*.[12] He wrote: 'Robert Dudley was born on 24th of June, 1532. The date of his birth is not given by any historian. I discovered it in one of his letters to Queen Elizabeth in which he says "This is my birthday".' However, Adlard does not give the year in which the letter was written, nor does he say where he found it. There is a further factor in that the Hilliard miniature in the National Portrait Gallery, London, was — according to the inscription— painted in 1576, the forty-fourth year of Robert Dudley's life. However, until the Adlard letter is found, one must assume that there is no very good alternative to Camden's date.

According to Robert Dudley, he first met Elizabeth Tudor in 1542 or 1543: 'I have known her better than any man alive since she was eight years old.'[13] It has been maintained that Robert Dudley and Elizabeth shared lessons with Roger Ascham as their tutor, but unfortunately there is no evidence for this. They were, however, both pupils of Ascham at one time or another. John Dudley saw to it that his children were well educated, and Ascham himself said as much. Ambrose and Robert in particular were given an education in society, as well as a formal education. They were often in attendance on the young Edward VI, and possibly shared lessons with him, since Ascham taught Edward to write. Robert Dudley disappointed him, however, because he preferred mathematics to Latin. As he wrote in a letter dated 5 August 1564 from London, when Robert was in Cambridge on an official visit with the Queen: ' . . . you did yourself injury in changing Tully's wisdom with Euclid's pricks and lines.'[14]

The year 1542 was one of the most prolific in the advancement of

John Dudley. He was made Warden of the Scottish Marches and Great Admiral for life. This was also the year of the Scottish expedition and the assault on Boulogne, which further enhanced his reputation as probably the country's ablest soldier. It was also the year in which he finally inherited his mother's title, and became Viscount Lisle.[15]

On St George's Day 1543 John Dudley was made a Privy Councillor and a Knight of the Garter, the following year Governor of Boulogne, and in 1546 ambassador to Paris. It came as no surprise, then, that when Henry VIII died in 1547, John Dudley was named as one of the sixteen regents who were to govern during the minority of Edward VI. Nor was it surprising — in view of what he stood to gain — that Dudley acquiesced in the designs of the young King's uncle, the Duke of Somerset, to turn the regency into his sole protectorate. In that year Dudley became Earl of Warwick and Lord High Chamberlain of England, but resigned his office of Great Admiral to Somerset's brother, Lord Seymour of Sudeley.

As an indication of how Warwick, as we must now call him, set about acquiring for himself a state suitable to his new rank, we have a revealing letter from him, written on 24 March 1547 to Sir William Paget, Secretary of State, asking for possession of Warwick Castle.[16] The last few lines of this letter are most revealing of the Dudley ambition: '. . . because of the name, I am the more desirous to have the thing'. The Dudleys were almost given to gloating over their possessions, which reached its climax in later years when Robert Dudley, by then Earl of Leicester, after parading in the insignia of the French Order of St Michel, held a great ceremony in St Mary's Church, Warwick, in 1571, then returned to his private chamber in the Priory at Warwick and sat alone in state for the rest of the evening. Proof of noble descent, as referred to in the last line of John Dudley's letter, seemed to be a constant preoccupation of the family, so that at times one feels they protested too much. In fairness to them, however, they were by no means the only family bent on proving their noble origins.

In August 1547 Warwick was put in command of the army sent to Scotland — though nominally it was under Somerset — and the victory of the Battle of Pinkie on 10 September was chiefly ascribed to him. In 1548 he became President of Wales, and in 1549 again served against the Scots, but was called away to put down Kett's rebellion in Norfolk. A letter written on this occasion to William Cecil (later Lord Burghley), dated 10 August 1549, shows a nice appreciation for the feelings of the demoted leader of the expedition, the Marquess of Northampton, and reveals Warwick to be not entirely a monster of ruthless ambition.[17] It is this that makes the Dudleys such difficult characters to come to terms with — especially John and Robert. In moods such as this they could be devastatingly charming and considerate — at least on the surface.

Warwick was in one of his better frames of mind at this time, and his handling of the fight at Dussindale won him a reputation for chivalry and generosity. On the other hand, one must not forget what Sir Richard Morrison, ambassador to Charles V said about him: 'This earl had such a head that he seldom went about anything but he conceived first three or four purposes beforehand.'[18] He may have handled Northampton with great tact, but for Somerset's feelings Warwick showed less concern. Confident of his military supremacy, and riding the crest of a wave of personal popularity among certain members of the Council, he now began to work against Somerset, to topple him from power. When he returned from Norfolk he summoned a group of friends to his house at Ely Place on 6 October, when it was asserted that Somerset was in open insurrection against the King and his Council. Daily meetings took place until 13 October, when Somerset was sent to the Tower, and power now passed into the hands of his rival. On 28 October Warwick became one of the six lords attendant on the King, and for a second time Great Admiral.

During the winter of 1549/50 he assumed yet more honours. On 2 February he became Lord Great Master of the Household and President of the Council. On 8 April 1550 he became Lord Warden-General of the North, but decided that it was more prudent to remain at Court for the time being, rather than take up an office that would require his absence at a time when his ascendancy was not totally assured. An equally absorbing matter at this time was a series of marriages, for which John Dudley had very precise plans.

Jane Dudley had borne her husband thirteen children in all: eight sons and five daughters, though two of the sons and three daughters died before they reached the age of ten, and Henry, the eldest son, died in 1544 at the Siege of Boulogne, aged nineteen. When John Dudley became Earl of Warwick, his title of Viscount Lisle therefore passed to his next son, John; Ambrose and Robert were now the second and third surviving sons respectively. John was already destined for Somerset's daughter Anne[19] (after his death she married Sir Edward Unton, by whom she had seven children; she later became insane). Ambrose was married to the heiress Anne Whorwood, and on 24 May 1550 John Dudley signed the contract for the marriage of Robert to the daughter of

Sir John Robsart, a Norfolk landowner.

Robert Dudley married Amye Robsart on 4 June 1550. The marriage took place at the palace of Sheen— now Richmond— in the presence of Edward VI, and the King recorded the event in his diary: 'Sir Robert Dudley, third son to the Earl of Warwick, married Sir John Robsart's daughter, after which marriage there were certain gentlemen that did strive who should first take away a goose's head, which was hanged alive on two cross posts.'[20] Despite the somewhat barbaric amusement that followed the ceremony, the banks of the Thames in early June made an ideal setting for such an event, especially in the mid-sixteenth century.

The day before, on exactly the same spot, the wedding between John Dudley and Anne Seymour had taken place. Despite the fact that Warwick had toppled Somerset from power the previous autumn, and had even committed him to the Tower, he had been set free, and on 10 April 1550 was once more admitted a member of the Privy Council. On 27 April the whole Council agreed to ask the King to restore to Somerset 'all his goods, debts and leases yet ungiven'[21] — this presumably included Sheen, where the wedding took place — and on 11 May the Council asked the King to admit Somerset again to the Privy Chamber, and soon after we find him entertaining the French ambassadors who came to receive the King's ratification of the ceding of Boulogne to their country for 400,000 crowns.

Warwick now had supreme power, he had no reason to hound Somerset to death, and therefore a family alliance commended itself. As yet the dynastic schemes he later formed had not presented themselves to him, so that his requirements for matrimonial alliances were not markedly different from those of any other nobleman of the day, namely that they should be with as influential and as rich a family as possible. In the case of Robert and Amye Robsart, it was true that she came of no great and influential family, but at that time Robert was only third son in order of seniority. He need not aim at such a grand alliance as his seniors, and on the financial plane, Amye Robsart was provided with a good dowry, which was adequate recommendation.

We do not know how the couple met for certain, but there is a strong possibility that it took place the previous year, at the Robsart house at Wymondham, when Robert went with his father to Norfolk to put down Kett's rebellion. There is a reasonable assumption, then, that it was a marriage of love. William Cecil, who had been Warwick's secretary, was to write in a memorandum in April 1566, regarding Robert Dudley's fitness to be consort to Queen Elizabeth, that the

Dudley-Robsart marriage was: *nuptiae carnales a laetitia incipiunt et in luctu terminantur* — carnal marriages begin with happiness and end in grief.[22] In other translations the force of the *a* has been taken as expressing negation, in other words without happiness, but this would seem not only contrary to the evidence of the time, but also to Robert Dudley's character. If his eye lighted on a pretty woman, there was no need for him to rush into matrimony. We may assume, then, that he was so far infatuated with Amye as genuinely to believe that he wanted to marry her. One must also bear in mind that Cecil was writing with the benefit of hindsight, and after Amye's death, the circumstances of which created a scandal throughout Europe such that the unfortunate woman could hardly have imagined.

At all events, the newly married pair then settled down in Norfolk, where for the next three years Robert led the life of a country squire — though he was no ordinary squire. His father-in-law had considerable local standing, and his father was now the most powerful man in England. In the eyes of tenants and neighbours he was obviously a person of some significance. The country life pleased him, for he enjoyed athletic pursuits, and continued to do so into his middle age. There was also the administration of his considerable and somewhat scattered estates to be taken in hand, and when the King appointed Robert and his father-in-law joint Stewards of the Manor of Castle Rising and constables of its castle in December 1550, they had official functions to fulfil locally.[23] In 1551 Sir John Robsart was appointed one of the Lord Justices and Lord-Lieutenants of the county. In 1552 and 1553 the appointment was renewed, along with the Earl of Sussex and Sir William Fermour, and Robert's name was added to the list. In this year (1553) Robert was also a Member of Parliament for Norfolk.[24]

Yet another Dudley, therefore, began to acquire a taste for public office and the attendant glamour, but no male Dudley — and certainly not Robert — was content to be a big fish in a small pond, or if so, then not for long. With his father virtual ruler of England, it was only natural that Robert should join those other members of his family with whom his father (Duke of Northumberland since 11 October 1550) had surrounded the King. One ought not forget the significance attached to a dukedom at this time. Apart from Norfolk, Suffolk and Somerset, there were no other dukes, and only one of these — Norfolk — was to survive into the reign of Elizabeth. Henry VIII had made his illegitimate son by Bessie Blount Duke of Richmond, but he did not survive adolescence. Elizabeth never created any dukes, and hesitated considerably before putting Norfolk to death. This puts into perspective the significance of Warwick's elevation and also, incidentally, that of George Villiers by James I which — apart from Northumberland's — was the first outside the royal family since the Wars of the Roses.

It was almost impossible for anyone to see Edward unless one or another of the Dudley family were present. Robert Dudley received his share of the benefits. On 15 August 1551 he was sworn one of the six Gentlemen-in-Ordinary to the King, and in October that year was of the party sent to welcome Mary of Guise, the Queen Dowager of Scotland, on her way to Hampton Court. During the Christmas Court of 1551/2, held at Greenwich, Robert was a constant participant in the tilting, much as his father had been almost thirty years before. On 27 February 1552 Robert was made Chief Carver, which office Henry VIII had given to his father, and which he had been carrying out since the previous Michaelmas. In June 1552 he was made Master of the Buckhounds for life by Edward.[25] We do not, however, hear of Amye having accompanied her husband to Court, but then that is not surprising, for wives did not necessarily do so, unless they held a specific appointment in the Royal Household.

From the start, however, there was a sense of isolation in Amye's situation, and this isolation was to become even more pronounced later when her husband became the favourite of Queen Elizabeth. Even then it was not thought particularly strange, in view of the Queen's dislike of feminine competition, and the devotion she expected from those women whom she was able to tolerate around her, until after the scandal of Amye's death — by which time people had the benefit of hindsight. There was, however, another factor with which Amye had to contend, and that was the extraordinary sense of family feeling that existed amongst the Dudley clan. It was summed up by Robert Dudley's nephew, Sir Philip Sidney, in his reply to the scurrilous pamphlet against his uncle which soon became known as *Leicester's Commonwealth*: 'I am a Dudley in blood, that duke's daughter's son,[26] and do acknowledge, though, in all truth, I may justly affirm that I am, by my father's side, of ancient, and well-esteemed and well-matched gentry, yet I do acknowledge, I say, that my chiefest honour is to be a Dudley . . .'[27]

Wherever there were Dudleys there was also the Dudley badge, the Bear and Ragged Staff. In the inventories of the contents of Robert Dudley's houses — for example Leicester House, Wanstead and Kenilworth — the bear and ragged staff, along with the cinquefoil, seem to have been almost everywhere. They were on bedcovers and cushions, on utensils and bookbindings. At Kenilworth they are still visible, though they evade the eye at first sight. On the charming Renaissance porch Robert Dudley added to the gatehouse, for example, what at first one takes to be simply perpendicular elements of the decoration prove, on closer inspection, to be ragged staffs, and what one assumes to be classical rosettes are in fact cinquefoils.

In the now destroyed portrait of Robert Dudley by Zuccaro, formerly in the collection of the Dukes of Sutherland, the armour was covered with ragged staffs. Even those who were only allied to the family by marriage were proud to wear the badge. The Longleat portrait of Lettice Knollys, Robert's third wife, shows the ragged staff as a ubiquitous element of the encrusted embroidery on her dress, and in the portrait of Henry Hastings, Earl of Huntingdon, who married Robert's sister Katherine, his armour is covered with ragged staffs, whilst a couple of bears and ragged staffs adorn each elbow. There is also Robert's own armour, still visible today in the Tower of London. The Dudley badge had become so common that at the height of Northumberland's power people would not have been surprised to see it on the coinage of the realm. On 3 October 1551 two yeomen of the guard made a declaration in which they said that they thought they had seen the coin of the realm stamped with the bear and ragged staff,[28] and one Thomas Holland, on a visit from Bath to London, just before the execution of the Duke of Somerset, was supposed to have shown his relations there a new shilling bearing the Dudley emblem. Of course there were counters made for internal use in the Dudley households, and it might have been one of these, or simply a badly minted coin.

At this time there was a great love of emblems and significant colours, which went hand in hand with an interest in heraldry and genealogy. White and green were the Tudor colours, for example, and when Elizabeth went to greet her sister Mary as Queen in July 1553, all her retinue were dressed in these colours.[29] When the quarrel between Robert Dudley and the Duke of Norfolk was at its height, their partisans went around wearing coloured laces to denote their affiliations.[30] The Dudleys, in common with many other families, came to prominence only with the Tudor dynasty. Had they not pushed their way to such prominence, others who were doing exactly the same thing might not have been so critical of their origins. To counter this criticism, Northumberland had a genealogical table drawn up with 128 quarterings on it, and in the Pepys Collection at Magdalene College, Cambridge, is a document entitled: 'Certain notes of divers matters gathered out of the records in the Tower that toucheth the ancestors of the Right Honourable the Lord Wa[rwick], son of the right noble and valiant prince John, late Duke of Northumberland'. On the title page is a coat-of-arms of sixteen quarterings surrounded by the Garter and surmounted by a coronet in colours.[31] Northumberland also bought the old seat of Dudley Castle from its impoverished owner and holder of the family title, known for his penury as Lord Quondam. There were other properties, too, such as Otford in Kent, which he acquired in 1551.[32]

In addition to this acquisitive streak there was also a vindictive one, both of which Robert Dudley inherited from his father. It is said that when Arundel had been removed from the Council and put in the Tower on 8 November 1551 — as recorded in Edward VI's journal[33] — Northumberland asked what his crest or cognisance was, and he was told that it was the white horse:

> 'I thought so,' quoth the duke, 'and not without great cause: for as the white palfrey when he standeth in the stable, and is well provendered, is proud and fierce, and ready to leap upon every other horse's back, still neighing and prancing, and troubling all that stand about him: but when he is once out of his hot stable, and deprived a little of his ease and fat feeding, every boy may ride and master him at his pleasure: so it is,' quoth he, 'with my Lord of Arundel.'[34]

The extract is from *Leicester's Commonwealth*, of which one of the constant themes is the way in which the Dudleys tried to do down the old nobility, and how for their part the old nobility resented the parvenus.

Northumberland obviously had immense drive and ambition, which brought his family so near to the crown and, for the second time in its history, so near to ruin. At the same time he was an excellent father to his children, and not only saw that they received a good education, on a par with the royal children, but he also knew how to make them happy — another characteristic that Robert inherited from him. This was an important factor in Northumberland's hold over Edward VI, for he brought the same qualities to his treatment of the young King. Unlike the parents of Lady Jane Grey — the Duke and Duchess of Suffolk as they became — Northumberland did not drink or gamble, and there were no arguments or blows in his household. There was no rumour or gossip about mistresses. His wife, Jane, was a devoted mother. It is not surprising, then, that the Dudleys were devoted to each other, and always worked in the family interest. A letter from Northumberland to his eldest surviving son about his debts is forthright, but basically kind, and concerned chiefly for the boy's welfare:

> I had thought you had had more discretion than to hurt yourself through fantasies or care, specially for such things as may be remedied and helpen. Well enough you must understand that I know you cannot live under great charges. And therefore you should not hide from me your debts whatsoever it be, for I would loathe but you should keep your credit with all men. And therefore send me word in any wise of the whole sum of your debts, for I and your mother will see them forthwith paid, and whatsoever you do spend in the honest service of our master and for his honour so you do not let wild and wanton men consume it, as I have been served in my days, you must think all is spent as it should be, and all that I have must be yours, and that you spend before, you may with God's grace help it hereafter by good and faithful service, wherein I trust you will never be found slack and then you may be sure you cannot lack serving such a master as you have, toward whom the living God preserve and restore you to perfect health, and so with my blessing I commit you to his tuition. Your loving father. Northumberland.

There is a postscript: 'Your loving mother that wishes you health daily. Jane Northumberland.'[35]

The Dudley men stuck together through thick and thin: they fought together, and they remained together in adversity. If the conduct of John, Viscount Lisle and Earl of Warwick after his father became Duke of Northumberland, did not match up to what one might expect of the eldest child, one must remember that he was really only the third son. He was quiet and dutiful, possibly not very robust, and distinguished chiefly in the loyalty with which he supported his father, and the dignity with which — unlike his father — he bore the calamities that overcame the family in the wake of the Jane Grey episode, and in which he and his brother, Guildford, were to perish. With the death of the seventh brother, Henry, at the Siege of St Quentin in 1557, Ambrose and Robert were the only sons left to see the reign of Elizabeth. It is strange that these two should be the ones to survive, because they so often acted together under their father's command, and although Ambrose eventually became the head of the family, Robert was by far the more brilliant of the two, and Ambrose almost literally adored him. Much later in their respective careers, when it looked as if Robert Dudley might be abandoned by Elizabeth and be wrecked in the troubled waters of the Netherlands campaign, Ambrose wrote to Robert in March 1586: 'Once again, have great care of yourself, I mean for your safety, and if she [Elizabeth] will needs revoke you, to the overthrowing of the cause, if I were as you, if I could not be assured there, I would go to the furthest part of Christendom rather than ever come into England again.' Ambrose then went on to reproach Robert — though in the gentlest of terms, it is true— for not answering his letters, and although he seems almost incapable of taking any initiative without Robert, his obvious faith in, and assurance of affection towards, his younger, brilliant brother, are touching:

> I pray you make me no stranger as you have done, but deal frankly with me, for that that toucheth you toucheth me likewise. I have sent you divers letters of great importance and as yet never had answer of them. Take heed whom you trust, for that you have some false boys about you. Let me have your best advice what is best for me to do, for that I mean to take such part as you do. God bless you, and prosper you in all your doings. In haste, this present 6 day of March [1586]. Your faithful brother. A. Warwyke.[36]

One of the key phrases of this letter — 'that that toucheth you toucheth me likewise' — might almost be taken as the collective motto of the Dudley clan. It certainly epitomised the nature of the relationship between Ambrose and Robert, and it was the whole motivating force in the way their mother struggled tirelessly on their behalf after the collapse of the Jane Grey plot. Such devotion must have been instilled into the children by their parents at a very early age.

In view of this, Northumberland's letter to William Cecil of 2 June 1552 about the death of one of his daughters may seem somewhat detached, even clinical in tone. One must bear in mind, however, that at this moment he was preparing to set out on a progress, he was at the height of his power, and he had to defend his rear during his absence from Court, since rumours were being set about that he had been ordered by the King to stay away. This same month of June, however, he had received from the King remission of a debt in 'sundry particular sums', amounting to £2,094 17s 3d.[37] The letter therefore explains to Cecil and the Lord Chamberlain why he thinks it unwise for his son or himself to come to the royal presence, lest they be contagious:

> Whereas I perceive by your letter of this instant, that, except the death of my daughter might seem dangerous and infectious, the King's Majesty's pleasure is that neither I should absent myself nor

stay my son; whereupon I have thought good to signify unto you what moveth me to suspect infection in the disease whereof my daughter died. First, the night before she died, she was as merry as any child could be, and sickened about three in the morning, and was in a sweat, and within a while after she had a desire to the stool; and the indiscreet woman that attended upon her let her rise, and after that, she fell to swooning, and then, with such things as they ministered to her, brought her again to remembrance, and so she seemed for a time to be meetly well revived, and so continued till it was noon, and still in a great sweating; and about twelve of the clock she began to alter again, and so in continual pangs and fits till six of the clock, at what time she left this life. And this morning she was looked upon, and between the shoulders it was very black, and also upon one side of her cheek . . . This [is] as much as I am able to express, and even thus it was: wherefore I think it not my duty to presume to make my repair to his Majesty's presence till further be seen what may ensue of it . . . [38]

Death was more common, and therefore more readily accepted, in those days. Certainly people lived in dread of an epidemic of the sweating sickness about this time — which is what Northumberland thought his daughter's illness had been. Only the day before he had had occasion to write to the Lord Chamberlain, and in the letter mentioned that the wife of his son Ambrose had also died.[39]

After the summer progress the burden of office began to take its toll of Northumberland. A letter to Cecil of 28 October 1552 ends: 'Scribbled in my bed, as ill at ease as I have been much in all my life.'[40] Again, on 7 December, he wrote to Cecil complaining of what he was suffering at the hands of his critics.[41]

It is illuminating that in this letter he harks back to his father, and the reasons for his execution, for at this very moment he must have been making use of his position for attacks upon the wealth of the Church in the name of the reformed faith — in phrases that sound remarkably like the Book of Common Prayer — and at the same time he was trying to convince himself, or at least others, that he was weary of life, and longed for a quiet retirement. In January 1553 the tone was still the same, whilst in the same letter calmly telling the Lord Chamberlain that he did not intend Princess Elizabeth to have Durham House, which he wanted to keep for himself.[42] And still the acquisitions went on. On 17 April 1553 Robert Dudley was given the custody of Thomas Philpot, lunatic, with all his lands, goods, etc., and one hundred marks,[43] and the same month his father was steward of all the honours, castles, manors, lordships, lands, etc., in Cumberland, Northumberland, Westmorland and York.[44]

Events were about to happen, however, that were to whirl the Dudley family to the edge of catastrophe for the second time in less than fifty years. By April 1553 Edward VI had had two eruptive illnesses from which he recovered, but tuberculosis was now apparent, and he developed galloping consumption. At the beginning of May his doctors said that he had only a matter of weeks to live. To some extent Northumberland would have been prepared for this, since a famous doctor from Milan, Girolamo Cardano, had made a private diagnosis of consumption in September or October of the previous year (1552). He had not dared tell the Privy Council, in case he were accused of high treason, but also because he had not been able to examine the King. Later he said: 'I saw the omens of a great calamity.'[45]

With such a crisis imminent, Northumberland had to take action. If Mary Tudor, the legitimate heir to the throne, were allowed to succeed, the Roman rite would be restored, and the Catholics and nobles whom Northumberland had offended would take their revenge. He knew that he would not have much difficulty in persuading the fanatically Protestant Edward — when the time came — that this would be undesirable, so that he was outwardly able to continue treating Mary as the heiress apparent, and so, he hoped, cause no alarm in that quarter.

When it came to Elizabeth Tudor, Northumberland had seen enough of her to realise that she would never be subservient to his will, despite the fact that on religious issues, at least superficially, they saw eye to eye. Elizabeth's distrust was well rewarded in the end, especially on the religious question, when Northumberland made his extraordinary confession on the scaffold, and announced that he had been a Catholic all the time. As a matter of policy he kept the princesses away from their brother in the last few weeks of his life, partly so that they would not realise how ill he was, and partly so as to isolate the King from his legal successors, so that the scheme Northumberland proposed to him would be more easily commended to him.

Quite simply Northumberland intended excluding Mary and Elizabeth from the succession. The precedent had been set for him by their father, Henry VIII, and it was this that Northumberland persuaded Edward to accept. He drew up a 'device' which excluded the two princesses in favour of the eldest granddaughter of Henry VIII's youngest sister Mary, which totally ignored the claim of Mary, Queen of Scots, granddaughter of the older sister, Margaret. Being a Catholic, however, Mary Stuart was as damned as Mary Tudor. The girl thus chosen was the ill-fated Jane Grey, whose mother, Frances Brandon — Duchess of Suffolk since July 1551 — was persuaded to step down in her favour. There was again a precedent for this in that Henry VII came to the throne whilst his mother, Lady Margaret Beaufort (through whom he made his claim), was still alive. Lady Jane Grey was then to be married to a Dudley son. At one stage Northumberland contemplated divorcing his heir from Anne Seymour, now that her family was no longer of use to him, but in the end he decided on his fourth surviving son, Guildford. One of the additional arguments against Mary and Elizabeth was that they would probably marry foreign princes, thus putting England under the domination of a foreign power, and probably a Catholic one to boot. This came true in Mary's case, and was seemingly always a possibility in Elizabeth's casting about amongst would-be suitors when she came to the throne.

Northumberland announced the engagement of the two people in the third week of April 1553, and a few days later two more engagements were announced. Jane Grey's second sister Catherine was to marry Lord Herbert, son of the Earl of Pembroke, and one of Northumberland's most powerful supporters, and Northumberland's daughter Katherine was to marry Lord Hastings, son of the Earl of Huntingdon. This triple union was to bind the Dudleys to the Tudors through the Jane Grey marriage, and to the Plantagenets through the Hastings marriage, since Hastings was the grandson of the Countess of Salisbury, niece to Edward IV, whom Henry VIII had executed in 1541. Through the Catherine Grey—Herbert marriage, Jane Grey's parents were allied to Northumberland's chief ally, and so it seemed the circle was complete. This last marriage was in fact annulled on the collapse of the Jane Grey plot, and Catherine then made a clandestine marriage with the Earl of Hertford, Somerset's eldest son.[46]

Jane Grey and Guildford Dudley married on Whit Sunday, 21 May 1553, and the other two on 25 May at Durham House on the Strand in London. Neither Mary nor Elizabeth was there, nor were the French or Spanish ambassadors. Even the spectacular triple nature of the weddings failed to alert many people to the audacity of the plot that Northumberland had hatched, though others — including Cecil — began to have an inkling of what was on foot. In Cecil's case he had not been helped by an illness which had kept him away from Court from 22 April to 2 June.

There were other indications of Dudley advancement evident, however, for those who noted such things. Lord Warwick and Robert Dudley had been given licence in May 1533 to retain one hundred men, and fifty men, respectively.[47] The patent for Robert is dated 17 June 1553 and is still at Longleat,[48] and in the same month he received the gift of the Manor of Corsy and Saxlingham in Norfolk, with a yearly value of £149 10s 4d.[49]

After the marriages, and once Northumberland's designs began to be apparent, it seemed as if the poor King, whose life had once been a matter of such concern, was now living too long. At one stage Northumberland dismissed the royal doctors, Thomas Wendy and George Owen, and brought in one of his own, together with a woman who gave the King arsenic, which may have stopped the haemorrhages, but probably hastened the boy's death. At all events, his own doctors were brought back, but it was too late. As long as it suited Northumberland's purpose, the pale face would be shown at the window of his room at Greenwich Palace, though who knew whether it were the King still hanging on to life, his corpse, or even a dummy? If and when he died, then his death must be kept a secret, Northumberland decided, until he had both Mary and Elizabeth in his power. When at last the poor boy did die, on 6 July in the presence of Sir Thomas Wrothe, Sir Henry Sidney (Northumberland's son-in-law), Doctors Owen and Wendy and a groom, Northumberland rapidly doubled the guards around the palace, took control of the Tower, and ordered a watch to be kept on all ports.

Mary had already been summoned before the death was officially announced two days later, and she had actually set off from Hunsdon in Hertfordshire, and reached Hoddesdon, when she was met by a messenger from Greenwich. Some person with her interests at heart, perhaps the Earl of Arundel whom Northumberland had treated so badly, or Sir Nicholas Throckmorton, warned her of the plan to capture her, so she turned about and fled first to Kenninghall in Norfolk, and then from there to Framlingham, a Howard stronghold also in Norfolk. Northumberland sent John, Earl of Warwick, and Robert his brother with three hundred horsemen to secure her person, but when they caught up with Mary's party the Dudley soldiers deserted to her and the brothers had to flee for their lives. John returned to London, but Robert went on to King's Lynn, a Protestant town in an area where he was a landowner, and there he proclaimed Jane Grey queen in the market place before returning to London also. Elizabeth, meanwhile, never even set off from

Hatfield. She too had been warned, probably by Cecil.

Yet another of the Dudley children now became involved, this time one of the daughters, the kindly Mary Sidney, wife of Sir Henry and mother of Philip, who was sent to fetch Jane Grey to Sion, so that she might be proclaimed queen on 9 July. The following day she made her entry into the Tower of London, a custom of sovereigns prior to coronation, but from which she was destined never to return. Up to this point Northumberland's plot seemed to those at the centre of it to have succeeded, but he had not counted on the amount of public support for Mary and the amount of hatred he had engendered for himself. Moreover, without the two princesses in his power, he could never have been truly safe.

Mary raised her standard at Framlingham, and men flocked to join her. Northumberland now knew that someone had to go out against her. If he left London he did not know what the Council might do behind his back, but the only other person to whom he might entrust the expedition was the Duke of Suffolk, Jane Grey's father, and she would not let him go. Having put her on the throne as his puppet, Northumberland was now disconcerted to find her acting like a queen. Moreover she refused to concede the title of king to his son Guildford, asserting — which was quite true — that only an Act of Parliament could confer that. Eventually Northumberland accepted the inevitable: 'Well! Since ye think it good, I and mine [the Dudley males] will go, not doubting of your fidelity to the Queen's Majesty, which I leave in your custody.'[50] As they left Northumberland was heard to remark to his companions: 'The people press to see us, but not one saith "God speed" us.'[51]

On 14 July Northumberland left London for Cambridgeshire with four of his sons — John, Ambrose, Robert and Henry. By the time they reached Bury St Edmunds there had been so many desertions that they were obliged to fall back on Cambridge, where Northumberland was Chancellor of the University. Robert Dudley was captured in a skirmish at Bury and taken to Mary's headquarters at Framlingham before being brought back to London. News now reached Northumberland that the Council had proclaimed Mary queen. He himself proclaimed her at the market cross in Cambridge, threw his cap into the air and money to the crowd, but it was too late. The Earl of Arundel, eager for revenge for the way in which Northumberland had treated him, came to arrest him, and he was taken into custody by Master Slegge, the University Sergeant-at-Arms, in the precincts of King's College, on 20 July. There was bitter irony in the text that Edwin Sandys, Master of St Catharine's and Vice-Chancellor, had chosen from Joshua I for his sermon the previous Sunday: 'According as we hearkened unto Moses in all things, so will we hearken unto thee'. That same day (20 July) Jane Grey's own father told her that she was no longer queen. On 26 July Robert Dudley was brought to the Tower to join the other members of his family who had left Cambridge on 24 July and arrived the day before him.

On Friday 18 August Northumberland and his eldest son were brought to trial in Westminster Hall (the other three brothers and Sir Andrew Dudley, Northumberland's brother, appeared the following day), and condemned on a charge of high treason. John Dudley Earl of Warwick merely said that he had followed his father and was therefore content to share his father's fate. He asked that, in spite of the fact that his goods were pronounced forfeit to the crown, his debts might be paid out of them. When sentence was passed on Northumberland, he specifically asked that: '. . . her Majesty will be gracious to my children, which may hereafter do her Grace good service, considering that they went by my commandment who am their father, and not of their own free wills. . . .'[52] In the event he proved right, though the Queen was perfectly justified in treating this with a degree of scepticism at the time. There was a certain element of pride, and the unquestioning acceptance of the devotion he took for granted in his children, but he offered a pathetic spectacle to the family he had inspired in this way and brought to such a calamity. In a letter to Arundel he grovelled to the Queen he had so determinedly plotted to dispossess, and asked Arundel to intercede on his behalf.[53]

This attempted political *volte face* was accompanied by another, this time a religious one. He had brought up his children as Protestants, and he had attacked and pillaged the Church of England. His career has been described as summing up 'both the ignoble side of Protestantism and the unresting cupidity of a class'.[54] He now declared that he had been a Catholic all the time. This incensed both the Catholics he had offended and the Protestants whose champion he had been taken for. He was executed on 22 August. Five days later the Queen sent a warrant to Sir Gilbert Dethick, Garter King of Arms, for the taking down of Northumberland's hatchments as a Knight of the Garter over his stall in St George's Chapel, and the draft for this warrant is still there today.[55]

That same day the anonymous author of the *Chronicle of Queen Jane and . . . Queen Mary* dined with Jane Grey in the Tower. She heard with amazement of Northumberland's recantation on the scaffold: 'Perchance,' the author said, 'he thereby hoped to have had his pardon?'

' "Pardon!" retorted Jane Grey. "Woe worth him! He hath brought me and our stock in most miserable calamity by his exceeding ambition." ' Pardon in such circumstances, she felt, would have been unthinkable: '. . . what man is there living, I pray you, although he had been innocent, that would hope of life in that case? Being in the field against the Queen in person as general?' [56] Despite the fact that she was not legally queen, Jane Grey had enough Tudor blood in her to know more of the business of royalty than any Dudley.

Although given plenty of advice to the contrary, Mary intended to be merciful. Northumberland, of course, as Jane Grey had pointed out, could not possibly hope for pardon, but Mary knew that Jane herself had been merely a pawn in his hands, and his sons had simply done their filial duty. Jane's parents, the Suffolks, were pardoned, and the Dudley sons, though still in captivity, were nevertheless still alive. Moreover their wives were allowed to visit them from time to time, as a letter from the Privy Council dated 10 September 1553, to the Lieutenant of the Tower, indicates, 'to permit these ladies following to have access unto their husbands, and there to tarry with them so long and at such times, as by him shall be thought meet; that is to say, the Lord Ambrose's wife, the Lord Robert's wife . . .'[57] Amye Robsart did not fail to do her duty as a member of the clan.

What tipped the balance against them, however, was the rising in January 1554 of Sir Thomas Wyatt in protest against Mary's determination to marry Philip of Spain. As the chronicler wrote: 'Note that on Tuesday the 23 January the Lord Robert Dudley, son to the late Duke of Northumberland, was brought out of the Tower to the Guildhall, where he was arraigned and condemned.' [58] The Duke of Suffolk had risen in support of Wyatt, but failed dismally, and in so doing signed not only his own death warrant but also that of his daughter and son-in-law. They died on 12 February, and Suffolk and Wyatt twelve days later.

Another victim of this chain of events was the Princess Elizabeth. On the morning of Palm Sunday, 18 March 1554, she was taken downstream to the Tower, since it was felt inadvisable to take her through the streets of the city. She remained there until 19 May when she left for Woodstock in the charge of Sir Henry Bedingfield. Philip of Spain was to arrive that summer for his marriage to Mary, and it was better that Elizabeth be well away.

There is a romantic legend that Elizabeth and Robert Dudley were able to meet in the Tower, and that their love affair blossomed there. Unfortunately there is no evidence for this, and indeed if what Robert Dudley himself said was true, they knew each other well enough before then for an attachment to be established already. Of course there were famous instances when love found a way, even in the Tower, but it is out of character from what we know of Elizabeth, even at this stage in her emotional development, let alone her political development. What may well be true, however, is that she was aware that Robert Dudley was sharing a captivity with her, even though they were kept apart, and this induced a feeling of solidarity with him that remained with her afterwards.

What is left of the time the Dudleys spent there is the emblem, carved on the wall of the Beauchamp Tower, showing the bear and ragged staff with a lion at the top of it, and underneath the words, 'John Dudle'. Then there are roses for Ambrose, honeysuckle for Henry, gilliflowers for Guildford and oak leaves — from the Latin for oak, *robur* — for Robert. There is also a verse:

> You that these beasts do well behold and see,
> May deem with ease wherefore here made they be,
> With borders eke therein there may be found
> Four brothers' names, who list to search the ground.

There is another inscription, showing an oak branch and the initials RD, which is usually attributed to Robert Dudley.

All this time the Duchess of Northumberland was working for the release of her sons. On 5 June she obtained permission for them to hear Mass in the Tower, provided they were kept incommunicado.[59] Her natural maternal instincts were reinforced by the fact that she, too, was a member of the Dudley clan, and despite the shock at the changes and chances of her fortunes, she soldiered on. As soon as she had been released from prison the previous August — almost so as to compile an inventory of her possessions for confiscation, it seemed — she had set out for Newhall in Essex, where Mary had taken up residence on her way to London to take possession of her throne, but the duchess was refused an audience and told that the Queen would not see her.

With the advent of Philip of Spain the next summer, however, and the Spanish members of his retinue, the duchess had more success. Hovering on the fringes of the Court, she made valuable contacts and eventually, on 18 October 1554, her sons were released. As Collins, in his *Sidney Papers*, stated: 'She was a lady of great piety, virtue and prudence, and by her solicitations, after the marriage of the Queen with King Philip, she obtained pardon for her sons, principally by the Spaniards, who accompanied him into England, as appears from her last will and testament . . .'[60]

The strain of the long captivity told on John Dudley, Earl of Warwick, and he died within a few days of his release, at Penhurst, the home of his brother-in-law, Sir Henry Sidney.[61] Ambrose now became head of the family, inheriting the titles of Viscount Lisle and Earl of Warwick. He did not officially take up his titles until later, however, when the act of attainder was lifted on 26 December 1561.[62] Ambrose also inherited the Manor of Hales Owen at his mother's death on 22 January 1555 (though Robert and Amye had it by 1558 when it was alienated to Thomas Blount).

Jane Dudley's funeral took place on 1 February 1555 in Chelsea Parish Church. She was buried 'with a goodly hearse of wax and penfils, and escutcheons: two banners of arms, and four banners of images, two heralds of arms, with many mourners. There was a majesty and the vallance and six dozen torches, and two white branches: and all the church hung in black and arms: and a canopy borne over her to church.'[63] Jane Dudley's monument remained in the church for almost four hundred years until the whole church was shattered by a German bomb in World War II.

After this, information about the Dudleys is especially scant. They were, after all, still attainted, and Protestants, one must assume, and Mary's persecution of those who refused to accept the return to Rome began in earnest in February 1555. It seems that the brothers may have attended some secret meetings in the vicinity of St Paul's in London that summer, for they were warned in July to leave the capital and keep away. However, the Manor of Hemsby, near Yarmouth, which Northumberland had settled on Robert and Amye in 1553, was allowed to pass to them in 1557, and when John Robsart died that year, they also inherited property from him.[64]

This is interesting, because there was a rumour that was said to have been repeated by the Princess Elizabeth herself, that when she was in financial difficulties during Mary's reign, Robert Dudley sold land so as to provide her with funds. Giovanni Michele, writing to the Venetian Senate in May 1557, said that, despite all her attempts at economy, Elizabeth was always in debt, and that she could ill afford the state that she was expected to keep up as heiress presumptive, let alone take into her service all the people who offered themselves.[65] There is also a later piece of evidence from the jeweller John Dymock, who was visiting the Swedish Court in 1562. When the king asked him why it was that Robert Dudley enjoyed such favour with Queen Elizabeth (as she was by this time), Dymock replied, 'When she was but Lady Elizabeth . . . in her trouble he did sell away a good piece of his land to aid her, which divers supposed to be the cause that the queen so favoured him.'[66] No evidence has been produced to support this claim, but we do know that in 1557 the Dudleys saw a chance for a return to favour and official recognition when Philip of Spain finally persuaded Mary to involve England in his war with France. The remaining three brothers joined his forces, with Robert as Master of Ordnance, under the Earl of Pembroke.

On 17 March Robert was sent home with despatches: 'The Lord Robert Dudley, having been beyond the sea with King Philip, came riding unto the queen at Court at Greenwich with letters.'[67] All three brothers distinguished themselves at the Battle of St Quentin on 10 August that year, but Henry was killed in the course of it, thus leaving Ambrose and Robert as the only two surviving brothers. On 30 April 1557 the title of Northumberland, as an earldom, had been given to the Percy family, when letters patent were issued to Thomas Percy for that cause.[68]

On 7 March 1558 the attainder on Robert was lifted, but he still failed to get back to the position he yearned for. There is a letter, dated 22 July 1558, to John Flowerdew, a relative of Amye Robsart by marriage, in which Robert Dudley talks of an estate at Flitcham. Syderstone, which had come to him from Amye's father, he now found was not adequate.[69] It took a great deal to content a Dudley once the tide began to run favourably for him. There is also, in the same collection, a letter from Amye to Flowerdew, dated 7 August, possibly 1558 or 1559. Robert Dudley had been called away, 'being sore troubled with weighty affairs', and his wife had forgotten to talk to him about several creditors before he left. So in her letter she tells Flowerdew to sell wool, even if it is at a loss, so that the people may be paid.[70]

The letter is inscribed 'from My Hyde's', who at that time had a house at Denchworth, near Abingdon. William Hyde, his brother, was MP for Abingdon, and Amye Dudley seems to have spent a lot of time with them. Robert visited her there, as we learn from the account books at Longleat. She had twelve horses at her disposal, and she moved around, to London, Lincolnshire, Suffolk and Hampshire. At some point, however, she decided to settle with her own household in the neighbourhood of the Hydes, and chose Cumnor. It belonged to Mrs Owen, and was let to Anthony Forster and his wife. Forster was the principal receiver of Robert Dudley's income at this time, and one of the controllers of expenditure. There was also, in addition to Lady Dudley herself, a Mrs Odingsell, who was a widow, and sister to Mr Hyde. She may have acted as companion to Lady Dudley. After Amye's death Forster bought Cumnor, and in his will gave first refusal of it to Robert Dudley, who bought it, though subsequently sold it to the Norreys family on 15 February 1575.[71]

Even if there was no actual estrangement between the couple, it would seem that they were hardly very close, either. However, the account books at Longleat show that Amye did not materially lack anything, even if she did not enjoy any longer the fullness of her husband's affection. She can hardly have failed to know where that was now directed. It was spoken of throughout the realm, at times almost as a matter of public concern. In such circumstances Amye doubtless thought it best to keep herself to herself, and if she became aware of an unfortunate illness, too, then all the more reason to do so.

Further light is shed on the domestic life of the Robert Dudleys at this period in the accounts kept by William Chaucy, now at Longleat. Robert won £12 6s 8d at tennis and £15 8s 4d 'at play',[72] which is insignificant, perhaps, when the sums passing through the books for one year amounted to £2,540 5s 6d[73] — except that he lost 'at play' £109 7s 10d.[74] By and large there is nothing particularly surprising in the items of expenditure for a household of the Dudleys' status, except that perhaps Amye never seems to have accompanied her husband to Court, whether it be at Windsor or in London, nor is there anything to indicate that she had any miscarriages or even conceived, let alone bear any children.

In the last few months of 1558 for many people it became a matter of waiting, of living in a twilight realm, as the life of the unhappy Mary ebbed away and the dawn of Gloriana waited to burst upon an expectant England. In the early hours of 17 November Mary died, and Robert Dudley, like the knight of romance, 'mounted on a snow-white steed, being well skilled in riding a managed horse',[75] and joined the stream of people hastening to Hatfield to kneel at the feet of the new Queen.

2

Death at Cumnor

... methinks I am here all this while, as it were in a dream, and too far, too far, from the place I am bound to be ...

Robert Dudley

Although he was not initially a member of the Council — that was to wait until 20 October 1562,[1] when Elizabeth was seriously ill with smallpox — the office of Master of the Horse which the Queen bestowed upon him at the outset of her reign ensured that Robert Dudley was virtually constantly by her side. When she left Hatfield to take up residence in London, and went from the Charterhouse (Lord North's home) to take possession of the Tower on 28 November 1558, Robert Dudley rode behind her,[2] and it was he who was sent to find out from the mathematician turned astrologer Dr Dee which would be the most auspicious date for the Queen's coronation (15 January 1559).[3] In the coronation procession itself, he led the palfrey of honour behind the Queen's litter, of which his brother Ambrose led the second horse. Robert was made a Knight of the Garter on St George's Day (23 April) 1559, and his 'stalling' took place on 6 June that year.[4] When a muster of the citizens of London took place on 1 and 2 July 1559 he was again present,[5] and when John, Duke of Finland, paid a visit to England that autumn, to ask Elizabeth's hand in marriage for his brother, Crown Prince Eric of Sweden, Robert Dudley took part in his reception.

The visitor landed at Harwich on 27 September, and on 5 October Robert Dudley went out with the Earl of Oxford to meet him at Colchester. When the party reached London it was met by the Marquess of Northampton and Lord Ambrose Dudley.[6] The Duke of Finland was lodged in the Bishop of Winchester's house in Southwark, and a fortnight later Robert Dudley gave a banquet for him at Court. On 27 October the two were godparents, along with the Marchioness of Northampton, to Sir Thomas Chamberlain's son. On 5 November there was jousting, in which Robert Dudley and the Queen's cousin Henry Carey, Lord Hunsdon, were the challengers, and Ambrose Dudley one of the defendants.

Such a position of potential power and privilege made Robert Dudley a target of those who had requests, either verbally or by letter, from the very outset of the reign. Some letters came from his own family, such as the one at Longleat from his sister Katherine Hastings, written in a fine italic hand from Sunninghill on 5 May 1559, asking her brother to esteem her husband Henry, 'though peradventure he useth not such flattering behaviour as many will do unto prosperity'.[7] Others came from abroad, such as the one from Genoa dated 20 July 1559, from Domenico Comicino (or Conncino), asking Robert Dudley to use his influence to obtain for him the renewal of a pension of £200 that had been granted to him by Edward VI, but which had ceased during Mary's reign: '. . . solo per opera e favore particolare del detto S̄ Duca vr̄o padre, quale poi mi fu suspesa dala serma Regina Maria.' [8] Comicino had served Robert Dudley's father, who had been the means of the granting of the pension in the first place.

Robert also began to have books dedicated to him. One of the first came in 1559, namely William Cunningham's *The Cosmographical Glass*, which has the Dudley arms on the title verso, and in the first initial of the dedication. It was one of the first books in English to include a description of America, and reflects Robert Dudley's lifelong interest in navigation and exploration, which he probably inherited from his father. Also that year, but dedicated to the Earl of Bedford as well as Dudley, was John Aylmer's *An Harborowe for Faithful and true subjects* . . . which was an answer to John Knox's attack on the fitness of women to rule. This shows another important sphere of interest for Dudley, namely religion, which must also have been inculcated at an early age, despite his father's denial of his Protestant ideals on the scaffold. We may also assume that Robert had had some reputation as a patron before these dedications were made, since they show him already identified as a source of further possible patronage.

The stream of requests, dedications and presents was to continue virtually throughout his life, and it was occasionally to produce a lighter note, as we see from a letter dated from Belvoir on 4 June 1560 and now at Longleat, from Henry Manners, Earl of Rutland, who wanted to send Robert Dudley a dog: '. . . one of the best dogs that ever has been in this country. Yet notwithstanding, for the enmity that some beareth your l[ordship], but specially towards me, they found means to steal the same dog, so as in ten days he could not be heard of, and besides that they did dye him of sundry colours.'[9] This letter also shows, incidentally, that as a favourite of the Queen Robert Dudley also had enemies from an early point in his career — enemies who were apparently only too ready to do him harm. They were soon to have plenty of ammunition put into their hands. In the autumn of 1560 his wife Amye was found dead in seemingly mysterious circumstances, and those ill-wishers needed little encouragement to turn the tragedy into a murder — particularly in view of the Queen's well-known affection for, and apparent infatuation with, Lord Robert.

In fact gossip had been rife for some time before that. As early as 18 April of the previous year (1559), the Spanish ambassador Count de Feria had written to King Philip II of Spain:

> During the last few days Lord Robert has come so much into favour that he does whatever he likes with affairs and it is even said that her Majesty visits him in his chamber day and night. People talk of this so freely that they go so far as to say that his wife has a malady in one of her breasts and the Queen is only waiting for her to die to marry Lord Robert.[10]

The St George's Day ceremony of 23 April had been described by Paolo Tiepolo, Venetian ambassador in Brussels — only on hearsay, however, from news from England — and he went on to say that Lord Robert was '. . . a very handsome young man, towards whom in various ways the Queen evinces such affection and inclination that many persons believe that if his wife, who has been ailing some time, were perchance to die, the Queen might easily take him for her husband'.[11]

At this time Count de Feria was replaced as Spanish ambassador by Alvaro de la Quadra, Bishop of Aquila, who reported to his master on 19 June that the Queen had given Lord Robert £12,000, 'as an aid towards his expenses',[12] but even he had to admit that the Queen constituted something of an enigma for him: 'I am not sure about her, for I do not understand her.'[13] The expenses of being a nobleman, and a prominent figure at Court, must have been proving almost beyond Lord Robert's resources at this point, and were certainly far in excess of his allowance for his official duties as Master of the Horse. In June he became patron of a theatrical company, and though it may not have taxed his financial resources at all, it required him to act on their behalf. A recent Privy Council proclamation had made it necessary for actors to have the permission of the mayor of a town, two Justices of the Peace, or the Lord-Lieutenant of the shire, before they were able to perform in a locality. Robert Dudley therefore wrote on behalf of his own company to the Earl of Shrewsbury, then President of the North, to ask for a licence for his men to play in Yorkshire. In so doing he guaranteed 'their being honest men and such as shall play none other matters, I trust, but tolerable and convenient'.[14] By the same Privy Council proclamation, plays were not to deal with matters of religion or state— such areas were far too sensitive to be left uncontrolled.

As we saw at the end of the previous chapter, there is evidence from the Longleat accounts that Robert was not neglecting his wife materially, and that the pair still maintained at least an outward semblance of domestic harmony. Even so, the gossip was mounting, and on 12 July that year (1559), De Quadra informed his king that the Bishop of Ely, who had been deprived, '. . . had words with Bacon and told him that if the Queen continued as she had begun to be ruled by those about her, both she and her kingdom would be ruined.'[15]

Of course outwardly there were other likely — or at least possible— suitors for the Queen's hand, such as James Hamilton, Earl of Arran and Duke of Châtelherault, or, much more important, the Habsburg Archduke Charles. In fact the latter commended himself much more to Robert Dudley, since Dudley was technically out of the running at this time, being a married man, and in order to promote it he rather unscrupulously made use of his sister Mary, the kindly Lady Sidney. One recalls the task her father gave her in escorting Lady Jane Grey to what proved in the long run to be her execution. Here the outcome was by no means likely to have been so tragic, but it still took advantage of Mary and her good nature. De Quadra wrote to Philip II's sister Margaret, Duchess of Parma, in Brussels where she was Regent of the Netherlands. This was the way in which he sent his despatches to Philip, and on 7 September 1559 he told the king: '. . . a sister of Lord Robert, called Lady Sidney, [said] that this was the time to speak to the Queen about the archduke . . . [She said I] must not mind what the

Queen said, as it is the custom of ladies here not to give their consent in such matters until they are teased into it.'[16] Not surprisingly, De Quadra felt that he ought to have some indication as to the authenticity of this story from Lord Robert himself, and naturally he was able to report that '[He] said in this as in all things he was at the disposal of my king to whom he owed his life.'[17]

Such encouragement emboldened the ambassador to broach the matter with the Queen herself, though her reaction took him somewhat by surprise: 'When I pressed her much, she seemed frightened and protested, over and over again, that she was not to be bound.' He came to the conclusion, not surprisingly, perhaps, that he must have been mistaken, but he could not imagine that both Lord Robert and his sister had been mistaken, and indeed Lord Robert maintained that he never thought the Queen would go so far. At this juncture the Swedish visit already mentioned took place, though on 13 November 1559 De Quadra wrote to King Philip that in his opinion both the Swedish and the Spanish proposals were all a waste of time: 'I had heard . . . veracious news that Lord Robert has sent to poison his wife.' In this case, foreign suitors were simply being used as a feint: '. . . until this wicked deed . . . is consummated.'[18] De Quadra was not the only one to be suspicious, however. There were plenty of English people who were of the same opinion. As De Quadra put it, on 18 November, 'He [Robert Dudley] has again been warned that there is a plot to kill him, which I quite believe, for not a man in the realm can suffer the idea of his being king.'[19]

By now Mary Sidney was aware of the part she had been made to play in this manoeuvre, and was angry with her brother. In fact, according to De Quadra, she said that even if it meant being sent to the Tower, she would speak her mind. Of course De Quadra may well have exaggerated her reaction, though in December he intimated that her husband, Sir Henry Sidney, had also been angry with Lord Robert. Since he was usually as devoted to his brother-in-law as the rest of the Dudley family were, Sir Henry's annoyance may have been expressed out of a feeling of solidarity with his wife. At all events, the breach was soon healed, and the star of their adored Robert continued to rise, both in favour and in fortune. He already had a warrant for £400 annually for the royal stable, dating possibly from 1560.[20] Then the Queen had given him lands in Yorkshire, as well as the Manor of Kew, in addition to which she now made him Lieutenant of the Castle and Forest of Windsor[21] and, from the financial point of view what was much more valuable, a licence to export woollen cloth free of duty.

It soon became obvious to De Quadra, however, that Lord Robert did not really want to see a match for the Queen with the Archduke, any more than he wanted any of the other possible suitors to succeed. On 7 March 1560 the ambassador declared that '[Lord Robert] is the worst and most procrastinating young man I ever saw in my life, and not at all courageous or spirited.'[22] Towards the end of the month he again wrote: 'He is laying in a good stock of arms and is assuming every day a more masterful part in affairs. They say that he thinks of divorcing his wife.'[23] During Cecil's absence in Scotland, negotiating the Treaty of Edinburgh, the Queen seemed to be shut up with Lord Robert for hours on end. Not surprisingly, rumours flew around. On 17 July Ann Dowe of Brentwood was brought before the justices for saying that the Queen had had a child by Lord Robert.[24] This can only have been a small indication of the rumours and gossip, some of which may well have reached Lady Robert Dudley herself. It seemed as if everything was conspiring to will something to happen. In Cecil's eyes things had almost reached crisis point, and on 11 September 1560 the Spanish ambassador wrote to the Duchess of Parma that Cecil had confided in him that he wanted to retire because ' he clearly foresaw the ruin of the realm through Robert's intimacy with the Queen, who surrendered all affairs to him and meant to marry him.' According to the ambassador, reporting an interview with Cecil after his arrival in Windsor on 6 September, Cecil heartily wished that Robert Dudley were in Paradise, but 'ended by saying that Robert was thinking of killing his wife, who was publicly announced to be ill, although she was quite well and would take care they did not poison her. He said surely God would never allow such a wicked thing to be done.' De Quadra went on: 'The next day [i.e. implicitly 7 or 8 September] the Queen told me as she returned from hunting that Robert's wife was dead or nearly so, and asked me not to say anything about it.'[25] De Quadra subsequently said that he had met the Queen the next day (again, implicitly 7 or 8 September), and she had told him that Lord Robert's wife was dead, or almost so, and the bishop added that nothing could be worse, as far as he was concerned, than to have Cecil in charge of the situation: '. . . but the outcome of it all might be the imprisonment of the Queen and the proclamation of the Earl of Huntingdon as king.'[26]

Since he arrived in Windsor on 6 September, and news of Amye's death did not reach there until 9 September, the effect of De Quadra's despatch was to give the impression that the Queen knew of the death before it had actually happened, but this is only implicit in his account, since he did not write it until 11 September, which seems a long time to wait to pass on such a potentially disastrous piece of news. Had he wanted to make the accusation direct, we may well assume that he would not have hesitated to do so. In any case, this was not chiefly the point at issue, and certainly not at the time. What mattered most was the fact that just when everyone had expected something terrible to happen, it did, and nothing could undo it. Robert Dudley may well have wanted his unfortunate wife removed, but the timing and manner of her departing could hardly have been more devastating in their effect.

Robert Dudley was also at Windsor when he was informed of the death of his wife at Cumnor, and immediately he sent Sir Thomas Blount on Monday, 9 September, to find out what had happened. As he was going towards Cumnor, Blount met one Bowes, a messenger, who was making for Windsor with the news that on the previous evening, that is, Sunday 8 September, Amye had been found lying dead at the foot of the staircase, but with no visible signs of hurt. Bowes also told Blount that on that day, since it was Abingdon Fair day, Lady Dudley had given orders that all the household was to go to the fair. At this Mrs Odingsell, the sister of Mr Hyde and the lady companion or housekeeper, remarked that it was not appropriate for people such as themselves to go to the fair on the sabbath, at which Lady Dudley apparently became rather angry, and said that: '. . . she [Mrs Odingsell] might choose and go at her pleasure, but all hers [her servants] should go.'[27] And go they did, leaving only Lady Dudley, Mrs Owen and Mrs Odingsell in the house.

Bowes continued his journey to Windsor, and Blount carried on towards Cumnor, but did not go there directly. He stopped at Abingdon, about four miles from Cumnor, and spent the night there at an inn. He told the landlord that he was making for Gloucestershire, and asked him what news there was locally. Naturally the death of Lady Dudley was uppermost in his mind, but when pressed to give his opinion, the landlord was reluctant to do so. He said that some people said well, but others said evil, and when pressed again by Blount, he said that he thought that it must have been a misfortune, since it happened in the house of Mr Forster, who was an honest gentleman.

The following morning, Tuesday 10 September, Blount picked up what talk he was able to in and around Abingdon and Cumnor, and then went to the house, where he heard substantially the same story from Lady Dudley's maid, Mrs Pinto. She felt that it could only have been an accident, because Lady Dudley was 'a good virtuous gentlewoman, and daily would pray upon her knees; and divers times I have heard her pray to God to deliver her from desperation.' This last remark made Blount prick up his ears. He asked Mrs Pinto whether she thought that Lady Dudley had an evil eye in her mind — i.e., any thought of suicide, but to this Mrs Pinto responded firmly, 'No, good Mr Blount, do not judge so of my words: if you should so gather, I am sorry I said so much.'[28]

Blount then set all this down in a letter to his master from Cumnor, dated 11 September and already quoted, which is now in the Pepys Collection at Magdalene College, Cambridge. He then went on to write that he had subsequently heard several things at Cumnor that had inclined him to believe that Lady Dudley had been rather distraught latterly. Furthermore, an inquest had already been opened by the coroner. Hardly had he despatched this letter than a messenger arrived from Windsor with a letter from Lord Robert, written on receipt of Bowes' news. Perhaps it seems strange that the husband did not go at once himself to the scene of his wife's sudden and mysterious demise. Indeed, did it not reveal a want of feeling verging on the callously indifferent? At the same time, he must surely have known that there would be many people only too happy to besmirch his reputation with such a crime — if crime there in fact was — and his presence could well be seen as having the aim of influencing a jury composed of simple country folk, and of inhibiting the discovery of the truth of the matter. Alternatively he might have been accused of having bribed them. In the circumstances, then, he probably did well to keep away at this point. Certainly the Queen sent him from her presence for as long as the shadow of accusation hung over him, and he took himself off to Kew. If we are to regard the letter to Blount as sincere, and there seems little reason for not doing so, then Robert Dudley was fully aware of all this:

Cousin Blount,

Immediately upon your departing from me, there came to me Bowes, by whom I do understand that my wife is dead, and, as he saith, by a fall from a pair of stairs: little other understanding can I have from him. The greatness and the suddenness of the misfortune doth so perplex me, until I do hear from you how the matter standeth, or how this evil doth light upon me, considering what the malicious world will bruit as I can take no rest. And, because I have no way to purge myself of the malicious talk that I know the wicked world will use, but one, which is the very plain truth to be known, I do pray you, as you have loved me, and do tender me and my quietness, and as now my special trust is in you, that you will use all devices and means you can possible for the learning of the truth, wherein have no respect to any living person; and as by your own travail and diligence, so likewise by order of law, I mean, by calling of the coroner, and charging him to the uttermost from me to have good regard to make choice of no light or slight persons, but the discreetest and substantial men for the juries; such as for their knowledge may be able to search honourably and duly, by all manner of examinations, the bottom of the matter; and for their uprightness will earnestly and sincerely deal therein, without respect. And that the body be viewed and searched accordingly by them, and in every respect to proceed by order and law. In the meantime, cousin Blount, let me be advertised from you, by this bearer, with all speed, how the matter doth stand; for, as the cause and the manner thereof doth marvellously trouble me, considering my case many ways, so shall I not be at rest, till I may be ascertained thereof: praying you ever, as my trust is in you, and as I have ever loved you, do not dissemble with me, neither let anything be hid from me, but send me your true conceit and opinion of the matter, whether it happened by chance or villainy, and fail not to let me hear continually from you. And thus fare you well. In much haste, from Windsor, this 9th day of September in the evening. Your loving friend and kinsman, much perplexed.

R.D.

There was a postscript: 'I have sent for my brother [i.e. brother-in-law] Appleyard, because he is her brother, and other of her friends also, to be there, that they may be privy and see how all things do proceed.'[29]

In addition to John Appleyard, who was the late Amye's half-brother, she had an illegitimate brother, Arthur Robsart. Appleyard was High Sheriff of Norfolk for 1558. Furthermore, Mr Norreys and Sir Richard Blount were both on the scene. The jury decided that 'they could find no presumptions of evil', but Lord Robert wrote from Kew on 12 September that he wanted a second jury to be summoned:

To deal . . . earnestly, carefully, and truly . . . to find it as they shall see it fall out. And if it fall out a chance or misfortune, then so to find; and if it appear villainy (as God forbid so mischievous or wicked body should live) then to find it so, and God willing, I shall never fear the day of prosecution accordingly, what person soever it may appear any way to touch; as well for the just punishment of the act as for mine own true justification; for as I would be sorry in my heart any such evil should be committed, so full it will appear to the world my innocency.[30]

The jury returned a verdict of accidental death, but it left behind it a cloud of suspicion and doubt that has not entirely been removed, even to this day, and which Robert Dudley never managed to evade for the rest of his life. Of course Amye might well have been going to die in any case, if modern medical opinions are correct about her probable cause of death.[31] She was known to have had a malady in one of her breasts — probably breast cancer — and this could have made her spine very brittle, to the extent that even walking, let alone a stumble or fall, could cause a spontaneous broken neck. The illness was already bad enough, but the additional fact that Amye knew that she was an impediment to her husband's advancement might have increased her depression, and even induced her to hasten a death that she may well have regarded as inevitable. That it should have happened when it did — when people were predicting that it would — was an extremely unfortunate coincidence. Whatever the truth of the matter, her death effectively dashed Robert Dudley's immediate hopes of aspiring to the Queen's hand, though — as was to happen so often with Elizabeth — he soon returned to favour, and the whole incident seemed to have been forgotten, which is remarkable in view of its potential implications. Robert Dudley had written at one moment to Blount: 'Well, cousin, God's will be done; and I wish he had made me the poorest worm that creepeth on the ground, so this mischance had not happened to me.'[32]

In a kind gesture, Cecil went to visit Robert Dudley at Kew, and the latter did not fail to appreciate what this meant:

Sir, I thank you much for your being here, and the great friendship you have shown towards me I shall not forget. I am very loath to wish you here again, but would be very glad to be with you there. I pray you let me hear from you, what you think best for me to do. If you doubt, I pray you ask the question, for the sooner you can advise me thither, the more I shall thank you. I am sorry so sudden a chance shall breed me so great a change, for methinks I am here all this while, as it were in a dream, and too far, too far, from the place I am bound to be; where, methinks, also, this long idle time cannot excuse me, for the duty I have to discharge elsewhere. I pray you help him, that sues to be at liberty, out of so great bondage. Forget me not, though you see me not, and I will remember you, and fail ye not . . . Your very assured

R. Dudley[33]

The effect of the news on the Dudleys was revealing. When it reached the Hastings family at Ashby de la Zouch on 17 September, Robert Dudley's brother-in-law was in the middle of writing a letter to him to accompany a gift of six venison pies: '. . . of a stag which was bred in the little garden at Ashby'. He was also anxious to learn: '. . . how the baking doth like you for I am in some doubt my cook hath not done his part'. Then the news arrived, and the best that one can say for what follows is that it makes adequate expression of condolence, but nothing about Lord Robert's personal loss, nor is there any reference to his sister Katherine, Hastings' wife, or her feelings.

> As I ended my letter I understood by letters the death of my lady your wife. I doubt not but long before this time you have considered what a happy hour it is which bringeth man from sorrow, to joy, from mortality to immortality, from care and trouble to rest and quietness and that the Lord above worketh all for the best to them that love him, well I will leave my babbling and bid the buzzard cease to teach the falcon to fly, and so end my rude postscript.[34]

Others were less nice in their reactions. Thomas Lever, writing to Sir Francis Knollys and Sir William Cecil from Coventry on 17 September, referred to the suspicion and muttering there about the death of Amye, and there must have been similar reactions up and down the country.[35] Perhaps Sir Francis recalled this in later years when he learned that his daughter Lettice was involved with Robert Dudley, and heard the rumours that were in circulation.

Amye's coffin was taken to Oxford on Friday, 20 September, and placed in Worcester College. On 22 September she was buried in St Mary's Church with much expense and pomp, though Robert did not attend. There is a legend that the twenty-year-old Edmund Campion was chosen to pronounce the funeral oration in English, since he was already well known for his eloquence, and this may subsequently have brought him to Robert Dudley's attention. Certainly he was much in evidence during the visit of the Queen to Oxford with Dudley in 1566.[36]

The mutterings continued, however, both at home and abroad, and the person of Arthur Guntor, who was to figure largely in later investigations, is first mentioned in the Cecil papers at this point.[37] In fact he stated quite categorically that the Queen was to marry Robert Dudley,[38] which is exactly what many other people must have been thinking and saying. On 26 October 1560 he said to one George Cotton that:

> . . . ere this my Lord Robert's wife is dead, and she broke her neck, but it is in a number of heads that the Queen will marry him. If she do, you shall see a great stir, for my lord is sure of the Earl of Pembroke, and the Lord Rich, with divers others, be ready, with the putting up of his finger, and then you shall see the White Horse bestir himself, for my lord is of great power, but a man shall have a ruffian with a dog to dispatch him out of a shop.[39]

In Paris the English ambassador, Sir Nicholas Throckmorton, was so appalled at the gossip that he sent his confidential secretary, Robert Jones, to England the next month (November) to let the Queen know exactly what was being said at the French Court. Probably the most disturbing was the remark attributed to the nineteen-year-old Mary, Queen of Scots, wife of Francis II, and at that point still Queen of France: 'The Queen of England is going to marry her horsekeeper, who has killed his wife to make room for her.'[40] When Jones finally had his audience of the Queen she stated that the jury had cleared both Lord Robert's honesty and her own honour,[41] but Jones detected that the Queen must have had time for reflection, for he maintained: 'Surely the matter of my Lord Robert doth much perplex her, and it is never like to take place.'[42] In confirmation of this he pointed to the fact that the Queen had contemplated making Lord Robert an earl, but when the necessary document had been drawn up and brought to her for signature, instead of taking up her pen, she took a knife, and cut it in ribbons, declaring that the Dudleys had been traitors in three generations.

The loss of face in the eyes of the other courtiers must have stung Robert Dudley almost as much as the loss of the earldom, and he remonstrated with the Queen, who patted him on the cheek and said: 'No, no! The bear and the ragged staff are not so easily overthrown!'[43] Later the Queen intimated that she might make him Earl of Leicester on Twelfth Night 1561, but again she held off, and in her heart she probably knew that it was still too soon to give him such an honour. For the rumours persisted. On 22 January 1561 De Quadra reported that Sir Henry Sidney had talked to him about using King Philip to promote Robert Dudley's marriage to Elizabeth, and that he would become the king's vassal. He also said that certain preachers in their pulpits were speaking about Amye Robsart in a manner that was prejudicial to the honour of the Queen.[44] Then on 27 February, the very next month, it was reported that one John White said that: 'Lord Robert did swive the Queen',[45] and it was not until 1567 that some of the immediate sources of intrigue were finally exposed with the examination of Appleyard and Huggins (*see* p. 104). Even then, the malicious gossip was to go on for the rest of Robert Dudley's life.

For his family, however, Robert remained a point of focus, as we see from a letter sent to him on 7 February 1561 by his sister, Katherine Hastings, in which she reminded him of her husband's impoverished state: 'I assure you when he shall go [to Court] he shall not be able to carry forty pounds in his purse to bear his charges the whole journey.'[46] It was important for any nobleman to keep up appearances in such a situation, but even more so for one who was of royal descent himself, and a member of the Dudley clan into the bargain. It was in the course of this year that Henry Hastings succeeded to the title of Earl of Huntingdon.

This year Robert Dudley used his influence with the Queen when he intervened in a dispute between the Inner and Middle Temples in London as to which should have control over one of the smaller inns of court. The Inner Temple, as a result, retained their control, and so the members voted that they would never be retained against Robert Dudley or his heirs, and that they would always give him legal assistance. They also placed his coat-of-arms in their hall, and that year their Christmas celebrations were dedicated to him. Moreover the association lasted throughout his life, and even in 1594 his widow was able to use it to obtain an admission for a candidate of hers.[47]

On 24 June — Midsummer Day — 1561, Lord Robert gave a party on the river for the Queen, and she invited De Quadra to watch the spectacle from her barge. He described it all in a letter to the King dated 30 June.[48] As the day drew on, and an atmosphere of jollity prevailed, Lord Robert suggested jokingly that, since the bishop was present, he could perform the marriage ceremony between Lord Robert and the Queen there and then. The Queen replied that she doubted whether the bishop's English was good enough, but the bishop himself took the thing seriously, and said that if the Queen would rid her realm of heretics, and she and Lord Robert brought back the true religion, then they might be married whenever they pleased, and he would be happy to officiate. On the same day that he wrote to King Philip describing this event, De Quadra wrote to Cardinal Granvella in Brussels: 'You will see by my letter to the King how we are going on. She on her part knows that it is to her interest to keep well with me, because with this love affair of hers she would be a lost woman if the King our master so pleased.'[49]

Next month, July, the Queen went on her summer progress into Suffolk. It was a difficult time. In France Mary Queen of Scots was now a widow, and had decided to return to Scotland. Pressures on Elizabeth to marry were, as ever, insistent. Her temper frayed, and in a conversation with Matthew Parker, Archbishop of Canterbury (according to what he told Cecil): 'She took occasion to speak in that bitterness of the holy estate of matrimony that I was in a horror to hear her.'[50] It was also a summer of terrible storms. In June the spire of St Paul's Cathedral had been struck by lightning and on the evening of 30 July, between 8 and 9 p.m., was seen '. . . as great thundering and lightning as any man had ever heard till past 10; after that, great rains till midnight, insomuch that the people thought the world was at an end and the day of doom was come, it was so terrible.'[51]

It was highly unfortunate, therefore, that Lady Catherine Grey should choose the arrival of the Court at Ipswich to reveal, first to Lady Seintlow — known better, perhaps, as Bess of Hardwick — and then to Lord Robert Dudley, that she had been secretly married to the Earl of Hertford, eldest son of Protector Somerset, and was now in an advanced state of pregnancy. However, not long after her wedding her husband had been ordered abroad, the clergyman who had carried out the ceremony was not to be found (since he was a Catholic priest this was perhaps not surprising), and the only witness — Lady Jane Seymour — was now dead. To crown all, the bride had lost her deed of jointure. Lady Seintlow was furious that Catherine Grey had made her privy to such information, and Lord Robert was equally annoyed, over and above the fact that she had gone to his bedroom at night, since that was the only time that she might be sure to find him alone.[52] The Queen had to be told, and since Lady Catherine was of the blood royal — in fact in her own eyes, and those of several others, she was heir to the crown — her eventual consignment to the Tower was almost inevitable. Lady Seintlow was also put there for a spell, which can hardly have pleased her. It must have been the fact of the potential heir to be born to Catherine Grey that aggravated Elizabeth's anger as much as the unauthorised marriage, especially in this turbulent and tiresome summer of 1561.

If he had not cares enough of his own with his personal problems, his demanding relatives, and other suitors at home, Robert Dudley was also rapidly becoming involved in foreign matters. A letter in the Pepys Collection from W. Herlle, dated 17 August 1561, commends to the Queen's notice Otto, Duke of Brunswick and Lüneburg, as:

> . . . worthy of her Majesty's pension for his wisdom, forwardness and goodwill to her Majesty's subjects. He is but about thirty-two, yet apt for all things, well proportioned, and of mean stature with a comely auburn beard. His country lies so hard upon the Elp's [sic] stream that upon time of service no place were more commodious. He has written several times to England, but received no answer. A letter would make such a man more careful to give larger intelligence of things.[53]

Herlle was travelling in the Low Countries, having already written to Robert Dudley from Antwerp on 12 July, and had then gone on to Amsterdam. Of course it was a time when almost all important figures — let alone sovereign rulers — maintained their own information services scattered across Europe. Robert Dudley's own father had done so. But this sort of opening might lead on to other things, and at this point in her reign, and indeed one might almost say for most of her reign, Elizabeth was anxious to avoid involvement on the Continent, certainly if it entailed the expense of armies. The Duke of Brunswick felt that he had been treated badly in the circumstances, since he had occasion to write later to Robert Dudley, from Langenhagen on 18 April 1563:

> I am astonished that you have not written to say whether the Queen wants my people or not. I do not think that my good will ought to be paid with ingratitude. Coming to my lands I would look for very good people, and I have now more than 2,000 or 3,000 soldiers thinking that the Queen would take me into her service. I put myself in your hands for an answer yes or no so that I may not remain with all the expenses, as I see that you are a very real friend. I pray you answer shortly.[54]

The duke continued to approach Dudley. On 24 November 1564, for example, he asked him to: '. . . show yourself in this affair, as you have promised by letters, a true brother and friend. I will serve you with my heart and blood when needed.'[55]

On 6 September 1561 George Gilpin wrote to Robert Dudley from Brussels,[56] and there is a strong possibility that a letter from Guido

Cavalcanti this year, also in the Pepys Collection, was addressed to him, too. Certainly Dudley had close ties with the Italian community in London and elsewhere, and Cavalcanti had been involved in negotiating the Treaty of Cateau-Cambrésis on Elizabeth's behalf. Although a Florentine by birth, Cavalcanti had considerable dealings with the Venetian residents in London. There was no official minister from Venice to England between 1537 and 1602, though in 1560 the Venetians living in London elected a Vice-Consul on their own responsibility. The Signoria soon put an end to the unofficial appointment. Cavalcanti's letter, which is not signed, but is almost certainly in his handwriting, recalls that when he was in England he often heard great lords there marvel that since the Queen's accession no one had been sent from Venice to pay their respects to the Queen on behalf of the Republic. As he took leave of the Queen she had alluded to this fact, expressing regret that she had been unable to maintain and increase the friendship which had once existed between her predecessors and Venice. Cavalcanti replied that the Signoria was of the opinion that the Queen would marry, and was therefore waiting to send an ambassador who would congratulate both her accession and her marriage at the same time. Since it now looked as if they had been wrong on the second point, it seemed too late to attempt to rectify the mistake over the first. To this the Queen tartly remarked that any time for correcting an error was better than none.[57]

If Robert Dudley were a serious candidate for the Queen's hand, then the letter might have had the effect of drawing him out. Whatever Dudley thought, however, Cavalcanti must soon have realised that what the Queen intended was a totally different matter. This ought to have stood him in good stead when he found himself some years later acting on behalf of Catherine de' Medici in the French marriage negotiations with Elizabeth. As far as any political overtones of this letter may have been concerned, however, it is difficult to see what possible political interest Robert Dudley could have had, and indeed subsequent evidence suggests that his involvement was only ever commercial. This would also be true of the majority of his dealings with the Italians in general. Either he employed them in his household, as messengers, artisans or in the specific area of horse breeding and training, possibly also as musicians; or he used their services, both as a patron and also as a client. Among the tradesmen's bills at Longleat, for example, are some from the goldsmith Benedict Spinola for the period 1562–6.[58]

Of foreign residents in London, it was not only the Italians with

41

whom Robert Dudley had dealings at this time. In 1561 the French preacher and writer Jean Veron dedicated to him his *A Most Necessary treatise of free will* . . . from which one appreciates yet again to what extent Dudley was seen as a focus for those looking for support, encouragement and protection, and especially when he was seen to be so much in the Queen's favour. And yet for Robert himself that favour did not extend as far as he wished. Whatever rewards he might have felt were his due from the Queen — and a step up in the degree of nobility would have been an obvious target for him — it was his brother Ambrose who was the first to achieve this. The patent is dated 26 December that year (1561), at Westminster, and Ambrose Dudley, knight, Baron Lisle, was elevated to the Earldom of Warwick.[59] Of course it could simply be regarded as royal permission to succeed to what was his due, since his father held both titles, and an act of restitution for his brother and two sisters had been passed in the previous reign.[60] In this way, however, and by waiting for a certain period, the Queen could maintain, if need be, that Ambrose's loyalty had been proved beyond question. As Lord Robert wrote to Lord Shrewsbury the following day, 'having reposed a special confidence in your lordship's friendship and good will towards my brother Ambrose and me, to participate unto your lordship these comfortable news; which are that it hath pleased the Queen's Majesty, of her great bounty and goodness, to restore our house to the name of Warwick, and as yesterday hath created my said brother earl thereof.'[61] In his *State Worthies*, David Lloyd remarked: 'His brother Ambrose was the heir to the estate, and he [Lord Robert] to the wisdom of that family.'[62] How right he was remains to be seen. Not to be left entirely in the cold, on 23 February 1562, Robert was made Constable of Windsor Castle, and on the 26th of that month he was assigned the Constableship of Warwick Castle, too, with the Stewardship of Warwick itself.[63]

Despite Lord Robert's opening up of relations with the French Protestants, he was still able to tell De Quadra in January 1562 that he wanted help from Spain, and on the terms already outlined, but by 8 May he was writing to Throckmorton in Paris about the possibility of Elizabeth sending aid to the Huguenots. Robert knew that the question was fraught with danger for the Queen, for open aid for the Huguenots would be tantamount to an act of aggression as far as the French crown was concerned. 'But,' wrote Lord Robert, '(Thanks be to God), she doth not so much measure common policy as she doth weigh the prosperity of true religion, as well to the world as for conscience sake.'[64] In view of

Robert's known sympathies in matters of religion later, we may assume that he was not being hypocritical in this letter, though he may well have been turning his religious sentiments to his own end, which would by no means have been beyond him.

He was often on the move at this time. In May 1562, for example, we have record of a payment of three shillings and fourpence made at Grimsthorpe, home of Catherine Willoughby, Dowager Duchess of Suffolk: '. . . to one of the Queen's stable which brought my mistress a horse to ride with my Lord Robert,'[65] and also this year, in the records of Beverley, is a note of twenty shillings paid to his bearward, and five pence for wine for him.[66] From the same source we have note of a much larger sum — £59 16s 11d — paid on two occasions for going to London to Lord Robert Dudley, '. . . as appears by two bills thereof'. There are some interesting 'resolucions', namely that the rents formerly paid to the Queen for '. . . the Dyngs, Westwood, etc.' are now payable to Lord Robert Dudley, but that for the Trinity Maison Dieu is still paid to the Queen. There are similar exchanges and agreements recorded elsewhere between the Queen and Dudley, and in this way he continued to build up his income so as to afford the state to which he had become accustomed.

Dedications also continued. William Fulwood's translation of Gratarolo, called in English *The Castle of Memory*, was dedicated to Robert Dudley, and also in this year Robert Fills dedicated his translation, *The Laws and Statutes of Geneva*, published in London, and J. Rowbothum dedicated his translation, from the French of Gruzar, of Damiano's treatise on chess. This was in fact the first English edition of this famous book, known in English as *The Play of the Cheasts*. Rowbothum also published, the next year, in 1563, an adaptation and translation, by William Fulke and Ralph Lever, of *The Most Noble, ancient, and learned play called the philosophers game*. Printed by Rowland Hall, there was a woodcut of Robert Dudley on the title verso. The verse around the illustration runs:

As reason rules Lord Robert's life with line of right wiseness
So doughty deeds cause Dudley's fame t'endure for age doubtless
The physiognomy here figured, appears by painter's art:
But valiant are the virtues that possess the inward part.
Which in no wise may painted be, yet plainly do appear.
And shine abroad in every place with beams most bright and clear.

No one could claim that the verse is distinguished, let alone original in its sentiments. On the other hand, one cannot simply dismiss it out of hand, along with most of the dedications to Elizabethan patrons. Often, when one cuts through the undergrowth, interesting facts are laid bare, and if it does nothing else, this particular verse shows that Dudley's standing was such at the time that people either disliked him or felt that he was worth flattering. It seems that very few articulate people simply ignored him. There was to be a further spate of dedications in 1563, notably Richard Grafton's *An Abridgement of the Chronicles of England*; William Fulke's *Goodly Gallery*; Thomas Gale's *Certain works of Surgery (chirurgerie)*, and Richard Rainolde's . . . *Foundation of Rhetoric*.

In 1562 Robert Dudley received an annuity of £1,000, to be paid out of tonnage and poundage, until the Queen should give him lands of equal value; three licences to export woollen cloth, and the estate of Sir Andrew Dudley, his uncle, whose will is at Longleat, and whose goods had reverted to the crown on his attainder in 1553. It is easy to overlook the more mundane aspects of Robert Dudley's existence when the surface was so full of splendour and excitement. All that had to be paid for, however, and when one delves beneath the surface the clues are there. There is a letter in the Pepys Collection, for example, dated 29 May 1565 from Anthony, Viscount Montague, in Bruges, about poundage and customs duties on cloths, and at Longleat an assignment, dated 27 March 1563, of patents for the export of woollen cloth and clothes, from Robert Dudley to the Merchant Adventurers of London.[67]

In June 1562 De Quadra's confidential secretary, Borghese, betrayed his master to Cecil. One of the matters discovered was that the bishop had had secret enquiries made in the Low Countries to discover what sort of loyalty, if any, Lady Lennox might be able to command amongst the Catholic exiles there to put her son Lord Darnley on the English throne. Margaret Douglas, Countess of Lennox, was the daughter of Margaret Tudor, sister to Henry VIII, by her second marriage to Archibald Douglas, Earl of Angus. Another matter was the things De Quadra had written to King Philip about the Queen and Lord Robert. De Quadra's defence was that he was only repeating what people were actually saying, and what indeed the Queen herself had told him. Apparently when returning from a visit to Lord Pembroke's house one afternoon with Lord Robert, the Queen was greeted by her ladies-in-waiting, who asked whether they were to kiss his hand as well as that of their royal mistress. She replied that they were not to believe all they heard. De Quadra went even further. He said that two or three days later Lord Robert himself told him that the Queen had promised to marry him, only not that year. Then the Queen had said that if she had to marry an Englishman, it should be Lord Robert. The ambassador then went on, 'I do not think, considering what others say of the Queen, that I should be doing her any injury in writing to his Majesty that she was married, which in fact I never have written, and I am sorry I cannot do so with truth.'[68]

If only Robert had been less consumed with his own ambition to marry the Queen, he might have used his knowledge of her character and weighed her words more carefully. She would marry, perhaps; but not this year. If she were obliged to marry an Englishman, it would be Dudley — but then at the time she was not obliged to marry anyone, despite the pressures being put on her to do so; and of course she never did. Lord Robert might profitably have repeated to himself the words that Elizabeth was said to have written on a window pane with a diamond at Woodstock: 'Much suspected, by me,/Nothing proved can be . . .'[69] The object of his desire, or mere ambition, was well schooled in the art of evasion, but it seems that his vanity dulled his senses to the fact. Was he really, as David Lloyd maintained, heir to the wisdom of the Dudley family — for if he was, then that wisdom in no way matched that of Elizabeth Tudor.

The next month, July 1562, a new stimulus was given to the Swedish marriage bid when John Keyle, an attaché to the Swedish embassy, arrived in London. As he reported back to Sweden:

> Lord Robert at my coming made very great search for me to some of his friends, that he might speak with me ere I dealt with the Queen and Council. But when he saw he might not, he wrought marvellously to have had me in prison . . . But he has troubled himself in vain, wherefore he is very angry, and now his cutters look as though they would do some hurt, and I have been warned to take heed.[70]

The Queen must have heard about this, because she rebuked Lord Robert in the Presence Chamber, in front of the Court, according to Keyle's report of 27 July, and he asked leave to go abroad. Of course Lord Robert had no such intention. He knew too well the truth of the saying *L'absent a toujours tort*.

There were, in any case, other matters on hand. Elizabeth had agreed that summer to meet Mary Queen of Scots at York. In the event the Council voted against it, but even if they had not done so, developments in France would have made the same decision for them. That July the Duke of Guise began to move against the Huguenots, and in the circumstances a Protestant monarch could hardly hold an official meeting with a member of that same house of Guise on her own — officially Protestant — territory. There were of course other considerations, too, such as the fact that the north of England was still largely Catholic, and the landowners there still held almost feudal sway. Moreover Mary had still not ratified the Treaty of Edinburgh, negotiated by Cecil, and continued to call herself Queen of England. It was the events in France, however, that carried the most force. Under the terms of the Treaty of Hampton Court the English were to garrison Le Havre on behalf of the Huguenots, and 3,000 men were to assist Condé in defending Rouen and Dieppe. Ambrose Dudley, Earl of Warwick, was to be in command of Le Havre.

Elizabeth wrote to the Queen of Scots on 15 October, explaining why England was intervening in France: '. . . to guard our houses from spoil when our neighbours' are burning.'[71] There was also the need to keep the Channel ports open for English traders and, not least, support for the Huguenots against the persecutions they were suffering for their faith. The letter ended: 'My hot fever prevents my writing more.' Five days earlier the Queen had taken a bath, in the belief that it would refresh her, and had then gone outside. Dr Burcot, a German who had treated Lord Hunsdon successfully, diagnosed smallpox, but the Queen refused to let him remain in her sight. That night she wrote to the Queen of Scots that she was so ill that the doctors thought that she would die. The Council was hurriedly convened, and it seemed as if their worst fears were about to be realised. The Queen was going to die without a successor having been named, since few expected her to survive this illness. Winchester seemed to favour the Countess of Lennox and her son Lord Darnley. Bacon and Hunsdon were probably for Lady Catherine Grey — who at least could provide the nation with an heir, and a male one at that — but for the fact that she was in the Tower, and for this reason Pembroke and Bedford, who might well have supported her, went along with Lord Robert Dudley in his support for his brother-in-law, Henry Hastings, Earl of Huntingdon, who was of Plantagenet descent. The one name that does not seem to have been canvassed was that of Mary Queen of Scots. Before any decision had been taken, the Queen recovered consciousness, and begged the Council to make Robert Dudley Protector of the Realm with a title and an income of £20,000 a year. She furthermore swore that although she had always loved Lord Robert dearly, as God was her witness, nothing improper had ever passed between them. She also asked that his body servant,

Tamworth, should be given £500 annually.[72] The Council agreed to her requests in her extremity, though luckily they did not have to decide whether or not to fulfil those promises. Lord Robert was, however, admitted to the Council on 20 October, though the Duke of Norfolk was also included. No doubt Cecil felt it necessary so as to keep the peace between them.

Dr Burcot was recalled, in spite of his justifiable reluctance to return to the spot where he had been insulted, and his treatment saved the Queen's life.[73] Unfortunately Lord Robert's sister, Lady Mary Sidney, who nursed the Queen, also caught the disease, and was disfigured in the way that the Queen miraculously escaped. As her husband wrote when he saw her for the first time after her illness: 'I left her a full fair lady, in mine eyes at least, the fairest, and when I returned I found her as foul a lady as the smallpox could make her, which she did take by continued attendance on her Majesty's most precious person.'[74] Henceforth Lady Mary was understandably reluctant to show herself much in public, and when at Court tended to keep to her own apartments. There were of course her children to claim her attention — Philip, Ambrosia and Mary, and the following year she was to give birth to Robert — and there was the delightful family home of Penshurst in Kent, and her husband's headquarters as Lord President of Wales, Ludlow Castle. Dr Burcot, for his pains, was made a grant of lands, together with a pair of gold spurs that were said to have belonged to Henry VII (see n. 73).

By 26 November 1562 the Queen was well enough to go out, for that afternoon Lord Robert and Lord Windsor — according to a letter from Henry Killigrew to Throckmorton — were in Windsor Park having a shooting match when the Queen came out with Lord Hunsdon's daughter, Kate Carey, and two other ladies — but dressed simply 'as a maid'.[75] The Queen is reported to have said to Lord Robert that 'he was beholden to her, for she had passed the pikes for his sake.' It is tempting to read into this somewhat enigmatic remark a connotation which, in the circumstances, it was not intended to have. Either way, however, it draws attention to the depth of her involvement with Robert Dudley. No matter how deep that involvement was — and the specific reference to Dudley's body servant Tamworth would seem to imply that it was to a considerable degree — we cannot assume that their union was sexually complete, certainly not if her words spoken during her illness are to be taken at face value, and one may assume that her supposed deathbed would be the one place where they ought to be so taken. Moreover her behaviour from a psychological point of view vis à vis Robert Dudley throughout her life was hardly consistent with that of a woman who had given herself totally to a man — even if the woman was Elizabeth Tudor, Queen of England.

As Parliament prepared to assemble in January 1563, the question of the succession and the Queen's marriage was the burning issue. At the opening service in Westminster Abbey the Dean of St Paul's, Alexander Nowell, preached before the Queen, and at her, declaring: 'All the Queen's most noble ancestors have commonly had some issue to succeed them, but her Majesty yet none.' Much more to the point was his reference to her late sister: 'For as the marriage of Queen Mary was a terrible plague to all England . . . so now the want of your marriage and issue is like to prove as great a plague . . . If your parents had been of your mind, where had you been then? Or what had become of us now?'[76]

There were plenty of problems to occupy the Queen's mind without Dr Nowell putting his somewhat rhetorical questions. For example, there were her troops in France. Although at first things did not go too badly, any expense on such a scale upset the Queen. On 23 January 1563 Ambrose wrote to Lord Robert thanking him for the fine horse he had sent him, and when he was riding that horse, with the token that the Queen had sent him round his neck, he imagined that he would do wonders.[77] In return he sent Robert the best setter in France. Then there was the matter of Catherine Grey. Lord Hertford had been sent to the Tower, too, on his return, though the two had contrived to meet and pursue their union, to the point where, on 10 February, she produced a second son. A commission under the Archbishop of Canterbury, with Lord Robert one of the members, was set up to examine the Hertford marriage, which was declared illegal; the children were therefore declared illegitimate, and the father was fined 15,000 marks for having seduced a virgin of the blood royal.[78] Yet another problem was the Queen of Scots, and Elizabeth's proposed solution produced what was perhaps the most surprising suggestion of all, and propelled Robert Dudley into one of the more curious episodes of his career.

In March 1563 Mary's Secretary of State, William Maitland of Lethington, came south to discuss with Elizabeth his queen's claim to the succession to the English throne, and the question of her second marriage. It came as more than a surprise to Maitland, however, when Elizabeth suggested, on 23 March, that Lord Robert Dudley would make a suitable husband for his mistress. Elizabeth then went on to say — according to De Quadra, to whom Maitland gave an account of the conversation — that she wished to God Lord Warwick had the grace and good looks of Lord Robert, then each could have one of the brothers.[79] The Earl of Warwick, she went on, was not ugly, either, nor was he ungraceful, but his manner was rather rough, and he was not so gentle as Lord Robert.

In purely diplomatic terms there was much to commend this as a solution. A French or Spanish union with Scotland would have been unacceptable to England, as would a union with a Catholic member of the English nobility. Thomas Randolph, the English ambassador in Scotland, saw the Dudley match as a means of establishing good relations between the two countries, though he had difficulties at first in persuading Mary herself, and then when he had achieved that, in persuading Lord Robert, which led him to exclaim: 'Now that I have got this Queen's good will to marry where I would have her, I cannot get the man to take her for whom I was a suitor.'[80] Some time later Mary maintained that, once she had overcome her own objections, Lord Robert informed her privately that the whole thing was a huge farce in any case.[81] As to the man himself, it hardly seems conceivable that he would for a moment have agreed to leave England and Elizabeth, in spite of the famed beauty of the Scottish queen. Nor did the lure of a crown hold sufficient attraction for him. If he was to have any crown at all it was going to be the crown of England. If the proposal was a farce from beginning to end, then it certainly was to enjoy a long run.

Meanwhile, Lord Robert's brother was having little luck in France. Despite his dedication and courage, Ambrose was not successful in Le Havre. Indeed, English intervention seemed to be having the opposite effect from what had been intended. Aid designed to help the persecuted Huguenots against the Catholics had simply served to unite both factions to repel the foreign invader. What finally decided matters, however, was not bravery or force, but disease. Plague broke out amongst the English garrison, and in early July the Queen ordered its withdrawal. She sent a letter to Lord Ambrose which praised the conduct of the English troops, and went on to say that, in spite of their failure, they had vindicated the crown of England once again in France by their bravery. In her own hand the Queen added: 'My dear Warwick . . . I will rather drink in an ashen cup than that you or yours should not be succoured by sea and land, yea, and that with all speed possible, and let this my scribbling hand witness it to them all.' She then signed it, 'Yours, as my own, E.R.'[82]

Ambrose's reply captures, even at this relatively early point in the reign, the nature of the relationship that bound Elizabeth to the men who fought for her, 'Most dear Queen and gracious mistress, I have received your letter, whereby I, with the rest here, may well perceive thy great care your Majesty hath of us all, and that, in respect of our lives and safeties, you do not regard the loss of this town . . . Your Majesty's most humble and obedient subject to the death, Warwick.'[83]

There was a letter for Lord Robert, too, dated 24 July 1563, in which Ambrose thanked God that he had been spared from the plague, since he would prefer, he wrote: '. . . rather to end my life upon the breach, than by any sickness . . . Farewell my dear and loving brother, a thousand times.'[84] Unfortunately the garrison brought the plague with it when it returned to England in August. In the ensuing epidemic De Quadra died, and Lady Catherine and Lord Hertford were removed from the Tower. The mother and her younger son went to her uncle, Lord John Grey, at Pyrgo in Essex, and the father and the older boy went to his mother, the Duchess of Somerset, at Hanworth.[85]

Robert did not wait until his brother was out of quarantine, but went to visit him, as he explained to the Queen in a letter written on 7 August. This meant that he himself could not now come to Court until he had observed the necessary quarantine. By 1 September Lord Warwick was cleared, as Luis Roman, a secretary, wrote to Cardinal Granvella in Brussels, whilst the arrival of the new Spanish ambassador was awaited: 'The Earl of Warwick entered here yesterday . . . He carried his right leg tightly tied up with taffety and a wide large red band of taffety as a support.'[86] The Queen also made Ambrose a Knight of the Garter in this year of 1563, and Robert, too, came in for some more royal bounty, for he was made High Steward of Cambridge (of which university Cecil was Chancellor), and in September she made him High Steward of Windsor, which carried the annual stipend of £1 6s 8d.[87] She also gave him lands in Lancashire, Yorkshire, Rutland, Surrey, Carmarthen, Cardigan and Brecknock.[88] Certainly there was now sufficient for a survey to be necessary, and at Longleat volume XVI of the Dudley papers is a survey carried out from 29 June to 3 October 1563. But of all the Queen's bounty, this year saw what was probably the most splendid and renowned of all her gifts, the castle of Kenilworth in Warwickshire. He began to embellish it and extend its accommodation almost immediately. The huge document that constitutes the letters patent is still at Longleat,[89] itself a worthy token, with its richly decorated borders, of the significant part Kenilworth was to play in Robert Dudley's life and ambitions.

3

A Husband fit for a Queen?

I have favoured him because of his excellent disposition and his many merits
. . . A thousand eyes see all that I do . . .

Queen Elizabeth on Robert Dudley

As the autumn of 1563 drew on, Robert Dudley was progressively more involved with the Scottish Court, as is evident from a letter to him from James Stuart, Earl of Moray, dated from Stirling on 17 November, in which he acknowledged receipt of Dudley's bill of remembrance, informed him that the Queen of Scots was in good health, and '. . . desireth from her the same of the Queen's Highness her good sister [i.e. Elizabeth].' Randolph, he said, was shortly to return, when Dudley would be more amply informed.[1] By 15 January of the next year (1564), Thomas Randolph was writing to Robert Dudley from Edinburgh, in unequivocal terms:

> I assure your lordship the worst I intend you is to marry a queen [but not, presumably, Mary] . . . The Queen [of Scots] hath recovered much of her health . . . I have wished this queen two or three of your lordship's geldings, fit for her own saddle; the other were so well liked . . . There is here good news of my Lord Warwick to be President of York. We think it no small benefit of good that two such earls as his lordship and my Lord of Bedford shall be placed so near unto this country [Bedford was given the command at Berwick] . . .

There was a postscript: 'Your lordship shall be shortly written unto in favour of my Lord Bothwell, whose suit is to be out of England, whereof I think there will come no hurt, for where he is, he doth no good nor never will.'[2]

Whether he was paving the way for the next letter or not, the Earl of Moray certainly wrote to Robert Dudley on 31 January 1564 from Edinburgh, to the effect that Elizabeth had held up Bothwell at Newcastle: 'I have understood of him his present estate wherewith he is annoyed and is willing, if it might stand with the [English] Queen's pleasure there, to visit other realms. I pray you to take consideration of his reasonable desires and at least for my sake to procure his liberty in the premises at the Queen's hands there.'[3] In the end Bothwell was granted permission to go to Scotland — or to leave England — with the eventual consequence we know well. Was it an error of judgement on Elizabeth's part, or a piece of cynical calculation?

It was not only the marriage of the Queen of Scots that involved Dudley that year, however; there was also that of the Queen of England herself. As early as 1 February 1564 Robert Dudley had himself been consulted about Elizabeth's marriage, as we see from a letter at Hatfield,[4] and there is another letter in the same collection from Cecil to Mundt, dated 8 September that year, about Robert Dudley as a future consort.[5] Cecil's most famous words (*see* pp. 8-9) only came later, however, in April 1566, when he set down his thoughts on the matter.[6]

Then there was news for Dudley from the Continent, and we see from various letters the standing he enjoyed there. On 29 March 1564 John Shers, who often wrote on foreign matters, sent a letter from Brussels,[7] for example, but what is important is the extent to which the correspondence reveals Dudley's position in the eyes of foreign rulers, and those of France in particular.

During the course of April 1564 there had been considerable correspondence between Robert Dudley and Sir Nicholas Throckmorton, ambassador to France, and his servant Thomas Barnaby, and from it we learn that Dudley seriously contemplated a visit to the French Court. It was the time of the Treaty of Troyes, which was signed on 6 April 1564, according to the ambassador's letter. The French were going to send Michel de Castelnau, Marquis de Mauvissière, to England in celebration of the event, though when Throckmorton wrote on 8 April 1564 to Dudley from Troyes, the name had not been announced:

I learn from the Duke d'Aumâle and other good horsemen that your rider Hercules [Trinchetta] is specially able to break a dogged horse [MS torn at this point].

I doubt whether it be meet for you to make so long a journey [as to Lyons]. Coming in journey it will be mid-June before you can arrive at this Court, and not much more haste is to be made if you come in post, because you cannot make more than four posts a day.

No one is yet appointed to take the oaths of each other's prince. I hear that you shall be grateful to the king if you come to do this office.[8]

As ever, interest in horses and horsemanship provides an immediate bond and topic of conversation, but one gets the impression that there was a genuine desire on the part of the French Court to see the man who had captivated the Queen of England. This is strengthened by the letter Thomas Barnaby wrote from Troyes on 14 April 1564:

I learn that the Italian esquire Hercules [Trinchetta] gives place to no other in breaking young and rough horses. He will be brought to you by De Mauvissière, who is sent to congratulate the peace [the Treaty of Troyes], and to see if he can induce you to come here. Employ your credit with the Queen that he may taste the same liberality as Mr Sommer [John Somer], who received from this King [Charles IX] a chain worth six hundred French crowns.

The peace is by most well liked here. The King and Queen mother desire you to be sent here to ratify it . . . My old master, though anxious to return home, will stay here if desired.[9]

On the same day Throckmorton once again wrote to Dudley. In order that Dudley should not disgrace himself — or the Queen of England — in the highly civilised world of the Court of France, Throckmorton went into detailed instructions as to what Lord Robert should and should not do, how he is to dress, and what clothes and effects he should take with him: 'You should send over a dozen fair and easy paced geldings, for you must make some presents. I think Mr Sommers will be charged to attend you on your journey.' It is also interesting that he mentions the fact that there was talk of bestowing the Order of St Michel, which was to be drawn out for some time, and created a slight problem since — unlike the Order of the Garter — women were ineligible for membership. This meant, then, that the French order would have to be bestowed on one of Elizabeth's subjects instead, which did not at all please her in prospect.

I see some inklings that the King will give you his order, and possibly exchange orders with our Queen. For plate you should stay upon these parcels, silver vessels for three messes — trenchers agreeable — a light basin and ewer — eight or ten slight cups — two leyers and no more, so as one horse may carry all, and be where you dine or sup — a light bed, and your silver vessel should not exceed three score pieces, the same to be trussed in leather bagettes on each side of the horse, and the rest of the plate to be also trussed upon the same horse. I will send Barnaby to you that he may be sorted in your livery. You should make no new apparel for the voyage, nor bring more suits of all kinds than besides your ordinary mail may be carried on one horse, for three or four comely suits will suffice as your voyage is in post.

The King has told De Mauvissière to bring him some good fighting mastiffs and two or three pretty curtals [horses with docked tails] that will gallop, and the Queen has told him to bring two or three geldings. These should be your presents to them if you come.

I think the commissioners shall have charge to speak of other matters; therefore sort yourself accordingly.[10]

All of which may well have been rather irritating to Robert Dudley, though meant in the best possible way by Throckmorton. The last comment, however, left itself open to all sorts of interpretations, and not especially reassuring ones as far as Dudley himself was concerned.

In the short term, however, matters hung fire, since by 26 April 1564 — by which time De Mauvissière was in London — Lord Robert's projected visit had been cancelled. As the Frenchman wrote to him: 'I am sorry that her Majesty is not sending you to France, but glad to know your affection for the King of France and the Queen Mother. I will inform them of your wish to give them a spaniel and mastiffs, and some cobs. I thank you for those which you have sent me.'[11]

As usual, the Queen's inability to make up her mind about things, or her reluctance to implement a decision once she had made it, exasperated those around her trying to keep the wheels of government turning. However, there was a matter nearer home to claim her attention in the month of April 1564, and one which came to touch Robert Dudley and his family also. John Hales, Clerk of the Hanaper or Chancery Exchequer, published a book entitled *A Declaration of the Succession of the Crown Imperial of England*. His stated aim was to have the claim of some successor to the crown recognised, so that England should never again see a repetition of the Wars of the Roses. Elizabeth's persistent refusal to marry, and consequent failure to produce an heir, especially in the wake of her attack of smallpox and the continual dangers from plague, made this even more imperative. Unfortunately for the Suffolk family, Hales came down in their favour — especially since Catherine Grey already had two sons. The Queen was understandably angry, and Hales was lucky to escape with only six months in prison. The ripples of royal displeasure continued to emanate, however, and almost inevitably they lapped around Robert Dudley's sister the Countess of Huntingdon, who was then at Court, and whose husband was a potential heir to the crown also. Although in later years the Queen was to be very fond of Katherine Hastings, *née* Dudley, on this occasion she was less benevolent and gave her, in Huntingdon's own words 'a privy nip'.

On her return home, he wrote to Lord Robert: 'How far I have been always from conceiting any greatness of myself, nay, how ready I have been always to shun applauses, both by my continual low sail and my carriage, I do assure myself is best known to your lordship and the rest of my nearest friends.' It was not his fault that he happened to have Plantagenet blood in him, nor that 'a foolish book, foolishly written' should have upset the Queen and brought down her anger on the head of one 'who desires not to live but to see her happy. What grief it hath congealed within my poor heart (but ever true), let your lordship judge.' He well knew, he went on, that Lord Robert's influence could effect 'far greater matter than this', and he asked his brother-in-law to use it on his behalf.[12] There is a letter from Robert Dudley to Cecil and Mason, dated 4 May 1564, about Hales's book and the Queen's wishes in regard to it. Rather than arouse people's curiosity by making too much fuss over it, the Queen decided to hush the whole thing up as quietly as possible.[13]

In June Cecil wrote to Robert Dudley that the Queen still had not decided whom to send to ratify the Treaty of Troyes, which meant that the King of France did not know whom to send either, since both delegations had to be of comparable rank and size:

> I doubt how the French King will resolve whom to send except he be advertised whom the Queen will send.
>
> I think Sir Nicholas Throgmorton shall be here before any shall be ready from here.
>
> I beseech you to inform the Queen that the two treaties must be delivered to the French Ambassador before Saturday at night.
>
> Being sent hither to-morrow signed by her, they may be sealed

here, and knowing her pleasure I shall deliver them to the French Ambassador on Saturday, having some doctor of the archives and a notary to testify the due delivery thereof. On Saturday at night I will wait upon you.[14]

The Queen did manage to make up her mind about one appointment, however, and that was who was to take the Garter insignia to Charles IX. She chose her cousin Lord Hunsdon, but on 15 June he wrote to Cecil in some anger that the actual Garter he had been provided with was much too big for the boy's leg, and the chains were so poor in quality that he would hardly have deigned to wear them himself. In the opinion of the French Court it would have been a terrible insult, as well as lowering the Queen's standing in their eyes. To this extent Throckmorton had been quite right in his instructions to Lord Robert. On the death of a knight, his insignia was also returned, so what about the chains that had belonged to Edward VI or King Philip of Spain? Hunsdon went on. Cecil must speak to the Queen about it: 'it touches her honour more than any chain or garter or George is worth. I assure you if I had such as my Lord Robert hath, he should have one of mine.'[15] In truth the inventories at Longleat mention several Garter chains, and in the extant portraits of Robert Dudley, he wears a variety of them, mostly richly jewelled. However, as Hunsdon rightly pointed out, it was not so much the articles themselves that mattered, as the Queen's honour. The Elizabethans had a much more positive and concrete conception of honour, which we are apt to ignore in an age when it is so outmoded as to have become almost beyond comprehension for many. Nevertheless it mattered a great deal at the time, it was highly sought after, but remained somewhat elusive, since it depended to a large extent on the reaction it evoked in others for confirmation that its owners had in fact acquired it. A better illustration than the career of Robert Dudley would be hard to find. His life was a quest for it, and in contemporary terms he certainly achieved it. Over the specific matter of the Garter, however, Hunsdon betrayed no animosity whatsoever to Lord Robert himself and only the day before he had written to tell him of the horse fair at St Denis where were gathered animals from all over north-west Europe. He wagered that if Lord Robert had been there he would have spent one, or even two, thousand crowns.[16]

During that same month of June 1564, Robert Dudley was in considerable correspondence with Italians about coming to work in England, and with members of the Italian community in London. We have already encountered Hercules Trinchetta, for example, as well as Guido Cavalcanti, and one relatively minor incident will indicate the depth of Dudley's involvement, which could— even so— touch much more important matters on occasion. A letter in the Pepys Collection dated 13 May 1564 addressed to 'his Excellency' is probably intended, on internal evidence, for Robert Dudley, though tears in the paper cast some doubt on the identity of the writer, possibly Salvestro Federi. The letter states that on Thursday 3 May the writer was sent for by Guido Cavalcanti, lately come to London, where were also one Ruleto, Ridolfi Damieno, Doffi, and Baptista Fortini. Cavalcanti informed Federi that the Queen had given orders that he was to leave the kingdom at once, whereupon he embarked the very next day at Margate, and after a dangerous voyage, reached Dunkirk. Here he learned on good authority that the Queen had given no orders for his departure, the truth being that 'these Florentines' had taken upon themselves too much authority, and done it for their own ends. As Federi held a patent from the King of Poland, he thought it very unjust that he should have been treated in such a way, and that they ought to be punished as well in person as in purse.

At his departure from England, Federi left a packet of letters with Antonio Bruschetto, in a cover directed to his Excellency. If they have not been received, Bruschetto must be asked to whom he consigned them. As a faithful servant of her Majesty, he must inform his Excellency that the Spanish fleet is said to be very large; good guard should be kept, and men in order and readiness in all the bands.[17] Certainly Sebastiano Bruschetto was a correspondent of Robert Dudley's, and also of Benedetto or Benedict Spinola, and both of them were engaged in obtaining the services of Italians for Robert Dudley and the Queen. On 13 June 1564, for example, Bruschetto wrote to Spinola in London, from Rome:

> We have good hopes that Ferrabosco will return to the service of her Majesty, and that by means of Signor Gurone, who has dropped a few words to a gentleman of Cardinal Farnese concerning his desire to do so. His father is no longer in Rome, so that the matter cannot be settled at once; otherwise he might have travelled to England with the Master of the Horse [Claudio], as he wished.

There is a letter from Rome, dated 22 April 1564, from Gurone to Benedetto Spinola, showing how extensive the ramifications of this network of correspondence were. Curiously, on the covering leaf of this letter the signature A. Warwyck is written several times.[18] Bruschetto's letter continues:

> As to a lady for her Majesty, Signora Lucia Bertana [a relative of Gurone Bertano?] has written to a lady of Bologna to enquire whether she would serve a great lady out of Italy, without mentioning her name. The matter cannot be in better hands than in those of the signora and the Duchess of Taliacozza. I have enquired about a lute player at Bologna, who is very celebrated and would be a fit person to serve the count [presumably Dudley, though he was not yet an earl].

There is a postscript: 'In my last I asked you to remit fifty crowns, which otherwise Gurone would have to pay. This proving inconvenient, we had recourse to Signor Pallavicini.'[19] One wonders whether this is a reference to Horatio Palavicino. Certainly the family, of Genoese origin, was well known in London. Four days later Bruschetto wrote to Lord Robert himself, apologising for not having troubled him with letters, but assuring him of his desire to serve him, and saying that he would do all possible to engage Signor Gurone's help in affairs relating to her Majesty and his lordship.[20] He also wrote on that same day to Spinola once more though, as he himself confessed, with relatively little to say:

> Only touching Ferrabosco, I have to say that either because the youth has shown himself too desirous to leave the cardinal [Farnese], and therefore has raised suspicion that he has been suborned by Signor Gurone, or for some other reason, not only is the cardinal changed towards the youth, but also towards Gurone, albeit, in truth, quite wrongly. For, as a gentleman versed in the customs of noblemen, he has moved very circumspectly, and before he said a word to the young man, he spoke to the cardinal; indeed, out of respect to him, he even made me keep back for more than ten days a letter written to Ferrabosco by your brother. So that, up to the present, we do not know what will happen as regards his going, especially as Signor Gurone holds his ground, and cares little for the anger of the cardinal, in the service of the Queen, knowing he has not merited it.

Amidst all this somewhat Byzantine intrigue, one nevertheless sees very clearly what the preoccupations of this comparatively small international group were, and how in certain domains individual interests ran right across — indeed in some cases quite contrary to — national interests. It is easy to ignore the realists such as Cecil and Walsingham, who saw beneath the glitter of Court life. And yet even in a letter such as this, every now and then more serious matters bubbled to the surface:

> Although they are both incensed with the cardinal about this, yet it has been said that after all he was able to entertain the young man well, and that money was not so plentiful in England or at the English Court that he could have any great hopes from thence. I tell you this to show you what is thought here about English affairs. To the same end, I will say that a few days ago, Signor Gurone being in discourse with the French ambassador, the ambassador said that the Queen was little enough loved in her kingdom; but whether he said this to sow discord for some end of his own, or had really understood as much, I do not know. But I think it well to inform you of all reports concerning her Majesty; whether or not they are of consequence, you yourself can judge.
>
> I do not begin to send advices to his lordship until you tell me whether to do so or not, but meanwhile will not fail to give you information of all that happens.[21]

On 24 June Gurone Bertano wrote to Lord Robert with advices from Rome,[22] and then the next day Bruschetto again wrote to Spinola:

> If the Master of the Horse does not appear as soon as his Excellency [presumably Dudley] and your honour expect him, it will not be to be wondered at, for the very evening before he was to start (that is six days ago) he was arrested by one to whom a horse had been sold by his means. The man complained that the horse was short-winded, and was determined that the master should make it good to him, declaring that he had taken the horse upon his word. I, and Signor Gurone also, believe that the matter sprang from another source, seeing that the Cardinal Farnese, as I wrote to your honour, was somewhat vexed with Signor Gurone on account of Ferraboscho [sic], and finding him hold his ground (as indeed he has cause), perhaps thought, by treating the Master of the Horse in this way, to put him to ridicule. Be that as it may, Signor Gurone has offered, sooner than that Claudio [Master of the Horse] should lose time here, to be bound for him as regards this controversy, and is sending him a quicker way, and Ferraboscho with him, but secretly, because, although he has had leave from the cardinal, he did not say that he wished to go to England, but merely to his home at Bologna.
>
> As Signor Gurone has sent his Excellency all the news, I will only add a few minor matters which he omitted . . .[23]

The references to the distinguished musical family of Ferrabosco are most interesting, because of the amount of cross-fertilisation that went on in the musical world at this time. Domenico Maria Ferrabosco (1513–74) was born and died in Bologna, though he was in Rome from 1551 to 1555 on the staff of the papal chapel, along with Palestrina. His son Alfonso is the one referred to here. He, too, was born in Bologna, in 1543, and died there in 1588. Nevertheless he came to England and was in the service of Queen Elizabeth, though he returned to Italy from time to time, and apparently only left in 1578 because he had enemies at Court, and there was some sort of fracas in which an Italian was killed. In all there were at least seven members of the family who gained distinction in one way or another as musicians, and the family stayed on in England after Alfonso's departure, so his son and grandsons carried on the tradition. There is an undated letter in the Pepys Collection from Petrucchio Ubaldini to the Queen which informs us that he had promised that Ferrabosco and Claudio Cavallerizzo would act an Italian comedy to please the Queen, but Ubaldini was unable to find more than a further three or four who were willing to act.[24]

Robert Dudley's involvement with foreigners was by no means restricted to the French and Italians, however, and there is a letter dated 30 June 1564 from the Burgomaster and Council of Antwerp that was to prove to have had a somewhat prophetic element twenty years later: 'We feel that we must thank you for your letter and the good will shown therein towards the Low Countries and this town. We hope the ancient amity between us and England may still be renewed, and that our Regent will meet your Court and nation in the matter of trade.'[25]

Robert, meanwhile, was being the successful courtier in England, for that same month of June the new Spanish ambassador, Don Guzman de Silva, arrived to take up his post. The Queen sent a message of welcome and compliments the day after his arrival, but Lord Robert had already sent one of his own. De Silva returned the compliment to Lord Robert, and at the same time asked him to let the Queen know that he would like an audience with her. When Lord Robert obtained this immediately, the ambassador was impressed. The Court was at Richmond, and at Longleat are the expenses of a masque held there on 10 June.[26] The ambassador missed that one, however, since he did not go from London to Richmond until 22 June. He thought it worthy of note, incidentally, that on that occasion he was met at the entrance to the Council Chamber by Lord Henry Darnley.[27] A week or two later, in the first week in July, De Silva was again in the Queen's presence at an evening entertainment in London, which included another masque, in which all the men were dressed in black and white. The Queen told De Silva that those were her colours. In some of the contemporary works on heraldry, they were also the colours of the perpetual virgin. De Silva was charming, and came to be well liked. Even so, King Philip would have liked him, with Lord Robert's help, to engineer the fall of Cecil.[28] It is to De Silva's credit that he not only realised that such a scheme was doomed to failure, but at the same time pronounced Cecil to be 'lucid, modest and just'.

On 10 July 1564 Henry Killigrew (Cecil's brother-in-law) wrote to Lord Robert from Paris, where he had gone as one of Lord Hunsdon's party, but had been granted leave to stay behind for private business. When he took leave of the king and queen mother they sent their commendations to Dudley, and requested his aid in preserving the friendship between England and France. Various other members of the clergy and aristocracy also sent their greetings.[29] In the eyes of the French Court Dudley was obviously a person of the highest importance, and was regarded as a great power in the land.

In the month of August the Queen paid a visit to the University of Cambridge. As its Chancellor — an office previously held by Dudley's father, John, Duke of Northumberland — Cecil made all the arrangements for the visit himself. There are details relating to the visit in the archives at Longleat.[30] The Queen was to be put up in the Provost's Lodge of King's College, and her ladies and doctors in the Fellows' Lodgings there. The Earl of Warwick and Lord Robert Dudley were to go to Trinity College, and Cecil would go to his own college of St John's. As Master of the Horse and Lord High Steward Lord Robert had his part to play also, and in reply to a letter from the academic body, assured them that the Queen fully appreciated to what extent they were trying to ensure the success of the visit:

> To my very loving friends, the Vice-Chancellor, with the rest of the fellows in the University of Cambridge: Touching the matter in your letters, for doubt of your well-doings to the good liking of the Queen's Majesty, I may very well put you out of any such doubt . . . nothing can with better will be done by you than it will be graciously accepted by her . . .

The letter then goes on to give Dudley's own assurance: '. . . with my friendship, every way to further you; with my purse, to assist and spend with you; and mine own self, at your commandments in all I may to honour and serve you.'[31] In the face of this sort of charm and courtesy, who could fail to be swept along on the general tide of good will and euphoria?

At 8 a.m. on Saturday 8 August, Cecil summoned the Vice-Chancellor and heads of colleges and informed them that the Master of the Horse was arriving that morning to see if they wanted him to do anything. They all met at King's College, where the Court would be located officially, and when Lord Robert arrived, the Earl of Warwick was with him. He inspected the Queen's lodgings, saw the chapel, and then went on to the Master's Chamber at Trinity. He was received with an oration, and gifts of two pairs of gloves, a confection of marchpane and two sugar loaves. A little after two o'clock in the afternoon, the Queen herself arrived.[32] There then followed five days of receptions, banquets and plays, interspersed with orations, dissertations and disputations, and the Queen listened to everything with intense concentration. So much so, in fact, that she almost wore herself out, and towards the end of the visit flagged visibly. A performance of Sophocles' *Ajax* by the students of King's had to be abandoned:

> Her Highness, as it were tired with going about the colleges and hearing of disputations, and over-watched with former plays (for it was very late nightly before she came to them, as also departed from [them]). . . could not, as otherwise, no doubt, she would (with like patience and cheerfulness as she was present at the other) hear the said tragedy.[33]

When it came to a farewell speech the following morning, to be delivered by the Master of Magdalene, the Queen had to ask him to excuse her, but she asked for a copy of his allocution to take away with her.

The visit was an unqualified success, but how did Lord Robert stand in the Queen's affection when the Court returned to London at the beginning of September? To many observers, both at home and abroad, and no doubt to Robert himself, it seemed that he had risen to such a position in the Queen's favour that nothing could now stop him. But there were at least two very serious obstacles in his way. The first came to nothing, though in one form or another it was to irritate Robert Dudley for years to come, namely the possibility of a foreign husband for the Queen. As De Silva remarked: 'I learn on good authority that Lord Robert has no chance, and the talk is now all about the Archduke.'[34] As to the official English view at that time, it is contained in a letter Cecil wrote 'by order of the Queen' to Sir Christopher Mundt, English agent in the Holy Roman Empire, on 8 September 1564. Mundt's task was to keep the possibility of negotiations for a match with the Archduke Charles on the simmer, but what is perhaps more interesting is that this letter reveals the second and more serious obstacle to Robert Dudley as a future consort for the Queen:

> His sole impediment is that he is by birth the Queen's subject. For that reason alone does he not seem to the Queen worthy to be her husband . . . Yet . . . on account of his eminent endowments of mind and body he is so dear to the Queen that she could not love a real brother more. And from this they who do not know the Queen as she really is, are often wont to conclude too hastily that he will be her husband. But I see and understand . . . that there is nothing more in their relations than that which is consistent with virtue and most foreign to the baser sorts of love . . . and this I wish you to believe and assert boldly amongst all when the occasion demands it.[35]

On the draft was the request: 'Please send this letter back to me for I am very anxious not to have published what I write in this affair.' And then towards the end of that month De Silva wrote, acting no doubt on information he had gleaned from the Marchioness of Northampton about the Queen: 'I understand, however, that she bears herself towards him in a way that, together with other things that can be better imagined than described, make me doubt sometimes whether Robert's position is so irregular as many think.'[36]

Lord Robert's marriage was to be the subject of even more speculation in the near future. That same month of September, the Earl of Lennox had requested permission from Elizabeth to go to Scotland to see about his estates there, which had been confiscated for his support of Henry VIII. This permission was granted, because it was assumed that he would not risk the security of his English estates, which were much more considerable than those in Scotland, by engaging in any activity that might be regarded as treasonous. At the same time, Sir James Melville came to London as envoy on behalf of the Queen of Scots to discuss her marriage to Lord Robert Dudley. That was his public mission, but secretly he was also to get Lady Lennox to seek permission for her elder son Henry Stuart, Lord Darnley, to join his father in Scotland. Mary, it must be remembered, was a granddaughter of Margaret Tudor, sister to Henry VIII, through her first marriage to James IV, King of Scotland, whereas Lord Darnley was a grandson through her second marriage to Archibald Douglas, Earl of Angus.

Melville suggested that Elizabeth should send the Earl of Bedford and Lord Robert to talk with Moray and Maitland. Elizabeth seized upon the order in which he mentioned the two, and complained that he seemed to make small account of Lord Robert by naming him, as Melville had done, second. Before he went back to Scotland, she went on, he would see Lord Robert made the greater earl of the two.[37] On Michaelmas Day, 29 September 1564, Robert Dudley was created firstly Baron Denbigh, and then Earl of Leicester.[38] Both the French ambassador and Melville were there, and the latter recorded in his *Memoirs* that the Queen could not restrain herself from tickling the back of Robert Dudley's neck as she put the mantle around his shoulders. The Queen then asked Melville how he liked her new creation, to which he replied with a suitably turned phrase, and then she completely surprised him by pointing to the bearer of the Sword of State, Lord Darnley, and saying: 'And yet you like better of yonder long lad!' The Queen had let him know that she was perfectly aware of what Melville was up to, though he was an experienced enough diplomat to assure her that no woman could prefer such a lady-faced boy as Darnley to a fine man like Lord Robert.

One evening after the ceremony had taken place, Melville was with the Queen in her bedchamber, with Cecil and Leicester, talking together at the far end of the room. The Queen opened a little cabinet, according to Melville, and showed him some of her treasures, amongst them some miniatures wrapped in paper. One was labelled 'My lord's picture'. Melville took up a candle and asked to see it, and discovered that it was Leicester's portrait. He asked to be allowed to take it to his queen, but Elizabeth said that it was the only one she had, and could not spare it. Looking to the other end of the room, Melville commented that she had the original with her. He then saw her take out a picture of the Queen of Scots, which she kissed — a gesture which inspired him to seize Elizabeth's hand and kiss it. He also noticed a huge ruby, so suggested that if she would not send the Earl of Leicester's picture, she might send the jewel. Thereupon the Queen put away her treasures, and said that if the Queen of Scots were to follow her counsel, in time she would get all that she possessed.[39]

At one point, as Melville was leaving Hampton Court by boat, Leicester accompanied him and said that he was aware that it seemed presumptuous of him to aspire to the hand of the Queen of Scots, and that it was all the fault of Cecil, who was trying to ruin him in the sight of both queens. Even so, it was widely assumed that his elevation to an earldom was to this specific end, as for example in Strype's *Annals*: '. . . and his preferment in Scotland (to match with that queen) earnestly intended.'[40] It almost seems that at this moment all the principal characters were playing an elaborate charade, and each one knew that the others were also playing a game, so that any extravagance was possible and yet had to be treated with caution, since it might just turn out to be serious. In the matter of Elizabeth's subsequent history of suitors this came to stand her in very good stead, though at the height of the Alençon courtship she almost went too far in the game, and had her bluff called.

Leicester sustained no material loss or neglect at this time, however, and the honours continued to mount up. On 30 December 1564, for example, he was appointed Chancellor of Oxford University, and on the very day that he was made an earl, Sir Thomas Smith, ambassador in succession to Throckmorton, had written to him from Avignon: 'This day at dinner De Mauvissière tells me that the King has chosen you knight and companion of the Order of St Michael.'[41] In fact Smith had not got his facts quite right, for as he wrote again on 21 October from Tarascon:

> At the coming hither of Jo[hn] Baptista [a messenger from Scotland] all the Court is full that you are, or shortly shall be, made duke. The County Rhyngrave cometh into England with the collar of this order to put into the Queen's hands to dispose of as shall be her pleasure. The King giveth you the prerogative of his voice.[42]

News seemed to travel fast on the international grapevine, and the details were not always carefully retailed. The Queen herself had cause to complain about it to De Silva as he reported on 9 October, less than two weeks before Smith's letter. She said, according to De Silva:

> I am insulted both in England and abroad for having shown too much favour to the Lord Robert. I am spoken of as if I were an immodest woman. I ought not to wonder at it: I have favoured him because of his excellent disposition and his many merits, but I am young and he is young and therefore we have both been slandered. God knows they do us grievous wrong, and the time will come when the world will know it also. A thousand eyes see all that I do, and calumny will not fasten on me for ever.[43]

Smith's letter to Leicester of 21 October had continued:

> Let the Queen have an eye to the practices in Scotland: they tend to
> the subversion of religion there, and the breach of the amity between
> us and that realm . . . I have sent piecemeal to you and Mr Secretary
> as they did occur, conjecture of their doings. You that be nearer see
> more, and do daily look to it . . . If I could have some light from
> thence, peradventure I should see more here. But no country is so
> still, I suppose, for advertising their ambassadors as ours is. I have
> written to the Queen and Mr Secretary, who, I am sure, doth
> communicate my letters to you. It is told here that he goeth, or is
> gone, to the emperor. If he be gone, open my letter to him.[44]

On occasion it seemed as if no scrap of information, no crumb of gossip,
was too insignificant to be recorded, and of course at times important
facts were made apparent in this way. One thing that one notices
particularly in respect to the ambassadors' communications to Leicester,
however, is that they have no compunction at all about making him the
recipient of all their grievances, too. The chief explanation for this lay in
the fact that he had the Queen's ear at only one remove, so that they
could make him their spokesman. This had the advantage that any royal
wrath reached them at one remove also. Smith wrote again from Nîmes
on 16 December 1564,[45] and then from Toulouse on 6 February 1565,
showing that as far as the French royal family was concerned, Leicester
was still very much at the centre of events:

> I have declared your message to the king and queen mother, who took
> it in good part. Where you offered to do what you could to entertain
> the amity between our Queen and them, the Queen said there was
> nothing they desired more. She trusted it would increase from day to
> day. I commended your geldings to them and especially the Queen's,
> who said she had heard that they were as fair pieces as could be seen.
> She hath sent for them.

There was an addition in another hand, dated 7 February 1565: 'De
Mauvissière hath started for England with a costly litter. Fair muletts
and camels for a present to the Queen. It will be past the middle of
March before he shall be in England.'[46]

At the same time, Leicester was closely involved with the French
Protestants, as we have already seen, and a letter from Beauvoir la Noche
to him, dated from Havre de Grâce on 5 February of the same year,
1565, runs as follows:

> The good will shown by you since we have been afflicted by civil war

emboldens me to beg you to induce the Queen to accomplish her promise. The hope we all have of this takes the admiral and his camp in a few days to Normandy to join the forces of England, to strengthen his Reiters by the aid promised by her Majesty. If this aid is deferred your experience can tell you how great will be the damage not only to France but to all Christendom.[47]

That winter of 1564/5 the Queen was not well. In December she had pains in her stomach, and aching limbs, which may have been gastric influenza. On 15 December Cecil wrote to Sir Thomas Smith: '[It] came to that which they call diarrhoea . . . for the time she made us sore afraid.'[48] It was in any case a hard winter, and the Thames was frozen over. De Silva was of the opinion that the weather had been hard on the weak: 'It has found out the Queen whose constitution cannot be very strong.'[49] She recovered, but the Earl of Leicester told him that she was very thin: 'It is true that young people can get over anything, but your Majesty should note that she is not likely to have a long life.'[50] Time was to prove him mistaken.

On 30 December 1564, Robert Dudley was made Chancellor of Oxford University.[51] He had apparently been appealed to this year on a different academic matter already. Adam Loftus, Archbishop of Armagh, and Hugh Brady, Bishop of Meath, petitioned the Queen for an 'academy to be erected in Ireland'. They wrote, therefore, to thank Leicester and Cecil for their furtherance of the same.[52] Apart from this, Leicester had already had dealings with the academic world at Cambridge, where he was High Steward, and at least one college at Oxford before he became Chancellor there, as early as 1560. In that year the governing body of Christ Church wrote to ask him for Thomas Sampson as dean in succession to Carew; or rather that Dudley would prevail with the Queen on his behalf.[53] As Chancellor, however, Leicester's role was now much more important, and indeed he took it seriously — as perhaps fitted a non-graduate of the university.

On 16 January 1565 he wrote to the university to the effect that on his election as Chancellor he had committed the election of his commissary to them, and being certified that John Kenall had been chosen by them, he went on: 'I cannot but make liking of him whom so many wise and godly in such sort have elected.' This was a tactful and flattering gambit. However, the same letter reveals that Leicester was also bent on reform. He had been assured, he went on, that they would consider his wishes as to reformation of want of preaching, diligent reading and hearing of lessons of all sorts, and comely and decent order of degrees.[54] Prompt action was taken, for on 23 January Roger Marbeck, Provost of Oriel, wrote that in reply to the Chancellor's letter certain had been chosen to take a survey of their statutes. The old statutes had been retained, he went on, 'excepting some which in part touched popery and superstition and be now by common consent utterly abolished.' Furthermore, Marbeck wrote, they had devised a few articles to the increase of public exercise in all faculties. The number of the divines, which Leicester had commanded him to certify, the commissary had got ready for him.[55] This exchange is interesting not only for what it reveals about Leicester's interest in the university and its function, but also about his interest in religion.

It is difficult to know how sincere Leicester's religious convictions were at this stage, or indeed throughout his life, and a consideration of them will be reserved for a later chapter. Initially, of course, it was almost inevitable that, as a courtier with access to the Queen, he should have been the recipient of requests in the scramble for offices that accompanied the return to the reformed rite under Elizabeth. There is, for example, an unashamed piece of lobbying from John Aylmer, whose piscatorial metaphor does nothing to conceal his boldness:

> Good my lord, if the Deanery of Winchester be not already swallowed up, let me among the rest of the small fishes have a snatch at the bait: if it be gone, I beseech your good lordship cast a hook for the Deanery of Durham that when Mr Hoorn is sped of a bishopric I may have that to serve God, my country and the Queen's Majesty in.[56]

A later request from William Alley, Bishop of Exeter, dated 18 February 1565, is concerned chiefly with mundane, secular matters, though still revealing the extent of Leicester's patronage and reputation in ecclesiastical circles:

> I request that the Earl of Leicester may be asked to obtain leave from the Queen for me to let certain out-houses and waste within the precincts of my palace, which stands me in yearly charges to repair. The net revenue of the see is not more than £300. I hope to dedicate to the earl a book which shall make open all the obscure, dark, hard and contrary places in the Scriptures under the title of *Anticimenon*. I send commendations to Sir John Chichester, praying him to have in mind Colum John.[57]

The bishop's confidence in his ability to elucidate the Scriptures is typical of the age, despite the fact that better men than Anglican divines have failed, then and since, to do just that. Leicester had already had dedicated to him, in 1564, a manuscript treatise on the study of history by Giacomo Concio (Acontius), and an anonymous translation, published by John Day, of Peter Martyr's *Commentaries*. The history of Peter Martyr himself is an admirable illustration of the upheaval caused by the Reformation. Born in Florence in 1500, he came to England at Cranmer's invitation and became Regius Professor of Divinity at Oxford in 1548. In 1530 he had been Abbot of the Augustinian abbey at Spoleto, but such were the changes and chances of that fleeting world that almost any metamorphosis was possible. He had acquired a wife on the way, a former nun whom he married in Strasbourg, where he was professor of theology in 1542. When his wife died in Oxford in 1553 she was buried in Christ Church Cathedral, near the tomb of St Frideswide. However, Cardinal Pole had the body disinterred, but in 1558 she was reinterred. By this time, however, the poor lady had become so mingled with the supposed remains of St Frideswide that the Catholic historian Nicholas Sanders was prompted to remark '*hic requiescit religio cum superstitione*' In view of Sanders' sympathies, it would be interesting to know just what he regarded as the religion and what the superstition. What one ignores at one's peril, however, is the extent to which religious convictions mattered at this time. After all, people were prepared to die for them, and did so in their hundreds. The Queen herself tempered her personal inclinations in the interests of national unity, and would probably have preferred a more demonstrably 'Catholic' ethos had she been able to choose. Leicester did not share her feelings on this point, and certainly by the time the vestments controversy broke out he had emerged as the champion of the more Puritan element.

There is a document in the Pepys Collection which dates possibly from 1559 and is endorsed: 'A remembrance to the Lord Robert Dudley concerning the preachers of the Gospel. To be considered.' It contains the names of 'certain godly learned preachers which have utterly forsaken Antichrist and all his Romish rags, besides divers whose names I do not presently remember and others that I know not'. The list is an impressive one, and contains such famous names as those of Miles Coverdale, William Whittingham (later Dean of Durham), Lawrence Humphrey or Humphries (President of Magdalen College, Oxford), Wyburne (preacher and reader at Northampton), and James Pilkington (later Bishop of Durham). It continues:

Whether these poor men (if they were but two) which for the zeal of God's pure religion, do refuse and reject Antichrist's liveries, receive and allow them, are to be preferred, let alone those that are godlywise judge: the one following the example of all Christ's faithful ministers in Germany, France, Scotland and all well reformed churches, to the abolishing of papistry and superstition: the other imitating Christ's sworn enemies (the papists) to the maintainance of popery and superstition.[58]

Perhaps Leicester acted on this advice. Certainly he is recorded as having gone to hear Pilkington preach at St Paul's Cross on 9 February 1560,[59] and later Pilkington wrote to him at some length about the wearing of vestments in 1564.

Briefly the controversy was over the wearing of vestments in church, which the Puritan wing of the clergy objected to, but which the Queen, in her desire for uniformity, and possibly also from her own inclination, wanted standardised and brought more into line with traditional practice. Matthew Parker had tried to compromise with the men who rejected such a policy, so that by the end of 1564 he was obliged by the Queen to issue an ordinance. William Whittingham, Dean of Durham, who owed his appointment to Leicester's influence, wrote to the earl on 25 October 1564. He had heard that an injunction compelling the clergy to wear the old 'popish' apparel, had either been passed or was at hand, and he requested the earl's intercession against it. He quoted from the Church Fathers in Latin, and even appealed to the example of Christ Himself, who would not suffer His disciples to wash their hands as the Pharisees did. He went on: 'If our apparel seem not so modest and grave as our vocation requireth, neither sufficient to discern us from men of other callings, we refuse not to wear such as shall be thought to the godly and prudent magistrates for these uses most decent.'[60] All of which seems very reasonable, though Whittingham was capable of a more impassioned appeal, and according to Strype in his *Life of Parker*, went even further: 'Alas, my lord, that such compulsion should be used towards us, and so great lenity towards the Papists . . . O noble earl, at least [length?] be our patron and stay in this behalf that we may not lose that liberty, which hitherto by the Queen's Majesty's benignity we have enjoyed . . .'[61]

It is perhaps hard for us to appreciate exactly what the vestments controversy meant to the men who had suffered for their faith, gone into exile, or even given their lives for it. Pilkington's letter to Leicester, also written in 1564, shows the depth of feeling among the clergy, and the very real dilemma that it placed them in:

> Not long since I was a suitor to you in the behalf of such ministers as be called breakers of common orders because they do not only forbear the Pope's doctrine but chiefly refuse to wear his livery, which is thought of some to be a disobedience to the Queen's Majesty and her laws. She has not more faithful hearts than of those that be thought so precise that in such small matters will not relent. As to your great commendation you did put yourself betwixt and helped to stay the displeasure conceived and intended, so I beseech you be not weary of well doing but continue your favour to such honest professors of God's truth that under your wings they may serve the living God purely, and that God's enemies the Papists have no cause to triumph against His people . . . what a wound to zealous men shall this be, to see one Protestant punish and persecute another because he will not wear the Pope's livery.

Allowing for a certain amount of bigotry, Pilkington put his case well. The next step in his argument is less easy to accept, however, though it shows the extent to which reform was fundamental to the establishment of the Church of England, and that it was not simply the child of a political necessity:

> The Papists would suffer no relics of our religion among them, and we shall strive how to maintain their inventions. Our sins and unthankful receiving of His word deserve a greater plague than this, but surely if this go afore, more will follow . . . Your wisdom can consider all the inconveniences that may follow the displacing of so many good ministers, seeing there is no greater store of them to be had. It is pity that no other apparel can be devised but this: for if it had not a show of the Pope's badge, they would most willingly receive any. The Lord open your heart to be a mediator for the utter suppressing of that punishment intended and give your Grace to find such favour that your words may take place.[62]

Pilkington rather weakens his argument by saying that it is not the apparel itself, but its associations, and that if it were not so, they would be happy to wear anything; but then the whole point was that it was precisely the Pope's livery — as they saw it — that they were being required to wear. In such circumstances, then, there could be little hope of compromise.

Leicester certainly seems to have had the trust of those who had most to lose in the controversy, but to outsiders there was little or no realisation — not at this stage — that he had any very pronounced views. De Silva, writing to his king in the January of the next year, 1565, said: 'I believe he desires to please everybody as he seems well disposed and has no inclination to do harm.'[63] Yet De Silva mentioned the vestments controversy in the same letter, and the earl's intervention. It would be true to say, however, that Leicester's support for the Puritans, and consequent dislike of the Catholics, if not formed already, began to crystallise from this time onwards, even if it did not entirely satisfy such out-and-out Puritans as the Earl of Bedford. Certainly by the time it came to the questions of the prophesyings in Northampton, he was clearly identified as a Puritan supporter, as we shall see later.

Bedford, who started out as a friend, and then became a relation through marriage, wrote to Leicester on 27 March 1565 from Berwick, where he was governor:

> You have recompensed your long abstinence from writing with a very friendly discourse and declaration of your great zeal for religion. I have heard of some speech used to a preacher in the pulpit. Albeit I think it not so much as it was said to be, yet do I wish it had been less or rather nothing at all; the thing was the more noted as it happened to so grave and learned a man.
>
> Touching my coming up I trust it be had in remembrance, so as soon after St George's Day I mean to set forward to communicate somewhat to you which I will not commit to writing . . .[64]

The previous month — February 1565 — saw the successful solution to a problem that had nagged at Leicester for more than a year. It chiefly concerned the recall of the English ambassador to Spain, Sir Thomas Chaloner. Chaloner had served Leicester's father, though in Spain he felt very much on the periphery, as we learn from a letter to Robert from Balbastro, near Montzon, Aragon, on 24 January 1564: '. . . if you here were as I am, knowing no more than I do, who once in five or six months receive not a letter from home . . .' Basically, however, the letter dealt with a matter of perpetual interest to Leicester in his capacity as Master of the Horse, namely the importation of suitable animals and the improvement of stock: 'Touching the licence for twelve jennets, I will motion it if by your next you still so desire . . . Your offer of dogs shall not be forgotten.'[65]

He little knew how long he would have to wait before his return.

By 7 June 1564 he had written to Leicester that he had had no indication whatsoever that a letter he had written to the Queen on 22 January 'by two hands' had arrived safely. He was therefore sending a copy to Leicester for him to see. The latter had, it appears, written to Chaloner on 22 March, a letter — according to Chaloner — 'in which I have imprinted the image of that noble duke your father's favour', towards him. He declared that Leicester's 'noble gentleness' had won from him 'a determinate mind to desire the continuance of my bond from the father to the son'. But by now Chaloner definitely wanted to be recalled: 'Set in your hand and favour that I be kept here no longer.' [66]

Robert Dudley wrote to him in Madrid on 15 July 1564, but the letter did not reach him until 26 September. The ambassador replied at once, partly stressing how critical his financial situation was becoming, and partly attempting to vindicate himself in the face of charges being made that he had not carried out his task adequately:

> Trade being stopped with Flanders I receive no bills of exchange, and you can judge how sweetly I pay for the money I borrow. I have things that I cannot write. If I had had, not so late, advice of things determined at home, I might have prevented things to a better issue. Now I fare like Cassandra, who was never believed. I am not ignorant what opinion some unadvised folks have of me for this or that. When I talk with a man of reason, as you are, I shall give such account of myself as blame shall not appear. When I come home I purpose to live a retired life to myself, my friends and my books. [67]

No sooner had Chaloner finished this letter than he received one from his servant Farnham, from which he learned that 'her Majesty gave no answer of any great hope of my recall'. This then provoked Chaloner to a passionate outburst:

> If I die here as sure this winter will make an end of me, then will they think of another for the place. All my things at home run to manifest rack, my receivers in the country keep my rents, and I am eaten up by interest. A new broom shall sweep clean; I am worn to the stumps. If her Majesty sends another here, the king will allow me to leave without waiting for his arrival.

The postscript is oddly different in tone, and interesting for the light it throws on the way foreign musicians moved around at that time:

> At Barcelona last March I heard one Fabricio Denti, a Neapolitan, son to Luys Denti, play on the lute. The father was offered of King

> Henry VIII 1000 crowns pension yearly to serve him. The father's play was mean, but his voice very sweet. The son's play for clean handling and deep music and parts, and excellent fingering is uncomparable of any I ever heard. He sings in a feigning [falsetto] voice after the Neapolitan fashion. He intends to come to kiss the Queen's hand. I recommend him to you.[68]

Unknown to Chaloner, however, relief was already at hand, and in a letter from Cecil dated 23 September 1564 he was informed that he was to be asked to stay on until the following spring, so as to accompany King Philip or his son in case either of them should go to Flanders. In Chaloner's opinion neither of them was likely to go within a year. However, the essential was that a date had at last been fixed for his return. As he wrote to the Earl of Leicester on 30 November, from Madrid:

> . . . In $3\frac{1}{2}$ years here I never had one penny of *ayuda de costas* [help with the expenses] besides my ordinary diet. The Bishop of Aquila, while in England, the cheapest place in the world, had besides his diet at three sundry times 9000 ducats in reward, besides the debt he incurred there of 17,000 ducats since paid of the king. I have been three years in Spain and am so sickly that I can scarce put pen to paper.

Chaloner then made some more reflections about the authorities, in a mixture of tetchiness and seeking for sympathy. Once more, however, it is the postscript that provides us with some fascinating details of the function of an ambassador and the breadth of Leicester's range of activities:

> If you wish, I can get the Queen's arms engraved in a ruby or diamond, which no other master save one I think in Europe can do.
> One Lewis Morgan is here, attendant on Mr Smyth, well known for his valiance at the assault of St Quentin. His suit appears by the enclosed. His pardon granted, he would return to serve the Queen. He says my lord Henry, your brother, whom God pardon, was his special good lord.[69]

Chaloner enclosed details of the murder of a David ap Llewellyn which had taken place at Brecknock in 1552 — all of which Leicester was expected to deal with. A further letter from Chaloner on 17 December, from Balbastro, shows that he was still waiting to be recalled,[70] but on

12 February 1565 he was able to write to Leicester from Madrid that he was 'packing to make home' the soonest he may.[71] It was Robert Huggins, however, who wrote to Leicester on 4 April from Madrid to let him know that Sir Thomas Chaloner had left for England on 2 March. He continued:

> The sending of the French order to you is much marvelled at; no one here having had it, they see a great amity between France and England. You are must praised at this Court. I hear this from Feria, who asked if it was true that her Majesty had determined to marry . . .[72]

A further sphere of Leicester's foreign activities in the early part of 1565 concerned Antwerp once more, and the Baroncelli family there. In fact Leicester was a godparent to Tommaso Baroncelli's daughter who was baptised Elizabeth as a compliment to the Queen. Though not as grand as the Medici family, the Baroncelli rise in the world was also due to banking, and their success in that field put them on a level with the aristocracy, and sovereign rulers were happy to acknowledge their existence. Baroncelli wrote to Leicester on 3 January 1565:

> I had hoped before now to have announced the accouchement of your fellow gossip [the Countess of San Segondo], and trust to do so, by my next. Your letter for her ladyship I have delivered, and written that I had commission from you to declare personally your good will towards her, which I hope to do after the accouchement of my wife and of her ladyship. If you have taken pleasure in having her as fellow gossip, she has not had less in having you.

As ever in much of this foreign correspondence, the topic then becomes consideration of horses, but also goes on to weapons, painting, and even gunpowder:

> I believe the geldings which you mean to send will be acceptable to her Highness, and the mares would have been brought from Holland to cross with those of the Prince of Orange, if the weather had not prevented. I am seeking for two white mares to go with the others. The arquebus for hunting will be ready in four days. I will tell you when the painter from Florence has started for your service, and if you send the pattern of the armour, I will see to it. I should like you to make interest with her Majesty that I may provide the powder. If your brother has tried the sample which I sent, I am sure he will have

recommended it to her Majesty. I should be glad to supply any armour.[73]

Leicester's reply is dated 16 January 1565, at the Court:

By yours of the 3rd I am glad to hear that her Highness has had my letter. The patterns of bodices which you have sent me for the Queen are beautiful, but not what she wants, having several of that make. She wants the kind used in Spain and Italy, worked with gold and silver. I desire you to make every effort that I may have the two white mares, in good condition. About the powder I am unable to give you any definite answer. I will send the pattern and measure of the armour.[74]

Near the end of January, on the 22nd, Pasquale Spinola wrote to Leicester from Antwerp with the news that Signora Baroncelli had given birth to a daughter, which Benedetto Spinola, his brother, had held at the christening ceremony on behalf of Leicester. The Count of Egmont was the other godfather, and a Signor Malgrani stood proxy for him, while the wife of Ludovico Nicolo stood proxy for the Countess of San Segondo. 'They gave the child the name of her Majesty.'[75]

Leicester had evidently sent a cup for the baptism, for on 21 February, Tommaso Baroncelli wrote to him to thank him:

Although I have had no letter from your Excellency, I have none the less cause to write this to thank you, if not so much as I ought, yet as much as I can, for the present you were pleased to send to your *comare* for Elizabeth, your spiritual daughter, for the which our gratitude is as great as her deserts are small. By it we shall keep you in perpetual memory, in the fashion of the Umbrian country, and when the Count of Agamonte [Egmont] returns from Spain, I shall pray him to dine or sup with us, and to measure how much the cup holds by quaffing it to your Excellency's health.[76]

As ever — or so it would seem — the business of horses crops up once more, with Bruschetto making a reappearance, as well as Signor Claudio, Leicester's Master of the Horse, and there is news of the arquebus, the armourer, and also the painter. Baroncelli had also sent the Queen a book:

I pray you to beg her Majesty to let me have two lines to say how she was pleased with the book I sent her . . . Mr Francis Bertie is coming here to make an end of the salt business . . . From Spain we have letters, and also some aid for the debts of her Majesty in this country, which has certainly come to a good resolution . . . It would be well if her Majesty . . . could be persuaded to come into this country. There is much need of it, on many accounts.[77]

Of course Elizabeth had no intention of going abroad, and it was only with great reluctance that she was to allow Leicester to do so some twenty years later. Nevertheless this atmosphere of courteous affability seems to characterise a moment when Leicester was beginning to find his feet, to use the opportunities afforded by his position and wealth, for patronage, for acquisitions, for developing his personality in the eyes of the world. However, 1565 was not destined to be pursued in this way. There were more serious matters on foot.

4

The Perfect Courtier

I cannot live without seeing you every day. You are like my lapdog.

Queen Elizabeth to the Earl of Leicester

On 30 December 1564 Cecil wrote to Sir Thomas Smith, English ambassador to France, to the effect that, 'The Earl of Lennox' friends wish that the Lord Darnley might marry with the Scottish Queen . . . But I see no disposition thereto in her Majesty, but she rather continueth her desire to have my Lord of Leicester preferred that way.' The plan had been discussed at Berwick, according to Cecil's letter, with Mary's half-brother the Earl of Moray and with Maitland. If Mary accepted this offer, then she would be recognised by the English Parliament as heiress presumptive. The letter continued: 'I see the Queen's Majesty very desirous to have my Lord of Leicester placed in this high degree to be the Scottish Queen's husband; but when it cometh to the conditions which are demanded, I see her then remiss of her earnestness.'[1]

On 5 February Randolph, English ambassador to Scotland, wrote from Edinburgh to Elizabeth that Mary seemed prepared to consider Leicester as a suitable husband, though he ought to have realised that the very words he quoted as being indicative of this were capable of bearing a very different construction, especially when seen in relation to Mary's past behaviour. She had said: 'My mind towards him is such as it

78

ought to be of a very noble man . . . and such one as the Queen your mistress, my good sister, doth so well like to be her husband if he were not her subject . . .'[2] In view of this, Randolph felt, Leicester's lack of enthusiasm was hard to bear. Nor was Randolph made to feel any more confident of bringing off the match when Darnley was allowed to go to Edinburgh that same month. In March there was a further blow to his hopes. News reached Scotland of a quarrel between Leicester and Norfolk, but what particularly dismayed Randolph was not only the nature of the incident, but the speed with which news of it had travelled. As he wrote to Sir Nicholas Throckmorton: 'What is most secret among you is so soon at this Queen's ears, that some would think it should be out of the Privy Chamber door where you are.'

There had been a long, simmering feud between Robert Dudley and Thomas Howard, 4th Duke of Norfolk, despite the fact that the latter's second wife, Margaret Audley, had been the wife of Leicester's brother Henry, killed at the Siege of St Quentin. Admittedly she herself died in 1563, so that the family connection had become tenuous to the point of invisibility. Though nominally a Protestant, Norfolk was the head of a family that was almost synonymous with Catholicism, especially in the north. Thomas Howard represented the old nobility, and bitterly resented parvenus such as the Dudleys — and even more so when they were the offspring of traitors. In the course of a tennis match between the two men that month, Leicester had taken the Queen's napkin out of her hand and wiped his face with it. Norfolk was outraged at this presumption, and threatened Leicester with his racket. Apart from anything else — for example, the very fact of such a commotion in front of the Queen herself — it was the familiarity between Leicester and the Queen that his behaviour revealed, which was so potentially damaging internationally. Norfolk also, it might be noted, was a potential suitor for Mary's hand, since he was now a widower for the second time, before he had even reached the age of thirty. With these two men, therefore, at loggerheads before her very eyes, and as the threat of a match between Darnley and Mary became more real, Elizabeth summoned the Council, and on 1 May 1565 had them sign a declaration that such a marriage would seriously threaten 'the sincere amity between both the queens'.[3]

On 4 April Robert Huggins had written to Leicester from Madrid, telling him that Sir Thomas Chaloner had left for England on 2 March. De Feria had expressed surprise that he had gone before his successor had arrived, and asked Huggins whether a successor had in fact been appointed, or if he knew who it was to be. Chaloner had been quite shrewd when he suggested that Elizabeth would save the cost of maintaining his successor for a space of three or four months if he was allowed to go early. He knew that it would appeal to her love of economy. Evidently Leicester had asked Chaloner to pay his respects to De Feria and his countess (Jane Dormer) before he left, which had been much appreciated by De Feria, and he also mentioned that the king was pleased that Leicester had been very civil to Diego de Guzman (de Silva), a fact which he had communicated in his letters to Madrid. Then the subject became horses, and it was noted that Chaloner had been given one by the king on his departure, with permission to take a further four for himself and twelve for the Queen. When the French ambassador left he had only been allowed to take six.[4]

Leicester's interest in horses and their welfare was reflected this year in the dedication to him of Thomas Blundeville's *Four Chiefest Offices belonging to horsemanship*. Another book this year was Thomas Cooper's *Thesaurus*, with the bear and ragged staff on the title page, a book which ran to five editions. And then there were others, such as Pietro Bizari's two poems *Ad Robertum Dudlaeum*, published in Venice; Arthur Golding's translation of the first four books of Ovid's *Metamorphoses* (there was an edition of fifteen books in 1567, also dedicated to Leicester); John Shute's translation of Pierre Viret's *The First Part of the Christian Instruction*, and John Stow's first set of *Chronicles*.

It is interesting that in Huggins' letter from Madrid there were references to Mary Queen of Scots and Darnley, indicating that the matter was being talked about there also. Huggins wrote again on 21 June 1565 from Madrid, thus keeping up the contact until the new ambassador had settled into his post.[5]

While hunting with the Queen at the beginning of May, Leicester met with an accident, and had to stay in bed. News travelled fast — and was exaggerated at the same time — for it had reached Bruges by 11 May, when Nicholas Wotton wrote: 'The first news of the fall of your horse under you made us more afraid than there was cause . . .'[6] Back at home, De Silva had been to visit Leicester on 5 May, when he found Maitland there also, soon to be joined by Cecil and Throckmorton. Maitland was to return to Scotland, and Throckmorton would accompany him. In the circumstances it had been felt that a more acute mind than that of Randolph was required to look after English interests in these delicate negotiations. Throckmorton had been replaced by Sir Thomas Smith as ambassador in France, and had done something of a volte-face as far as Leicester was concerned. His reaction to the scandal

surrounding the death of Amye Robsart from Paris had condemned
Leicester and offended the Queen. Through Bedford and Sidney, however, the breach had been healed, and even before he left Paris he had
asked Leicester to be godfather to his son. Back in England, Throckmorton wanted power, which included a seat on the Council, and he saw
Cecil as the most formidable opponent to pursuing that aim. Alignment
with Leicester seemed by far the most sensible course of action in the
circumstances. At all events, when Throckmorton arrived in Edinburgh
he realised that the Queen of Scots was determined to marry Darnley,
and that matters had gone too far for there to be any reasonable hope of
retrieving the situation. As he wrote to Leicester on 21 May 1565:

> I know not whether I may more com[mend] your fortune, your
> wisdom, or your immeasurable d[evoti]on to the Queen's Majesty.
> For I am sure one of these or [them] all have stayed you from a great
> inconvenience as never to give yourself over to like any other than the
> queen's Majesty. If solicitations of many . . . if persuasions and
> severe commandments of her Majesty, from time to time, if evident
> presumptions and manifest assurances of your never enjoying her
> Majesty and contrarywise probable arguments and vehement tokens
> were offered to move you to take hope that this queen was like to be
> yours, as I know there was divers and sundry; if all these respects then
> and many more could have enchanted you to al[low?] of this matter
> for yourself, you have been very unhappy . . .

Throckmorton then stressed how lucky Leicester was not to have forfeited the favour of Elizabeth for the dubious favour of Mary. People
were saying that if Leicester had been more forthcoming, then Mary
would have been his. More than that, Mary would not have found
herself in the position that she was vis à vis Darnley if Leicester had come
forward. Certainly this seems to have been Randolph's view, and Mary
herself was even now taking this line, though laying most of the blame
at Elizabeth's door: '. . . she her[self] doth not altogether accuse you,
nor excuse you [but?] chargeth the Queen's Majesty with the whole
. . .' In other words, Mary was maintaining that since she had agreed to
take Elizabeth's advice, then it was all Elizabeth's fault. In Throckmorton's
opinion the situation was past remedy: 'I think it meet to advertise you that
the matter betwixt this Queen and the Lord Darnley is too far past to be
broken, for though the consummation of the marriage be deferred, I am
sure it is indissoluble without violence. And . . . I do wish that her
Majesty may use the matter to her own most advantage and surety.'[7]

In June De Silva received a letter from King Philip — written on 6 June — in which the latter declared that the marriage between Mary and Darnley was one that was favourable to Spain's interests, and that they ought to be supported. If they would only control themselves, and not be precipitate, then the king would help them. De Silva was not to let this be known at the English Court, of course, but to make sure that the news got to Mary.[8]

For Leicester, June saw at least one piece of business — though a relatively small one — satisfactorily concluded. On 29 March that year Leicester had been addressed by Anna, *née* d'Oldenburg and Delmenhorst, Countess Dowager of East Friesland, from Emden on behalf of her son, John. He had been promised 2,000 *écus au soleil* (£600) yearly by the Queen, but the first year had passed without any payment being made. The letter therefore made request that payment and letters patent be sent to Antwerp or Emden.[9] A subsequent letter of 21 June thanked Leicester for having commended her son to the Queen, and requested that he should receive just compensation for his expenses in hiring colonels for her Majesty in 1564.[10]

In the first week of July Leicester was up and about again, and came into violent conflict with Thomas Radcliffe, 3rd Earl of Sussex. Once more the Archduke Charles was being put forward as a suitor for the Queen, and Sussex was to go to handle the negotiations. Despite the fact that Charles was a Catholic, Sussex was in favour of the match because he believed that the Queen would be likely to produce an heir from it. He felt, however, that Leicester would be working against him, behind his back, and so fell into an open quarrel. The seemingly omnipresent De Silva reported: 'I am told that when the Earl of Sussex . . . speaks to the Queen about it she tells him that Lord Robert presses her so that he does not leave her a moment's peace, and when Lord Robert addresses her, she says the same thing of the Earl of Sussex, and that she is never free from him.'[11]

Despite Throckmorton's vision of a match between them, the summer of 1565 did indeed represent a low-water mark in the state of the relationship between Leicester and Elizabeth. On her side there was distress at the death of her beloved Kat Ashley. The Queen always took the death of those to whom she was attached badly, and naturally this became more pronounced as the years went by. Then there was the problem of the Queen of Scots and her marriage to Darnley. In May Darnley had been made Earl of Ross, and in July Duke of Albany. On 29 July Mary had him proclaimed king in Edinburgh, and on the same day married him. It was, after all, Leicester who had encouraged Elizabeth to grant permission for Darnley to go north in the first place. Certainly De Silva noted in July that: 'He seems lately to be rather more alone than usual, and the Queen appears to display a certain coolness towards him.'[12] In August, when the Court was at Windsor, Cecil wrote to Sir Thomas Smith in Paris: 'I will in a few words give you some light. The Queen's Majesty is fallen into some misliking of my Lord of Leicester, and he therewith much dismayed.'[13] The same month he wrote in his diary: 'The Queen's Majesty seemed to be much offended with the Earl of Leicester, and so she wrote an obscure sentence in a book at Windsor.'[14]

There may have been previous disagreements between Leicester and Elizabeth which had passed without comment. This one was so serious, however, that it could not escape notice. It is difficult to see what caused it, apart from the baleful influence of Mary Stuart and her marriage to Darnley, for which, in some very ill-defined way, Elizabeth may have held Leicester responsible. Or perhaps it was simply that as the seventh year of her reign drew to its close, Elizabeth had become more mature in her reactions to men. She saw Leicester in a somewhat different light — possibly even in his true light, which was no longer the image of the knight on horseback. To a certain extent it was to be his tragedy that he did not seem to realise this, and indeed he had very good reason for not doing so, for the Queen's mood did not prevent her from continuing to give him signs of favour. On 3 August, for example, he was permitted to keep one hundred retainers, by a document that is still at Longleat.[15] This was to remain true for the rest of his life. No matter how much Elizabeth raged, the rage was soon forgotten when it was occasioned by Leicester, and his material situation never once suffered as a result.

There certainly was a new element for him to contend with, however, for the Queen was seen to be flirting with Thomas Heneage, who had become a Gentleman of the Privy Chamber in 1560, and Sir Henry Sidney told De Silva that, in his opinion, his brother-in-law Leicester 'had lost hope of his business'.[16] He felt that the Queen did not intend to marry, and that in itself was a terrible thing for the country, for if she were to die without an heir, no three persons in the realm seemed to agree about who should be her successor. Another view, taken by some and reported subsequently, as for example by Strype, was that: 'The Earl of Leicester now fell into some misliking with Queen Elizabeth. And he was therewith much dismayed. (The cause seemed to be, for not liking the Queen's marrying with the Archduke.)'[17] Yet the same account, slightly earlier reported that 'The Earl of Leicester furthered the Queen with all good reason to take one of these great princes. Wherein surely perceiving his own cause not sperable he did honourably and wisely . . .' At all events, Throckmorton seems to have encouraged Leicester to try and find out whether the Queen would marry him or not, and if not, then support the Archduke Charles. There is in the Pepys Collection a letter dated July 1565 from the Emperor Maximilian II, from Vienna, thanking Leicester for 'his service in promoting that matter with the Queen',[18] and he was Charles' brother. Cecil told Smith, moreover, that: 'My Lord of Leicester hath behaved himself very wisely to allow of it.'[19] That was, incidentally, about the same time that he wrote in his diary about the 'obscure sentence' written by the Queen.

Meanwhile, Leicester indulged in a flirtation of his own. At the beginning of September — acting once more, according to De Silva, on Throckmorton's advice — Leicester made up to Laetitia or Lettice Knollys, Viscountess Hereford. One day the flirtation was to blossom into a full-blown romance, and Lettice was to become Leicester's wife. His choice was unfortunate, to say the least. Although she was a cousin of the Queen — her grandmother, Mary Boleyn, was Anne Boleyn's sister — Elizabeth could not stand her. De Silva described her as 'one of the best looking ladies of the Court',[20] which goes some way to explaining why. Although the Longleat portrait may not make her a classic English beauty, it expresses a good deal of the attraction she obviously possessed. As if to underline what he was up to, Leicester asked permission to 'go to stay at his own place as other men did'. After three days this had the desired effect. The Queen summoned him, there was a furious quarrel, and then the inevitable reconciliation. De Silva had heard that both Cecil and Sussex had interceded on behalf of Leicester, though neither of them was a true friend in his heart of hearts. Heneage discreetly left Windsor, though not for very long.

September saw the arrival in England of Princess Cecilia, sister to King Eric of Sweden. She had married the Margrave of Baden, on condition that she came on a visit to the Queen of England. At the same time, of course, she would have the opportunity to press her brother's suit for the Queen's hand, but she was in any case very keen to meet this Queen of whom she had heard so much. She wrote to Elizabeth begging her to accept a little ring: '. . . not measuring her affection by this mean offering. If the ring holds together and does not break, so will also her poor service never break.'[21] A letter from the princess dated 12 May 1565 had reached Leicester from Danzig, in which she thanked him for

YOW THAT THESE BEASTS DO WEL BEHOLD AND SE
MAY DEME WITH EASE WHERFOR HERE MADE THEY BE
WITH BORDERS EKE WHERIN ...
4 BROTHERS NAMES WHO LIST TO SERCHE THE GROWND

The carved inscription recording the time spent by Robert Dudley and his three
brothers in the Beauchamp Tower at the Tower of London, imprisoned for their
part in the Lady Jane Grey conspiracy.

An illustration of Elizabeth's coronation procession shows clearly how close the
Dudleys were to her at the start of her reign. Ambrose leads the second litter
horse, and Robert the palfrey of honour.

Probably painted by Steven van der Muelen when Dudley was in his early thirties (*c.* 1560-65), this portrait captures admirably the nature of the man who held so much attraction for Queen Elizabeth.

Ambrose Dudley, Earl of Warwick, Robert's elder brother, but a much less colourful character than his junior. Elizabeth placed great trust in him, and he was widely known as 'the good earl' for his nature.

Dudley's signature on a letter written in 1564, before he was created Earl of Leicester and began to sign himself differently. His flamboyant hand echoes that of the Queen herself. (Dudley papers Vol. I, f. 6).

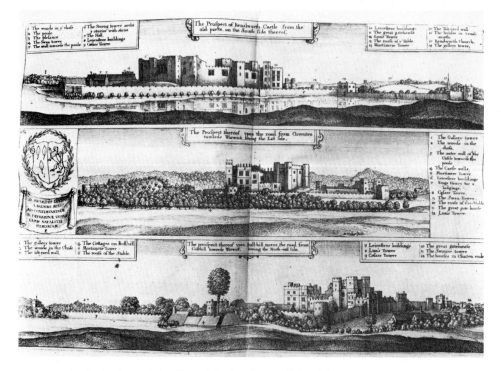

Hollar's views of Kenilworth before it was slighted in the Civil War. The extent of Leicester's buildings at right, centre and left of the three views can be clearly seen, as well as the lake in the top view.

The entertainment on the lake at Kenilworth during the queen's visit in 1575 has not been depicted, but it must have been very similar to the one shown here, which took place at Elvetham in Hampshire, 1591.

The huge barn that Dudley built at Kenilworth, within the castle walls, seen here prior the recent restoration, as it appeared in 1959. Little else remains of his vast amount of building on the site.

An illustration from Turberville's *Book of Hunting* which was originally published in 1575, the year of Elizabeth's visit to Kenilworth and participation in just such a deer hunt as the one depicted here.

A section of Marcus Gheeraerts the Elder's representation of the Garter Procession of 1576. Dudley is seen second from the left, and his brother Ambrose on the far right.

Another section from Gheeraerts' Garter Procession. Here we see Elizabeth, preceded by the Sword of State, against a backdrop of Windsor Castle.

Nicholas Hilliard was a protégé of Dudley at one time, and painted this miniature of him in 1576, the year before Hilliard went to France. The artist named several of his children after members of the Dudley family.

An illustration to Spenser's *Shepheards Calender* of 1579—the March eclogue—in which he made an indiscreet reference to Dudley's wife, Lettice, and so incurred his patron's wrath, leading to banishment to Ireland.

his commendations of her to the Queen, which had been communicated to her by George North, and she took the opportunity of sending some *munuscula* (small gifts) which she hoped might be accepted.[22]

By the time she reached England, the princess had been travelling for eleven months. Moreover she was pregnant, and within a week of giving birth. In order that the royal visitor might be suitably lodged, the Earl of Bedford's house in the Strand was taken over, since he was absent in his post as Governor of Berwick. According to the report of the Spanish ambassador, the lady created something of a sensation when seen in London.[23] The Queen was at Windsor, but came to see her just before the son was born, and agreed to be godmother. The name Edward was chosen, along with Fortunatus, for there had indeed been a happy issue out of all his mother's afflictions. The christening ceremony took place at the end of the month, and was carried out with great magnificence in the chapel at Whitehall.[24]

On 12 October Sir Thomas Smith wrote from Nantes to the effect that he, too, wanted very much to be recalled: 'For my coming home I never desired it more, and am sorry that England should be destitute in time of peace of men to succeed me.'[25] He was still there in November, for he had occasion to write to Leicester on the 22nd of that month, this time from Tours, interceding for his man Charles Wilson, who had been charged with piracy.[26] The earlier letter conveys Smith's view of the Queen's marriage, and his lordship's role in the affair: 'For mine opinion betwixt Homefriend and Lovealien ye take it right. But of all I cannot like the opinion of Agamias and Spitewed, for it is the source of the ruin and trouble of our realm and will be the final disturbance of her Majesty's good designs.' He was sorry that neither he nor his wife had been at home when the Queen visited his house, but looked forward to the time when he would welcome her, and Leicester, there in person:

> I am glad that the Queen took my poor house at Ankerwick, but sorry that my wife was not there at that time to entertain her Highness. That you write that the Queen was merry there recompenseth all. And I pray God I may once see her Majesty merry there, and your lordship together. Then I shall reckon my house twice sanctified and blessed.[27]

Another correspondent during this month of October was Francis Russell, Earl of Bedford. Not that it was a new correspondence, by any means. We have already seen, for example, how Bedford's Puritan sympathies had drawn him to Leicester in March that year, but it increased in frequency at this time, partly because Bedford was yet another person who felt that Leicester was a useful connection at the centre of power, when he himself felt so much on the periphery, but also because they were soon to be united by family ties. Many of the letters in the Pepys Collection[28] are much the same as those in the Calendar of State Papers, Foreign, but the one of 7 October — though also having its counterpart in the State Papers — is interesting for the alarm it expresses to Leicester. Bedford had heard from Cecil that the Queen was pleased with him at Berwick, and yet he had also heard from Melville that she intended sending the Earl of Sussex with troops to aid the Lords of the Congregation. He protested against being superseded in this way, since he was willing to spend his goods, lands, blood and life in the cause of God, the Queen, and the peace of both kingdoms. He therefore requested Leicester's interest to avert the discredit.[29]

On 24 October Bedford wrote to find out the date of his daughter's marriage to Ambrose, Earl of Warwick,[30] and the ceremony in fact took place on 11 November.[31] From Leicester's letters to Bedford one has the distinct impression that not all the efforts of the bride-to-be, her father, the intending bridegroom, or even the Queen herself, would have been of any avail without the favourite himself at the hub.[32] In the event he gave away the bride in her father's absence, and it may just have been that the Queen and her favourite found, in fussing over this marriage, some compensation for the one they were unlikely ever to be able to arrange for themselves. Anne Russell was Ambrose's third wife, and it was a cause for deep regret that they never had any children. In fact Ambrose's only recorded child John, by his first wife, died before his mother.

Leicester's involvement in his brother's wedding continued beyond the actual ceremony, for on 1 December the Earl of Bedford wrote to him again about the jointure for his daughter.[33] This letter is also interesting for the light it throws on the extended stay of the Princess Cecilia: 'If the Lady Cecilia lies not in my house herself, I pray that order may be given for the removing of her train which as I hear be but a homely company and in as homely manner do use my house, breaking and spoiling windows and everything.' He repeated the request to Cecil on 7 December: 'I heartily pray you help that my house there may be rid of certain rude guests that spill and spoil everything in the same.'[34]

By the end of the year it seemed that Leicester was well and truly back in favour, and that his old ambition of marrying the Queen had flickered into flame once more. Certainly De Foix, the French ambassador, was of that opinion, as he communicated to Catherine de' Medici on 27 November 1565: 'The friendship and favour of the queen towards the Earl of Leicester increases daily.' De Foix went on to relate that Cecil had told him that the Earl of Leicester had paid him a visit in his rooms, and informed him that he was not only a suitor to the Queen, but felt that he was more likely to succeed than anyone else. He therefore asked Cecil to give up any plan he might have for marrying the Queen to a foreign prince.[35]

In their attempt to prevent a Habsburg alliance, Catherine de' Medici and Charles IX of France wanted to encourage Leicester, and when they heard that he had expressed a wish to visit France, they forthwith issued an invitation. By the time this arrived, however, the quarrel between Leicester and the Queen had been patched up, and he was much less keen to leave the Court. When Elizabeth heard De Foix's account she asked Leicester to his face, in front of the ambassador, whether he wanted to go. It was not only the prospect of his absence that upset her, but also the fact that he appeared to have been making plans behind her back. This was certainly the appearance it bore, because of the delay in posts. Leicester was caught in an awkward situation. The Queen, moreover, seemed to be determined to make the most of it. With barely concealed malice, that seemed to owe not a little to Mary Queen of Scots, she said that she could hardly send a groom, a horsekeeper, to wait upon so great a king. She then seemed to thaw, and said: 'I cannot live without seeing you every day.' Barely giving Leicester time to assimilate this apparent compliment, she went on: 'You are like my lapdog, as soon as he is seen anywhere, the people say that I am coming; and when you are seen, they may say, in like manner, that I am not far off.'[36]

Leicester had been put in his place with deadly accuracy. As a realist he knew that whatever apparent room for manoeuvre he might have from time to time, when he strayed too far he would quickly be brought to book — and the alternative was one he hardly wished to contemplate. He had far too much to lose. On 19 December De Foix wrote: 'Leicester has very much urged the Queen to decide upon her marriage by Christmas. She, on the other hand, has desired him to wait until Candlemas [2 February], and then she will satisfy him.'[37] The ambassador had, moreover, heard it said that the Queen had promised to marry Leicester in the hearing of witnesses. De Foix was not the only one. On 28 December Catherine, Dowager Duchess of Suffolk, wrote to Leicester from Edenham in a curious mixture of flattery and would-be maternal admonition:

> I was once minded to have sent such a new year's gift as Mr Bertey [her husband, Richard Bertie] told your lordship I had devised to the Queen's Majesty, or if not that none other than ordinary money, for that I could frame no certain device to that purpose which I most desired, because the planets reigned most incertainly, now I hear to my great comfort of some better aspect, but if it was so far forth as the friendly report is abroad, I have just cause to hinder that which I would most willingly further, seeing you have so far proceeded without either the knowledge or any means made for your mother's consent, and therefore unlawful before me, which ought with [?] the first to have the participation of the first fruits of your felicity as naturally I most feel the first sorrows of any your infelicity, wherefore I wish your lordship as well as any mother her child, but my blessing I will withhold till your better amendment upon pain whereof I desire your lordship to have my most humble duty in remembrance to her Majesty, and so I leave your lordship to the eternal God. Your lordship's loving mother and assured friend to my power. K. Suffolk.

Her husband did not neglect to add his postscript: 'According to my promise I intend, God permitting, to wait upon your lordship this next term, in the mean season and ever I remain your lordship's humble at commandment, R. Bertie.'[38]

One may think that the duchess's claim to be regarded as Leicester's mother was somewhat tenuous, but the prospect of having him as royal consort was an understandable attraction. Two days later, on 30 December, a person with a more immediate claim to kinship, the Earl of Hertford, wrote to Leicester from Sir John Mason's: 'Knowing that you are the appointed means that in the end shall gain unto us our prince's over long wanted favour I beseech the employing of your credit for us and that you will help the afflicted that still seek your mediation to our Queen.'[39] There is also a letter in the same collection from Anne, Duchess of Somerset, to the Queen on the same subject, pointing out that by now her son had been in prison for over four years.[40] The marriage was destined to remain subject to royal disapproval, however, for the rest of Catherine Grey's life, though this was not to last much longer. She died early in 1568, and the Queen gave money for her funeral.

With so much talk of marriage, Leicester was on particularly dangerous ground. He could ill afford to wreck his own chances by trying to promote the cause of others. Not only did the Queen resent the marriages of those near her, but her own words to Leicester were so cryptic. As De Foix was forced to conclude, in his letter of 19 December, 'If she thinks fit to disengage herself, no person will call her to account, or give testimony against her.'[41] At this time English common law recognised two kinds of espousal. *Sponsalia per verba de praesenti* was a declaration by both parties that each took the other at the time as spouse, and was legally binding, no matter what change in circumstances took place, and it amounted to full marriage, whether the union was consecrated subsequently or not. *Sponsalia per verba de futuro* was simply a declaration of intent to marry at some future date, and was not absolutely binding. However, if the couple had intercourse, then the marriage became binding. As Henry Swinburne wrote in *A Treatise of Spousals*, not published until 1686, though written approximately a century earlier, '. . . if a man contract spousals conditionally with a woman . . . and . . . in the meantime he have access to her, as to his wife, these doubtful spousals do thereby pass into matrimony.'[42] Of course this common-law attitude would have been based on canon law that was in operation before the Council of Trent altered it, and which therefore was not held to be valid in a Protestant country such as England. Nevertheless the ecclesiastical view was much the same in a writer such as William Perkins,[43] and this throws particularly interesting light on Elizabeth's behaviour, not only at this point with Leicester, but also subsequently with the Duke of Alençon. The question of the Queen's marriage was to continue to occupy thoughts and passions in the New Year of 1566, and bring Leicester into conflict with his long-standing rival the Duke of Norfolk.

Initially, however, the round of Court life continued. On 13 January a summons was issued from Westminster requiring Leicester's attendance at Windsor for the installation, two days later, of the French king, Charles IX, as a Knight of the Garter by his proxy 'Lord Rambuliet' — Jacques d'Angennes.[44] Then, at this time, the Queen fell down a short flight of steps; but though very shaken, and somewhat lame, she was able to receive De Silva by 27 January. Candlemas came and went, but there was no marriage with the Earl of Leicester. In fact De Silva had heard that at a Council meeting held two days later, the Duke of Norfolk had seen fit to recall to Leicester that he had maintained that he was not seeking the Queen's hand, and that she had stated plainly that she had no intention of marrying him. He then went on to say that it was for this reason that the Council had reactivated negotiations with Archduke Charles. If these were protracted and it was generally felt that Leicester was in any way to blame, then his situation, Norfolk stressed, would be a highly awkward one. For this reason, if for no other, Norfolk advised Leicester to support the Council in its endeavours. Caught in a very tight corner, Leicester bowed to pressure and said that he would indeed support the initiative, if it could be arranged in such a way that the Queen did not imagine that he had done it out of any lack of determination on his part, for this 'might cause her, woman-like, to undo him'.[45]

Later that same day, De Silva had an audience of the Queen, who was going to Greenwich on the morrow, and she had nothing but praise for Leicester. In his next letter De Silva added his own remark: 'She, in her part, deals with them in a way that deceives them all! When she speaks to the Duke [of Norfolk], she says one thing, and when to Lord Robert, quite the contrary.'[46] Things had indeed been difficult at Court during January, to the point where, again according to De Silva, Leicester's adherents began wearing blue or purple, and Norfolk's yellow. There was also a very murky story, which only came to light later, that at about this time someone approached Amye Robsart's half-brother, Appleyard, in an attempt to bribe him and get him to denounce Leicester as Amye's murderer. When the Order of St Michel was eventually bestowed, it was on Leicester and Norfolk — not Sussex, as Leicester is supposed to have suggested — and this was no doubt an attempt on Elizabeth's part to strike a balance between the two factions.

A shaky truce then ensued, and in February Leicester was away from Court, for Throckmorton wrote to him on the 19th of that month from Baynard's Castle: 'Take heed by your hasty coming that you do not wrap yourself into the whole burden of the matter.'[47] At this point the Queen was insisting that the Archduke must change his religion — at least secretly — and any apparent intervention by Leicester would again threaten him with the accusation of having harmed the good of the realm. It was indeed a trying time. Then on 14 February the Earl of Bedford had written to Leicester from Berwick to commiserate:

> For your own estate I am glad it is better than some would have it, yet I am sure not so well as some of your friends could wish. Touching my daughter I wrote to her that I had heard somewhat, though not so much as I feared, and glad I am you have put me out of that doubt . . .'

With it went the almost inevitable requests: 'Remember the best means for my coming up against St George's Day and let me put you in mind for Mr Randolph [for the Postmastership] . . . His only trust is that you will stick by him.'[48]

On 25 February Randolph wrote from Scotland to say that the marriage between Darnley and Mary Queen of Scots had failed, and that both Darnley and his father, Lennox, were plotting against the queen and her assumed lover, David Rizzio.[49] Randolph went on to prophesy that Rizzio would be murdered 'within these ten days' — a prophecy that came true on 9 March, though not quite as soon as he had expected.

On 17 February Anna, Lady Hungerford, wrote to Leicester from Exton that her sister, the Countess of Feria, had written from Madrid and told that one Morgan Roberts, who had Leicester's licence to go to Spain, had 'unhonestly used his tongue towards you and other noblemen, and has reported our Queen's Court more like a stews than a place of degree and virtue. This with a great deal more he reported in the Count of Feria's house, and had warning to use himself more circumspectly . . .'[50] Then Bedford wrote again on 21 February from Berwick to protest that at Lady Day the garrison would be a year and a half behind with its pay, and the men were in great necessity. He was almost of the opinion that someone in London had deliberately created this situation to spite him, and did not care if it was the devil himself who came, provided he brought the money with him.[51]

A further suppliant, in a letter of 28 February, was Sir James Croft, writing from the Minories. Croft had a long and varied career in office, despite being in the pay of the King of Spain for part of it. He wanted Leicester to confer with Cecil and move the Queen to grant him a full pardon. He had been banished from Court for a year, lost an office worth £1,000 annually, and 'otherwise hindered' to the value of £5,000. He then went on to list all the service he had rendered in various capacities, both at home and abroad, yet now he was forced to beg for a living or sell his inheritance in order to maintain the countenance of a poor gentleman.[52] In due course the Queen restored him to favour, and made him Comptroller of the Household.

In March 1556 Leicester's sister Katherine was ill, so he went to Ashby de la Zouch to visit her. As ever, there were those who wished to interpret this absence from the Court as a desire to touch the Queen, and one cannot totally rule out the possibility, for the Queen had a new flirtation at this time, on much the same lines as the earlier one she had had with Heneage. Thomas Butler, Earl of Ormonde, had been brought up at Court during the reign of Henry VIII, but during that of Mary he had gone over to pacify his Irish tenants. He soon found himself at loggerheads with the Earl of Desmond, and there is a letter in the Pepys Collection from Ormonde to Leicester, dated from Dublin on 23 November 1564, in which Ormonde complains of Desmond.[53] The next year Ormonde came to England to plead his case, and spent the next four years there. De Silva said that he was 'an Irishman of good disposition, thirty years of age', and on 20 March 1566 the French ambassador, De Foix, wrote: 'The Earl of Ormonde is in high favour with Elizabeth, though he has neither ability nor means to maintain his ground; Leicester is, nevertheless, under some apprehension.'[54] By May the Queen's attentions to Black Tom, as he was known, provoked Dr Young, Archbishop of York, into warning the Queen that her behaviour was causing scandal. Not surprisingly this enraged her. Moreover it was known that Dr Young was a friend of the Earl of Leicester. Luckily the latter was able to mediate in the matter, but it did not encourage a friendship between Leicester and Ormonde. When Leicester went to Ashby, then, he had not given a date for his return. The Queen wrote to ask him to come back, and he replied by requesting a further fifteen days' leave, whereupon the Queen told him to return forthwith.

Possibly the earl had intended paying a visit to the Earl of Shrewsbury if he had spent more time away in the north, for a letter from Wingfield in Derbyshire, dated 3 April 1566 expresses George Talbot's regret that he had not seen Leicester.[55]

April also brought to an end the visit of the Margrave and Margravine of Baden — the Swedish Princess Cecilia. What had begun as a romantic and charming interlude had turned into broad farce. Leicester had already received a letter from the Margrave dated 3 February 1566, from Baden, thanking him for his kindness to his wife and son in England, and requesting further services for them, and hoping to be able to make some return. He then added, somewhat cryptically, that his wife would be able to explain her husband's position.[56] He had in fact come to Calais, and was waiting on the other side of the Channel for her, but he then crossed over, and on 4 April wrote to Leicester from Rochester: 'I have been arrested by mean merchants to whom, if justice were done, I owe nothing, and have been put into the common prison here. I shall have my revenge hereafter.'[57]

The mayor of Rochester sent a letter to the Queen, asking that either the Margrave might be told that he must abide by the laws of the land, or else the town might be released from the responsibility for holding such a difficult prisoner. The Queen paid his debt and the Margrave left. His wife, however, remained behind until 29 April, and at one point creditors boarded her ship and threatened to lay hold of some chests which did not in fact belong to her, but to her ladies. One happy outcome of her visit was that her youngest maid-of-honour, Helena Snakenborg, who was only fourteen when she arrived in England, remained to marry the Marquess of Northampton in 1571. He only lived six months after the marriage, being considerably older than his bride, and she survived to become one of the Queen's closest friends, and chief mourner in her funeral procession.[58]

Throughout May and June the Ormonde issue continued to irritate Leicester, and the vestments controversy made its appearance once more, this time exacerbated by a new attack on preaching, and Laurence Humphrey appealed to Leicester on 2 June for help:

> Being informed that it is the Queen's pleasure that this decree against the refusers of the prescribed apparel without reservement shall proceed, I leave it even to the final determination of Him that is Governor of all churches in all causes ecclesiastical as well as temporal . . . Two things only I would wish: liberty of preaching without living generally . . . secondly, for the licence to answer this new examination of a book lately set forth in the name of the ministers of London . . . I trust the Queen's Majesty at her coming to Oxford shall have no cause in that respect to be offended with me or any in the university. Wherefore as I have once been tolerated by her goodness as others have been hitherto, so I wish your lordship to bear with me still in your university, and obtain that old freedom may be renewed.[59]

Two days later he wrote to Leicester again, but this time together with John Pierse, lamenting the decay of 'readings and disputations' at Corpus Christi College, and requesting Leicester to stir the Bishop of Winchester, founder and ordinary of the college, to remit enquiry to 'such grave and learned person as will reform the same'.[60] But on 12 June Humphrey wrote, from Rycote, on his own account about the stopping of preaching: 'As misery groweth, so mercy is to be sought . . . I crave your lordship this friendship, that I may be advertised . . . that it may be lawful for me yielding up . . . my livings most obediently, yet to continue in my vocation with pains, though without profit of the Church's goods . . .'[61] In fact Leicester subsequently recommended him for the Vice-Chancellorship, as we shall see.

Humphrey was not the only one to be troubled by the preaching controversy, however, and that same month of June 1566 Thomas Cole, Archdeacon of Essex, had cause to write to Leicester also:

> I have sent particulars of my May Day sermon at Chelmsford to Mr Christmas as you willed. If you have perused it, I hope I shall not be blamed, but thought to be a good subject. I spake nothing in that sermon, or any other since to the prejudice of the order taken, but rebuked those who said that the Queen minded to erect Popery again because of this order of apparel; my sermon was to hinder nothing the order of apparel, but to hinder the disorderly talk and impudent conceit of the Papists, which by reason of this order rumoured that they should have their Mass again. I am accused because my adversaries think that I dare not come to my answer for want of conformable apparel. If you examine them, they neither remember the text nor any circumstance appertaining to the same. The days are perilous: there are many quarrels against them that preach the truth. I hear that you are this week to be with Mr Stonarde in the forest, and would wait upon you. I beseech you that by the bearer I may hear somewhat of your pleasure in my case.[62]

As well as doctrinal matters, Leicester was, as usual, involved in matters of preferment and benefice. At the beginning of June, for example, William Aubrey wrote to him from Bruges. He had heard that the Bishop of St David's could not be induced to give him rights, or accept what Aubrey considered to be any just conditions. He wanted Leicester to help his friends, since he was so far away, and the bishop had so much power in his distant diocese.[63] In mid-June it was the Deans and Canons of Windsor — a body by no means noted for their humility or respect for niceties. On this occasion, however, even they treated Leicester with care:

> As our answer to your first request for our manors and parsonages in Somerset was not liked by you in all points, for ourselves we can be well content in consideration of your goodness towards us to accept one hundred marks only in the name of a fine and also to enlarge the term to ninety-nine years. Howbeit for the abatement of the yearly rent of £60 we think us of duty so bound to our posterity that we may not otherwise defalk any part thereof except by your honour's good means they and we may be eased of that great burden of our tenths

which being now but grievous unto us may haply thereafter be scant tolerable by them. The obtaining whereof though my Lord of Northumberland and other my lords of the Order lately here with us have promised their help, yet shall we accept the same as your honour's only doing and be ready with any pleasure or service we can do to requite the same.[64]

A further issue about leases was with New College, Oxford, and on 29 June Dr Thomas White wrote to Leicester: 'I and my company have with one assent granted you the lease of the parsonage of Adderbury, Oxon. If the election either of Mr Foster or Mr Danvers to the preferment be referred to the college, Mr Danvers will never obtain it, as he has been told. Whoever enjoys the lease shall have cause to thank you.'[65] As if to make this quite clear, thirty of the fellows signed a letter to Leicester saying: 'We and every of us granted you the lease of Adderbury, and it is not true that if we had free choice, we should have given the lease to Mr Danvers, for the names subscribed being a majority were in favour of Mr Foster.'[66] Such was one aspect of power. Who knows what potentially murky doings this somewhat too emphatic declaration may have hidden.

In June and July a renewed source of trouble came from a different quarter, namely the Earl of Sussex. At a council meeting Leicester told Sussex that he was responsible for Shane O'Neill's rebellion in Ireland. Naturally this incensed Sussex, who had been Lord Deputy in Ireland until 1564, and who said that it was Leicester, on the contrary, who had provoked the rebellion through his letters to O'Neill, and the two men almost came to blows. There is in fact a letter in the Pepys Collection from O'Neill, Earl of Tyrone, to Dudley (as he then was) dated 29 February 1564, in which he thanks the latter for his letters and messages of goodwill that he had received via Sir Thomas Cusake, and asks for further friendship and despatch of his business.[67]

On 19 June 1566 Mary Queen of Scots gave birth to her son James, and Melville hastened south with the news. He went first to Cecil, at his house in Cannon Row, and it was Cecil who took the tidings to Elizabeth, who was then at Greenwich, and dancing after supper when Cecil arrived. As reported by Melville — who was not there — Elizabeth's reaction was the bitter remark: 'The Queen of Scots is lighter of a fair son, and I am but a barren stock.'[68] Whatever her personal reaction to the news, certainly the birth of the prince put a very different complexion on Scottish affairs. By the next day, however, when

Elizabeth received Melville, the Queen had recovered her equanimity sufficiently to offer him her congratulations, and to agree to be godmother to the baby.

During the course of this year Leicester was granted a licence for twenty years to export all manner of wood and timber growing in Shropshire, and the lordships of manors in Worcester, Hereford, Gloucester, Somerset, Dorset, Denbigh, Brecon, Warwickshire, Hertfordshire, Bedfordshire, Norfolk and Lincolnshire.[69] At Longleat a whole volume (XVII) is devoted to the survey of lands made on 29 June this year,[70] and in the same collection are details of a sale of jewels to Leicester worth £1,400 on 12 July, to be paid by 12 January 1567.[71] Also at Longleat are tradesmen's bills, from Benedict Spinola for goldsmith's items and William Heron and Nicholas Lezard for painting, spread over a period from 1562 to 1566.[72] Dedications of this period included John Barthlet's *Pedigree of Heretics*; Thomas Danett's translation of *The History of Philip de Commines* (though not actually printed until 1596); John Jones' *A Dial for all Agues*, and Thomas Nuce's translation of Seneca's *Octavia*.

The French ambassador De Foix had now been replaced by La Forêt, who was on good terms with Leicester because it was in the French interest to encourage Elizabeth's marriage to the latter in order to prevent the Austrian match. On 6 August La Forêt had a conversation with Leicester, in the course of which the latter made the statement already quoted about having known the Queen since she was eight years old, and that she had always maintained that she would never marry. However, if she were to marry an Englishman, then Leicester believed that he would be the man.[73]

Certainly that summer there was a great deal to suggest that the favourite was as high in the Queen's affection once more as he had ever been. As part of her summer progress the Queen was to visit Oxford, of which university Leicester was Chancellor. In the middle of August Leicester was at Kenilworth, to be on hand to supervise arrangements for the visit, and the young Philip Sidney, his twelve-year-old nephew, was brought over from Shrewsbury School. By the third week in August the Queen was at Woodstock. On 27 August Leicester went hunting there with the Spanish ambassador, De Silva, in Woodstock Chase, and the latter reported, 'I talked with Leicester for a long while on the way, trying to direct the conversation as I usually do to his own affairs. It is easy to see he has not abandoned his pretensions by the manner in which he treats the matter.'[74] The Queen herself was that day unwell.

The Court was to arrive at Oxford on Saturday 31 August, and two days before Leicester and Warwick, with their brother-in-law the Earl of Huntingdon, went to make sure that all was well for the visit. They met Cecil in the quadrangle of Christ Church, but it began to rain so heavily that they were obliged to go indoors. Luckily the weather improved for the great day, and on the evening of 31st the Queen came by coach from Woodstock. There was the inevitable presentation of dignitaries, amongst them the Puritan Dr Humphrey or Humphries, whose garb inspired the Queen to remark: 'Master Doctor, that loose robe becomes you mighty well; I wonder your notions should be so narrow.' But, perhaps unwilling to cast a shadow over the proceedings at the outset, she added: 'But I do not come to chide.' She then went into Christ Church Cathedral, where a *Te Deum* was sung.[75]

An accident during a performance of *Palamon and Arcite* marred the visit. A staircase and part of a wall collapsed under the throng of undergraduates, three of whom were killed. Cecil had specifically acted to prevent this sort of thing happening when the Queen visited Cambridge two years previously. Nevertheless the play was repeated without further mishap the next night. When Elizabeth returned to Woodstock after the visit, some of the young men were summoned to debate in Latin before her — impromptu because the Spanish ambassador had expressed the opinion that without practice the young men would not make a brilliant showing. Edmund Campion was among them, and although he had spoken at Amye Robsart's funeral in 1560, his connection with Leicester really blossomed from this time. When Campion came to dedicate his *History of Ireland* to Leicester in 1571 he wrote:

> There is none that knoweth me familiarly but he knoweth withal how many ways I have been beholding to your lordship . . . How often at Oxford, how often at Court, how at Rycote, how at Windsor, how by letters, how by reports, you have not ceased to further with advice and to countenance with authority, the hope and expectation of me, a simple student.

Elizabeth also visited Kenilworth at this time, '. . . where she was magnificently entertained'.[76] And then, on the return journey to London, Leicester and the Queen, with only certain members of the retinue, stayed at Rycote, the home of Sir Henry Norreys and his wife Margery, whom Elizabeth called 'mine own Crow'. In early September the place has a timeless quality of peace and calm, and here in the friendly intimacy of a house they came to know well together, the tensions created by cares of State must have slipped away. It was perhaps no coincidence that Leicester's last letter to the Queen, some twenty-two years later, almost to the day, was written from this house.

Whilst this idyll was going on in England, however, Robert's brother-in-law Sir Henry Sidney was enduring agonies in Ireland. As he wrote from Drogheda on 5 September: 'Ah! my dearest lord that you could find in your heart to lose one of your fingers to have me at home; God defend that you should lose any one joint for me, but I would that I had lost a hand that I were delivered of this cursed charge . . .' He went on to remark with bitterness that in spite of all his incessant toil and labour for the good and quiet of others, he was slandered and in disgrace with his sovereign: 'Help me home speedily, or Almighty God dissolve my troubled spirit from my overtoiled body . . .' Ireland had already been the despair of lesser men than Henry Sidney, and was to continue to be so for many years to come. In a reference to Leicester's sister Mary and her children, Sidney made a final plea: 'As you love me and the issue of your worthy sister help me out of this wretched land or I shall shortly die, for, before God, I feel myself half dead already of very grief and toil . . . pardon my shaking hand; I fear I am entered into a palsy.'[77] For brother-in-law Leicester, however, enjoying the Queen's company amid the rural delights of Oxfordshire, Ireland might as well have been on the other side of the globe. Even this autumn idyll, however, must have seemed worlds away when, towards the end of the month, Parliament began to reassemble, and the Queen's marriage was uppermost in everyone's minds.

Parliament had been prorogued for three years, and when it assembled at the end of September, there was a determination to discuss and, it was hoped, settle the question of the Queen's marriage and the succession. In the Council it was Norfolk who broached the subject on 12 October, though he met with an angry retort from the Queen. The following week, when the Commons began to consider the subsidy bill, the matter was discussed openly. In all fairness to them, when they had adjourned in 1563 Elizabeth had promised to answer their petition, and they were still waiting. The message therefore went to the Queen from the Commons via the Council that no subsidy would be voted until they had some sort of satisfaction. On 22 October it was the turn of a deputation from the Lords, under the leadership of the aged Marquess of Winchester, who made their own representations to the Queen at Whitehall. Receiving no comfort from the Queen, a combined deputation from both Houses, with Norfolk as their spokesman, put their case to the Queen. De Silva's account of the event runs: 'The Queen was so angry, that she addressed hard words to the Duke of Norfolk, whom she called traitor or conspirator, or other words of similar flavour. He replied that he never thought to have to ask her pardon for having offended her thus.'[78] Not surprisingly, De Silva went on to report that the Queen had subsequently denied that she had ever spoken to the duke in this way. He also maintained that Leicester, Pembroke, Northampton and the Lord Chamberlain (Sussex) had all spoken to her, and Pembroke in particular had pointed out to her that it was not right that she should treat the duke in such a way, since he and the others were only doing what they thought right for the good of the country, and giving their considered opinion on what they thought best for her, too. Even if she chose to ignore their advice, it was still their duty to offer it. To Pembroke she retorted that he talked like a swaggering soldier. Northampton's matrimonial problems were such, she pointed out, that it had required an Act of Parliament to disentangle them, so let him look to himself before he started on her. As for Leicester — her sweet Robin— she had thought, she said, that if all the world abandoned her, he at least would not. He swore that he would die at her feet. She merely remarked that that had nothing to do with the matter. So much was she enraged that Elizabeth was contemplating telling them to consider themselves under house arrest, but she calmed down a little and merely told Pembroke and Leicester not to appear in her presence.

On 5 November the Queen eventually agreed to receive a deputation of thirty members from each House, whom she told that she hoped to marry and have children — with a large hint in the direction of Archduke Charles— but that she would not risk the danger of naming a successor. The speech turned out to be one of her most famous, as she uttered the immortal words:

> Though I be a woman, yet I have as good a courage, answerable to my place, as ever my father had . . . I will never be by violence constrained to do anything. I thank God I am endued with such qualities, that if I were turned out of the realm in my petticoat, I were able to live in any place in Christendom.

In the face of such oratory, there was little the assembled members could do. Elizabeth was not going to rely on words alone, however. Having played for time to prepare her strategy, she was back in control, and she now had a master stroke to play. The subsidy under consideration was to be paid in three parts, but she told both Houses that she would forgo the third part, knowing that if the money were in her subjects' pockets, then it was as good as in her exchequer. This virtually pre-empted any further moves from Parliament, except that there was a suggestion that her promise to marry be incorporated in the preamble to the subsidy bill in its published form. This would have the effect of proclaiming to the nation at large what the Queen had undertaken to do. When the draft was put before her for her signature, she wrote at the foot of it: 'I know no reason why any of my private answers to the realm should serve as a prologue to a subsidy book, neither yet do I understand why such audacity should be used to make without my licence an act of my words.' In the published version it simply incorporated a reference to 'the great hope and comfort' that the members felt on hearing the Queen's gracious promise to marry when it was convenient.

After such a display of her aversion to marriage, Leicester ought to have realised that the crown matrimonial would never be his. It says much for his vanity, his determination and his relentless ambition that he would not accept that reality. In the aftermath of this battle with the Queen his disgrace, if it is to be termed so, lasted into the new year of 1567. Meanwhile, he continued to deal with the day-to-day claims on his attention. On 10 December there was an after-effect of the Queen's visit to Oxford when Thomas Godwyn, Dean of Christ Church, wrote to him, along with seven others, from Oxford, to the effect that:

> The charge of the Queen's repair to the university and her abode with us is more than our church is able to bear. You affirmed that the whole university should be partakers of the burden. We therefore pray you will address letters to the Convocation that either by the university in common, or the colleges proportionately, we answering our portion may be unburdened.[79]

Then on 19 December Dr John Man, the English ambassador in Madrid, wrote that he was 'in extremity for money. Consider my case or recall me.'[80] Man's appointment had not been viewed well from this consideration right from the start. Robert Huggins had written to his brother-in-law John Appleyard from Madrid on 4 March 1566: 'Mr Man, the English Ambassador here, wants all things meet to supply his place . . . Yet I understand that this foolish man has as great allowance of the Queen as any of his predecessors; one quarter of it would suffice him . . . You may be able to tell Lord Leicester that some other man should be sent.'[81] Man himself had written to Leicester on 4 November

1566 from Madrid,[82] and the letters were to continue into the next year, for there are in the Pepys Collection letters from 18 February 1567 and 3 March that year,[83] but in April 1568 Man was still pleading with Leicester for his return.

From a very different quarter, when the Vintners' Company petitioned the Queen for a fresh charter, their previous one granted by Edward VI having been repealed in November 1566, they felt it worth their while to petition Leicester also. Certainly a new charter was granted the following year.[84]

As long as Leicester was in disgrace with the Queen, however, all such requests were subordinate to his own needs, and the chief of these was to restore himself to his former position as soon as possible. In January 1567 the Court was at Nonsuch in Surrey, and De Silva reported, 'the Earl of Leicester not being in very high favour with the Queen just now, I was walking out of her chamber when she called me back, and said she should be glad if I would show some love and friendship to Lord Robert as I used to do.'[85] De Silva assured the Queen that any apparent lack of goodwill in his demeanour towards Lord Robert was not born out of any dislike, but merely out of consideration for the Queen herself. Any reserve on De Silva's part towards Leicester was wholly motivated by the Queen's own state of mind, therefore. Before the end of the month, however, the breach must have been healed; and the Court returned to London.

About that time Leicester received a letter from Lady Mary Grey, written on 25 January from Chequers, that must have made him ponder on his own situation. Having secretly married the enormous Thomas Keys, the Queen's Sergeant-Porter, and thereby incurring the Queen's wrath, Lady Mary wrote: 'I understand by my very good lady the Lady Clinton of your lordship's good will in procuring the Queen's Majesty's most gracious favour towards me . . .'[86]; she then went on to beg that, as Leicester had begun, so would he please finish, and thus bring about a complete reconciliation with her royal mistress.

More momentous events were soon to break any hopes of a lasting solution to the Scottish problem when news reached London that in the early hours of 11 February, a small house on the outskirts of Edinburgh at Kirk O'Field had been blown up and Lord Darnley had been strangled. But the murderers had bungled it, and instead of Lord Darnley being destroyed in the explosion, he tried to escape and was caught in the garden, along with his servant. Mary had in fact written to Leicester only three days before, on 8 February:

We have at all times but specially by the declaration of the bearer our servant Robert Melville at his late return understood your good mind always shown to the increase and entertainment of the amity and mutual intelligence betwixt us and our good sister the Queen your sovereign whereof we give you hearty thanks and effectuously pray you to continue . . .

In the Queen's own hand she added 'Your good cousin, Marie R.'[87] The receipt of this letter may well have sent shivers down anyone's spine, and if one is to judge by Leicester's later reactions to Scottish events, he would have concurred with what Thomas Barnaby wrote to him from Paris on 1 March 1567: 'Your letters tell us of the strange and sudden disaster which of late hath happened in Scotland. Pray God the tragedy may have no more acts but one.'[88]

According to De Silva, writing on 17 February 1567, the very same night that the news reached London, Leicester sent his kindly brother Ambrose, Earl of Warwick, to the Earl of Hertford 'to offer him his services in the matter of succession', whilst he himself went off to approach Hertford's mother the Duchess of Somerset.[89] Leicester had realised that at one stroke Mary had sacrificed whatever hopes she might have had of succeeding to Elizabeth's throne, and a new successor was therefore to be found. Once more Catherine Grey seemingly became a valuable pawn, though at the time she was in the custody of Sir Owen Hopton at Cockfield Hall in Suffolk, and destined to live for barely a year longer. In fact the successor was already there, in the shape of the infant James in Scotland, though in that unhappy and unruly kingdom, no one would have expected that he would live to inherit both kingdoms.

The changed situation created some strange speculations. At this time Leicester was in correspondence with Sir Henry Norreys in Paris, and on 1 February Norreys wrote to him,[90] then again on 18 February: 'By your letter I am not only satisfied of your godly disposition touching religion, but can shew [it] if any such things should happen as an alteration of religion . . .'[91] There is a further letter of 1 March, as well as 8 and 10 March.[92] Whether or not there was any possibility of changes that could have induced Norreys to make such a statement, one must not forget that even without the events in Scotland, conflict in matters of religion persisted at home. On 28 February 1567, for example, John Scory, Bishop of Hereford, wrote to Leicester:

The Papists, who have watched me to have me in a trap, and know, as well as I do, what I say and do in my own house, now think that they have won the field, and intend to undo me at the next assizes. I desire you to be a mediator for me to the Queen to dispense with, or pardon my rash doings.[93]

Scory had merely sent a letter to five or six rural deans, asking them to give what help they could financially to a new residentiary, but there was a law in existence from the reign of Henry VIII, relating to Wales and the Marches, forbidding such a move. It was this law that was being invoked by Scory's enemies against him.

Other dealings in religious matters at this time concerned principally the matter of patronage. On 16 March, for example, John Jewell, Bishop of Salisbury, wrote to Leicester commending George Coryat, BA of New College, Oxford, to the vicarage of Helmarten,[94] and the next day Leicester himself wrote to the University of Oxford recommending for the Vice-Chancellorship Drs Humphrey, Tremayne, Westfaling or Caulfield.[95]

At the end of April and beginning of May, Leicester was away from Court at Burton, for one place, and also at Norwich, and Throckmorton kept him in touch with events. On 30 April, for example, he wrote to tell him that since his departure it had been bruited that the Queen of Scots had been married at Seton to Bothwell before her journey to Stirling.[96] In fact the marriage did not take place until 15 May, though the so-called abduction of Mary had taken place on 24 April. When Throckmorton himself had had to be away from Court, then Leicester's brother Ambrose was in charge. As Throckmorton wrote, on his return to Westminster, on 10 May,

You shall understand what the Queen wishes you to hear from her through your brother who was in charge in my absence. Lady Stafford sees no cause in matters within her reach why you should hasten hither. The storms which were up here lately are now so appeased that it seems there was no rough sea.[97]

What exactly the rough sea might have been is difficult to say. Whilst he was at Norwich, staying with the Duke of Norfolk, with whom he was on good terms at the time, Leicester received a letter from the Queen which may have set out the 'many ways' in which he might have offended. As he wrote to Throckmorton: 'If many days' service and not a few years' proof have made trial of unremovable fidelity enough, without notable offences, what shall I think of all that past favour which in such unspeakable sort remained towards me, thus to take my first oversight as it were an utter casting-off of all that was before?'[98] Leicester was indeed afraid that his star had fallen.

Cecil also kept in touch at this time, and wrote on 15 May, 'wishing myself to be with your lordship at Burton, to be your messenger to Stamford, where I am informed this May to grow a sovereign medicine for my gout.'[99] Behind the scenes, however, was taking place the examination of one William Huggins, which was a curious, delayed echo from the Amye Robsart affair, and brought to light some interesting details. As Throckmorton himself wrote, in the letter quoted from above:

> By Mr Blunt's [sic] writing, you shall understand what hath been proceeding touching Appleyard. Huggon [sic] is sent for, after whose examination I think the matter shall suspend until you return. Lord Arundel remains here about that business. Lord Pembroke has shewed himself in this and in the handling of it your assured friend. Your well-willers would have you go through now with this matter
> . . .

The letter concludes: 'This night a fair lady lodges in your bed.'[100]

In fact Thomas Blount's letter tells at length what had happened. He had been summoned to a meeting, at which the following were present: Pembroke, Northampton, Arundel, Clinton and Cecil, who asked Blount what John Appleyard, Amye's half-brother, had said to him in a matter touching Lord Leicester. Huggins had apparently told Leicester that Appleyard had been 'practised with by certain persons', so Leicester sent Blount to Appleyard to try and find out who these persons were. At first Appleyard would say nothing, nor would he write, since his letters had been opened. Blount paid a second visit to Appleyard, however, and this time, although Appleyard still would not 'deliver over', he said that he would tell Blount about the matter as a friend, so he shut the door and began: 'Mr Blount, if I would be a villain to my lord I could have money and friends great and good . . . There came to me a man, as I judge, a waterman, into the garden at Hampton Court, and delivered me a letter wherein I was called to come over the water alone . . .'

Appleyard went on to tell how he had debated with himself, and then decided to go. He met a man like a merchant, who pledged him to secrecy, and told Appleyard that he had come on behalf of certain persons who knew that he was 'ungently handled at my Lord of Leicester's hands'. If Appleyard would join them in bringing certain charges

104

against Leicester, then he would have no need of gold or silver. The first of the charges was responsibility for the death of Amye, and the second the fact that Leicester had been the sole hinderer of the Queen's marriage. Despite the offer of a lump sum of £1,000 down, and as much as Appleyard might require from time to time, he said that he answered this man: 'my Lord of Leicester is better my good lord than he is reported to be . . . I will neither for gold or friend stand against him, but am and will be his to death . . .'

Blount then asked Appleyard to go with him to Leicester and tell him who the people were and what charges they would make against him, as well as the name of the merchant. Appleyard agreed to this, except for naming the merchant — though he would 'point him out with his finger'. All of this Blount reported to Leicester, but Appleyard did not put in an appearance, and so Blount went back to see him. On the way he met Huggins, who said that he had told the earl how he had observed all that had transpired between Appleyard and the merchant, and had gone up onto the leads at Hampton Court to get a better view. There were also two men 'in tawny coats' standing apart. Appleyard would not tell Huggins the merchant's name either, but he said that the other men were Norfolk, Sussex, Thomas Heneage and others. Huggins said that he 'judged naught of the matter in view of the goodness of them named', but promised to get Appleyard to tell Leicester.

When Appleyard still failed to go to Leicester, the earl sent Blount a message from Greenwich, where the Court was then in residence, and told Blount to bring Appleyard to him there. This time Appleyard came, and when he arrived he found Northampton with Leicester, who became so angry with Appleyard 'that it seemed that, if they had been alone, he would have drawn his sword upon him. He bade him depart and to Blount said that he was a very villain.'[101] From Cecil's own examination as recorded in the papers at Hatfield, it appeared that Appleyard 'had not been satisfied with the verdict of the jury at her [Amye's] death; but that, for the sake of Dudley, he had covered the murder of his sister'. Appleyard's explanation, when pressed to it, was that though he would not say categorically that Dudley himself was guilty, he thought that it would be no difficult matter to find out who the guilty parties were.

We may leave the last word on the matter to Sir Henry Neville, who wrote from London to Sir John Thynne, the builder of Longleat, on 9 June 1567:

On Friday in the Star Chamber was Appleyard brought forth, who showed himself a malicious beast, for he did confess he accused my Lord of Leicester only of malice: and that he hath been about it these three years, and now, because he could not go through with his business to promote, he fell in this rage against my lord and would have accused him of three things: 1. of killing his wife;.2. of sending Lord Derby into Scotland; 3. for letting the Queen from marriage. He craved pardon for all these things . . . My Lord Keeper answered that . . . in King Henry VII's days, there was one lost his ears for slandering the Chief Justice: so as I think his end will be the pillory.[102]

This was not to be the last that was heard of the matter for all time, however,[103] for the story has fascinated people ever since, and echoes continue to make themselves heard even today.

5

Plot and Counterplot

. . . marriage, as it is lawful, so it is convenient for such as cannot otherwise contain.

Robert Dudley

As the summer of 1567 drew on, events developed apace in Scotland. On 15 June Mary capitulated at Carberry Hill; she was first taken back to Edinburgh, and then imprisoned in Lochleven Castle on the island in the middle of the lake. Whatever Elizabeth's feelings about the foolishness of Mary's behaviour, these were overshadowed by the fact that a monarch had been deposed and subordinated to the will of her subjects, though Mary did not abdicate immediately. There was, in Elizabeth's eyes, an all too dangerous precedent established. Certainly Elizabeth was very reluctant to let matters rest there, and Leicester was inevitably closely involved with her in her reactions to developments.

Sussex was still in Germany, as we see from a letter to Leicester written from Ulm on 25 July,[1] but of more urgency at this time must have been the Scottish business. Throckmorton had gone to Edinburgh, and from there he was able to appreciate that not only was Elizabeth's somewhat peremptory attitude towards the Scots damaging the cause of the very person she was attempting to help, namely Mary, but it also ran the risk of pushing the Scots back into the arms of the French. As he wrote to Leicester on 24 July: 'If the Queen will still persist in her former opinion towards the Queen of Scotland (unto whom she shall be able to do no good) . . . these lords and all their accomplices will become as good French as the French king could wish.'[2] It would not matter very much to the French which side they found themselves on when they got there, and they were certainly not set on rescuing Mary at all costs.

Two days later Throckmorton again wrote to Leicester: 'It is to be feared lest this tragedy end in the person of the Queen violently, as it began in David's and her husband's.'[3] In this Throckmorton was correct, though he would no doubt have been incredulous had he been told at that point by whose command Mary would eventually die. As it was, however, he desired to be recalled, '. . . seeing I do nothing here but spend the Queen's money'. Normally that would have been reason enough to recall someone if considerations of economy were allowed to take precedence over all else, as they might well do with Elizabeth, but for the time being Throckmorton had to stay. On 6 August Leicester wrote to him, acting as the Queen's mouthpiece, telling Throckmorton that he was 'to use all means to let the Queen of Scots know the Queen's great grief for her . . . the Queen takes the doings of these lords to heart, as a precedent most perilous for any prince.'[4] This cut little ice with Throckmorton, who replied: 'The way to amend this Queen's fortune and treatment is for the Queen of England to deal more calmly in her speech of them than she does.'[5]

Towards the end of October Sussex sent Henry Cobham, brother to the Lord Warden Cobham, back to England, requesting guidance in the marriage negotiations with Archduke Charles. Naturally this touched Leicester closely, for as ever, a successful conclusion would see an end to his own hopes. It is said that it was at Leicester's prompting that Bishop Jewel of Salisbury preached at St Paul's Cross against idolatry at this time, in an attempt to stir up anti-Catholic hatred, and in the Low Countries there was the all too plain message of Alva's cruel repression as a warning to those who might be tempted to encourage a Catholic consort for the Queen.

Norfolk was for the match, but was away from Court because of illness. Cecil wrote to him at the Queen's instigation, and asked him to let them have his opinion. He declared that he approved of the idea, and felt that if the Archduke were to be allowed his private chapel, this would be a small price to pay if the succession were thereby to be ensured. He then hit out at Leicester and his followers, saying that not all 'earnest Protestants were . . . making religion a cloak for every shower . . . naming one thing and minding another.'[6] The letter Norfolk wrote to the Queen, also dated 15 November, was somewhat different in tenor. If the Archduke were to profess his religion openly, he might constitute a threat to the unity of the nation, and this was to be avoided at all costs. On the other hand, it was equally reprehensible to let the whole project die: 'If this, then, should not take place, what present help is there of any other, as delay on your Majesty's marriage is almost an undoing of your realm?' He did not miss the opportunity, either, for protesting against 'mythical devices', and attempts by Leicester's party to ruin his reputation, for he was 'nearly counted a papist'.[7]

Leicester had the support on the Council of Knollys, Pembroke, and possibly Bacon, whereas with Sussex and Norfolk away, Cecil had the Lord Chamberlain Howard, Lord Admiral Clinton, and the Comptroller Rogers. It is doubtful, however, whether the outcome would have been any different had the others been present. Moreover Leicester continued to improve his standing and his financial situation. On 20 November 1567, for example, he was made High Steward of Reading, with an annual stipend of £1,[8] though with considerably more than mere monetary value attached to the office.

Eventually, however, in December 1567, Elizabeth wrote to Sussex and put an end to the matter on the grounds that she was unable to allow the Archduke a Catholic establishment. Sussex was convinced that it was Leicester who had been the leader of the action against the match with the Archduke, and said, 'If it should ever please God to put into my dear mistress's heart to divide the weed from the grain . . . she may, if she will, make a happy harvest.' The failure to bring the negotiations to a successful conclusion was one thing, but through his absence Sussex also lost the presidency of the Council of Wales to Leicester's brother-in-law Sir Henry Sidney, who continued in office, despite the fact that he was more and more ill with gall stones. Not only had the Queen promised the office to Sussex — or led him to expect it — but Leicester had also promised to support his candidacy, only to fall back on his brother-in-law. Time dealt kindly with Sussex, however, for the death of Archbishop Young of York in 1568 made was for the earl, and the presidency of the Council in the north was a more important post than that of Wales.

All this time, it is easy to forget, Leicester continued to fulfil his day-to-day task as Master of the Horse, and he did so with conscientious application. Among the tradesmen's bills for this year at Longleat, for example, are amounts paid out for 'stuffs for the Queen's litter'.[9] Even so, as most other people saw him, he was still one of the most important people in the kingdom. Before the end of 1567 de la Mothe-Fénelon became French ambassador to England, and reported that the Duke of Norfolk and his father-in-law the Earl of Arundel had spoken to Leicester in serious terms about his relationship with the Queen. If Leicester could say quite definitely that the Queen would marry him, then they would support him, but if not, then his behaviour was improper. All that Leicester could say was that the Queen had shown him such affection that he had been led to hope that she would marry him, but he was unable to say categorically that she would do so. Moreover, this was a considerable affront to Leicester, and the fact that he did not react violently to this rebuke indicated — at least to Cecil — that he had never possessed the Queen and could not, as a consequence, fall back in confidence on her total support.

The new year of 1568 did not therefore open on a very auspicious note for Robert Dudley. On 27 January the unhappy Lady Catherine Grey died; the Queen contributed £76 for her funeral in Salisbury Cathedral. Her sister Mary who, as we have seen, committed the same matrimonial folly, suffered in the same way, but was to live for another ten years. Two days later Sir Henry Norreys wrote from Paris.[10] Leicester had spoken to Sir Thomas Gresham on Norreys' behalf, and also to the Queen, to lend him 1,000 crowns, but the main concern was finding suitable messengers. Norreys wrote again on 30 March and 8 April,[11] but when he wrote on 30 April he still had the same problem:

> By your letter of the 9th I find you know the insufficiency of him whom necessity causes me to use. Hitherto he has served me as I might very ill have spared him, and has cast himself into such danger as I could get none other to do for love or money. Yet I am not so addicted to my own opinion but am to be ruled by your direction.

Of couse Leicester may have had very good reasons for not trusting Norreys' messenger, though in view of the problem the poor man had in finding someone, that did not make his task any easier. What is also true is that if Leicester took a dislike to a person, or they crossed him, then he was usually implacable in his hatred of them. This is one of the early examples, and they appeared to increase as he grew older. Norreys went on to write about religious troubles in France, and added a postscript: 'I praise God for the great justice that I hear done there by your honour to the disobedient in causes of religion.'[12] It was no coincidence that when the Bishops' Bible was published this year, there was a portrait of Leicester on the title leaf before the Book of Joshua, which was the beginning of the second part.

Norreys was not the only Englishman on the Continent to appeal to Leicester at this time. On 4 April Dr John Man wrote in desperation from Madrid: '. . .[I] beg you to help to rid me out of this disdainful country. I had liever serve the Queen in a right base place at home.'[13] Then nearer home, Richard Onslow wrote on 8 May 1568 about the problems caused by the lack of a Chancellor for the Duchy of Lancaster. There was no precedent for the office being carried out by a commission, and the lack of a successor in the post was creating difficulties.[14] As far as Cecil's relationship with Leicester was concerned, things seem to have improved, however, for De Silva had written in February that he had heard that a rapprochement was expected to take place between the two men, and that they would work out something together for the question of the royal succession.

Then on 17 May, having escaped from Lochleven, having been defeated at Langside, and having crossed the Solway, Mary Queen of Scots landed at Workington. Sir Francis Knollys the Vice-Chamberlain was sent north to take control of the situation. There was an unfortunate incident on his arrival. Mary had asked for some clothes, since she had arrived literally in what she stood up in, and one of Elizabeth's maids — probably with no very precise orders — had put together a totally unsatisfactory selection. When this was opened in Knollys's presence he was covered with confusion, and tried to explain the matter away to Mary. It was then thought prudent to remove her from Carlisle to Bolton Castle, though initially Mary was treated with deference, and Leicester, as Elizabeth's Master of the Horse, took on the same responsibility towards Mary. There is a leter from Knollys to Leicester from Bolton Castle, written 'late in the night' and dated 1 August 1568, asking Leicester to send two or three horses for Mary's own saddle.[15] If Mary was virtually destitute, then Leicester certainly was not. This year he acquired the manor of Middlefoy in Somerset, and the considerable sum of £1,303 2s 1d for the surplus value of trees on manors he had exchanged with the Queen.[16]

Meanwhile the regular correspondence with Norreys in France continued,[17] though some of the letters from this period merely double official ones in the Calendar of State Papers Foreign. There was also one from Sir Henry Lee in Ausbruck dated 3 July,[18] and from John Mersle from the Low Countries dated 5 September.[19] There were also the usual letters about patronage. On 16 June, for example, the Dean and

Chapter of Christ Church, Oxford, wrote to Leicester as Chancellor of the university about one of their vicars who had been deprived of his house,[20] and on 2 August Edward Lord Hastings wrote from Loughborough to inform Leicester that he had granted Killigrew the stewardship that Leicester had asked for him on his behalf, '. . . and am glad to have pleasured him, both because he is so faithful a servant to you, and for the liking I have to all his race for their truth toward your lordship. Resting as you will command me without spot or wrinkle . . .'[21] Such a letter is of interest because it shows that no matter what struggles were going on at the very seat of power, Leicester was nevertheless a person held in great awe by many of the lesser nobility, his family and, even more so, by the populace at large.

A new name figures in the Pepys Collection at this juncture— that of Lord Cobham. He had written to Leicester from Cobham on 3 and 13 August about troop movements on the Continent,[22] but on 5 September we learn that his wife had been Leicester's guest at Kenilworth: 'The courtesy you have shewn to my wife at Killingworth [*sic*] bids me always to serve you. I am glad to hear that you have passed these dangerous months without sickness.'[23] He was, of course, referring to the possibility of plague which was at its most rife during the summer, especially in towns and cities. Elizabeth went on progress as usual, though this summer she seems to have kept to the home counties, largely because of the unsettling presence of the Queen of Scots in Yorkshire.

After considerable thought, Elizabeth decided to appoint a commission to look into the affair of Mary Queen of Scots, and investigate the charges that she and her subjects were making against each other. The commission met at York in October, and Elizabeth appointed to it Norfolk, Sussex and Sir Ralph Sadler. Lord Herries and the Bishop of Ross acted for Mary, and Moray and his party were their opponents. However, little progress was made at York, so Elizabeth decided to move the proceedings to Westminster. The size of the commission was increased by the addition of Leicester and Warwick, Cecil and Bacon, and a summons was sent to the earls of Northumberland and Westmorland— the Percys and the Nevilles— to attend also. As Catholics, and the most powerful forces in the north, they must at all costs be kept in check. But there was also a rumour, which the French ambassador had repeated to Elizabeth before the end of October, that the Duke of Norfolk, a widower for the third time, was himself thinking of marrying Mary. Although nominally a Protestant, as head of the Howard family his ties with Catholicism were strong. Any alliance with the northern earls could have terrible implications for Elizabeth if he were in fact to marry the Queen of Scots, go into open rebellion, and bring about a Catholic uprising.

In its turn the Westminster Conference ground to a standstill, and Elizabeth asked the Duke of Norfolk to his face what he thought about a marriage with Mary. He of course replied that he hated the idea, though if, at some future date, he was persuaded that it was for the benefit of the realm and the safety of the Queen, then he might change his mind. Norfolk's tragedy was that he was not the person, either by temperament or intellect, to play this sort of game with any reasonable hope of success. Not that Leicester was — in the last analysis — to have success in his particular ambition, either, but he was more of a survivalist, more of a realist. Perhaps in some respects he was even more truly ambitious than Norfolk, and knew that there was a time for all things.

On the surface, however, life went on very much as before. A letter from Norreys in Paris dated 6 September 1568 gives details of paintings to be sent to Leicester:

> . . . Yesterday one Du Court, valet of the king's chamber, said that according to his promise to you he had drawn her Majesty's picture, one of his master, and two of your honour. He sends them by Pierre Roulet, secretary to the Queen of Scots, a crafty fellow and greatly of Lorraine's counsel.
>
> The bearer's business considered has caused me to write more liberally, nothing doubting that he will unrip [?] my letter.[24]

The problem of finding suitable letter bearers was always recurring, and from the next letter in the Pepys Collection we learn that Thomas Barnaby, who had been persuaded to stay in England after falling foul of the French authorities, had returned, but had once again been arrested. He was originally Leicester's servant, but loaned to Norreys the previous year:

> I shall have much to do to have my letters come safely to your hands. They have already imprisoned one, taking away his letter which I sent to her Majesty, which as yet I cannot recover. Your servant Barnaby is still prisoner only for sending a letter to Mr Steward. The letter they have of mine is of importance; the taking of the man was strange in time of peace. I wish they may find the like there in England.[25]

On 19 October Thomas Percy, Earl of Northumberland, wrote to

Leicester requesting an answer by the bearer, his cousin Vavasour, to his suit for licence to travel abroad. In the circumstances this was a request that had to be treated with a certain amount of circumspection, since Northumberland was regarded with suspicion in official quarters, and that suspicion was to be proved warranted in the near future. Northumberland then went on to refer to 'the matter of the mines, in which judgement was on the Queen's side', though his counsel had not seen the records, which 'moved most of the best learned to think his title good'.[26] Elizabeth was not over nice when it came to such matters, and this did not set a good example to Leicester, who was capable of hounding people with litigation. Ten days after Northumberland's application it was the turn of Robert Horne, Bishop of Winchester, explaining that his delay in coming to Court was caused by the bad weather, and sickness in his household. He took the opportunity to confirm that he would give an advowson to one of Leicester's chaplains.[27]

An event which created a completely new web of complications around Leicester was the arrival in England of Odet Cardinal de Châtillon, brother to Admiral Coligny, in the autumn of 1568. Despite having become a Protestant, and having taken a wife, Châtillon remained a cardinal. He had arrived in England, as William Lord Cobham had reported to Leicester, on 10 September, and was destined to stay for some time.[28] By 4 November Acerbo Velutelli, a merchant, became involved. He had been bringing wine from France for the cardinal and an acquaintance of Leicester's, Franchiotto, but the wine had been seized at sea. First of all Franchiotto wrote to Leicester,[29] and then the cardinal followed, with two letters on successive days — 6 and 7 December — from Sheen.[30] He said that the matter touched him so closely that he would not be easy until it was all sorted out. From his side he had written to his brother the admiral and De Condé in La Rochelle, the Protestant stronghold, but he wanted Leicester to take action, too, and sent the letter via Velutelli, who could no doubt add his own explanation where necessary. It needed the intervention of Sir Thomas Gresham before things were appreciably clearer, however, and when he wrote to Leicester on 29 December he explained that the cardinal had taken sixty-nine tuns of wine from Velutelli, which cost him some £500. He had promised to pay at La Rochelle, and apparently Leicester had promised to send some of his own men there to receive the money. In view of the dangers by land and sea, however, Gresham said that Velutelli now wanted the earl to see him paid in London in four or six months' time, and the cardinal to be bound to Leicester or Gresham himself for payment.[31] At first sight it seems amazing that important and busy people could find the time to be involved in such relatively insignificant matters, but as far as Leicester himself is concerned, it is instructive in revealing his desire to serve and be recognised as the person who sorted things out, and also the extent to which he was involved with commercial ventures, especially with the Italian business community in London.

The day after Gresham's letter, on a much less domestic note, Louis de Bourbon, Prince de Condé, wrote to Leicester from France to thank him for what he had heard by Mr Steward of his good will to the cause of French Protestantism and said he hoped to repay him for it. He requested Leicester to assure the Queen of the gratitude of his party. He would send, in five or six days, a despatch to her relating their successes, the enemy having retreated with loss of men and baggage. Cardinal Châtillon, he concluded, would communicate news of it.[32] This letter highlights one of Elizabeth's constant worries, created by her position as a Protestant monarch close to mainland Europe which made her the focus of appeals for moral, financial and military assistance from all those who struggled against Catholic oppression. The first kind of assistance was not too difficult to supply, for it cost nothing, and could be given in relative secrecy. The other two were a very different proposition, however, for she had financial problems of her own, and military aid would not only seriously undermine her persistent assertion that she had no territorial ambitions, but risked massive retaliation from much larger powers. Even having dealings with rebel leaders was open to interpretation by those in power as interference in the internal affairs of the state in question, which of course it was to a certain degree, though at the same time the religious issue was one that inspired feelings of strong solidarity, and tended to cut right across national divisions.

None of this made life any easier for official representatives at Catholic courts, however. Norreys kept up his despatches to Leicester from Paris all through this period. Often, as on 8 December, for example, they closely echoed official despatches,[33] but on other occasions they contained news of internal affairs in France, as on 14 December,[34] which were related in addition to, or in a manner slightly different from, the official reports. Sometimes they cut across the two. A letter from Norreys dated 1 January 1569 follows the one in the Calendar of State Papers Foreign, but then has a totally personal addition: 'I beseech your honour to have in good remembrance Mr Francis Parlandes who very friendly travailed for a licence for Nicholas your cook to transport wine for your provision, as also the pains to search out the mullets I sent you.'[35]

What strikes one about the correspondence of this period is the way in which matters of relative insignificance rub shoulders with issues vital to the very existence of the status quo in England. We find, for example, Estienne Perret, in London, writing to Leicester on 14 December 1568 in Italian requesting payment of money on account of a lottery,[36] or Gilles de Ville, also in London, writing on 18 December about some chamber furniture he wished to sell for £800. Her Majesty had ordered Sir Nicholas Throckmorton to bargain with the late Postmaster, probably Sir John Mason who died in April 1566, for some pieces, and therefore he had induced Madame d'Egmont to write to Leicester to bring them before the Queen. In consequence of troubles he would now accept £450. If this price were accepted, he would send for the money, being too ill to leave the house.[37] On the other hand, there are letters from John, Lord Herries, about Mary Queen of Scots,[38] as well as from John Leslie, Bishop of Ross, about the government of Scotland,[39] and one has a glimpse of the enormous network that Leicester was part of — sometimes constructed deliberately by himself, but also built up almost in spite of himself — simply because he was what he was.

A letter from Edward Horsey from Southampton, for example, dated 20 December 1568 is, on the surface, an account of the taking of treasure from a Spanish ship in the Hampton River,[40] but it rapidly takes one out of the private domain and into what soon became a national crisis with many facets to it. The ships in question (there were four) had taken refuge in Plymouth Sound and Southampton. Their treasure was intended to pay Alva's troops in the Low Countries, though since it had been advanced by Genoese bankers, it remained their property until Alva received it. When the Council discovered this, they approached the bankers' London agent, who said that the Queen of England's credit was much better than that of the King of Spain, so the chests were taken off the ships and up to the Tower of London. By way of retaliation, Alva imprisoned such English merchants as there were in the Low Countries at the time, and impounded their goods. The English replied by doing the same to Spanish merchants in England, who had much more to lose than the English in the Low Countries had.

The new Spanish ambassador, Don Guerau De Spes, was placed under arrest, also. There is a letter from him to Leicester, dated 23 November

1568— shortly before this incident— in which he said he was sending his servant, James Burques, to impart certain matters of moment on his behalf, and hoped that Leicester would give credence to what he said.[41] Tact was not De Spes' chief asset, as it happened, and indeed there were those who wondered how he ever came to be an ambassador at all. He was a fanatical Catholic, and at times revealed an ill-judged disdain for the English government.

The closure of Antwerp to English ships, and the threat of more reprisals from Spain, began to backfire on Elizabeth. As ever, when things went wrong it was the fault of her advisers, but when they went well she took all the credit. It was unfortunate that the responsibility now fell on Cecil. It was his fault that the merchants of the City of London were experiencing these setbacks in their trading ventures, and it was fuel for those members of the Council who felt that, having been in office for ten years, he now ought to resign. As a contemporary wrote: 'Many did also rise against his fortune, who were more hot in envying him than able to follow him, detracting his praises, disgracing his services and plotting his danger . . .'[42]

Allied to this general current was the fact that Leicester was of the opinion that it was Cecil who stood in his way of marrying the Queen; though of course all the others — Norfolk, Pembroke, Northampton, Arundel, Lumley, Northumberland and Westmorland, as well as Winchester — had a variety of reasons why they might wish to see Cecil put down. The idea was that Cecil would be charged at the Council meeting in the Queen's absence with being a bad adviser, arrested and despatched to the Tower, much as Thomas Cromwell had once been. But the Queen and Cecil found out about this in time; the Queen summoned a Council and so scotched the plan. Later, when Cecil, Norfolk and Northampton were in the Queen's chamber one evening before supper, Leicester came in and Elizabeth upbraided him for the way in which the Council had acted. Leicester replied with an attack on Cecil, but the Queen was not to be shaken in her support of the Secretary, and Norfolk said to Northampton: 'You see, my lord, how the Earl of Leicester is favoured as long as he supports the Secretary, but now that for good reasons he takes an opposed position, she frowns upon him and wants to send him to the Tower.'[43] This was reported on 8 March 1569, and despite the fact that Elizabeth had made it quite clear that she would not abandon Cecil, the plot continued. De Spes reported that on three separate occasions in April when the others had been ready to take action, Leicester had 'softened and said he would tell the

Queen'.[44] One person, at least, had learnt his lesson.

After the failure of the anti-Cecil plot, the project to promote a marriage between Norfolk and Mary Queen of Scots developed further. Leicester gave it his support because it meant that the question of Elizabeth's marriage would then cease to be of very much importance — so he imagined — since Mary already had a son. There would then be no more foreign suitors, and the field would be left open to him. Or so it might seem.

Mary had been placed in the care of the Earl of Shrewsbury at Tutbury early in the year. The somewhat reluctant host wrote to Leicester from there on 7 January 1569, complaining of the short notice he had been given and expressing the apprehension with which he contemplated his new responsibility:

> I received advertisement from Mr Secretary at Nuneaton twenty miles from Tutbury for my stay at home till I hear further of the Queen's Majesty's pleasure. The Queen of Scots coming to my charge will make me soon grey-headed. May it please her Majesty to give me leave to come to speak with her though I tarry not past a day. If I might know the certain day of the Queen of Scots coming here, I could leave such directions with my officers that they should be as well done as though I were there present, and I think if come from the Court but a day or two before her coming it will be best.[45]

Two weeks later his countess, better known as Bess of Hardwick, wrote to Leicester, also from Tutbury, complaining of the time it took for letters to reach her about the arrival of Mary, though she hastened to add that she would, however, go without her own comfort rather than disobey Queen Elizabeth.[46] But Mary was there for the foreseeable future, and giving herself to the idea of marriage with Norfolk. That Leicester was party to at least some of the plans is revealed by a letter to him from the Regent James Stuart, Earl of Moray, dated 11 March 1569 from Stirling, on the very question of Mary.[47] Well might Henry, Lord Hunsdon, have written from 'Cold Berwick' on 15 January that he would like to hear how Leicester's hawks were doing, were it not for the fact that he thought that Leicester was so busy he was having small pleasure of them.[48] Others were content simply to offer advice. Sir Ralph Sadler wrote from the Duchy (of Lancaster) House at the Savoy on 21 March advising what the Queen ought to do in the current situation, assuming no doubt that Leicester would communicate the same to her.[49]

It was almost a relief to turn to the wide range of business that had occupied him since the beginning of the year, for as controversial as some of it was, it did not touch him anything like the way that matters of royal marriages did. On 7 January, for example, Sir William Dormer wrote to him from Westminster about his daughter Anne, Lady Hungerford, who had been charged with attempting to poison her husband in 1564, and with committing adultery with William Darrell between 1560 and 1568. He had no doubt, he wrote to Leicester, that the allegations against his daughter would prove untrue, and he was persuaded by his counsel 'that little advantage is to be had for these defamations'. He resolved therefore '. . . to have such expedition used as may stand with the orders of that court, and, she once cleared, to bring the whole matter into the Star Chamber to have order of redress for such slanders. From the earl's favourable inclination she has conceived just cause of comfort.' Her sister, now the Duchess of Feria, would take similar comfort, he concluded. In fact Lady Hungerford was cleared, but her husband failed to pay the costs, and so was sent to the Fleet.[50]

Leicester also involved himself considerably in Church and in university business. On 15 May 1569 Leicester was planning to take Cardinal Châtillon to Oxford on a visit, so Dr Thomas Cooper, Dean of Christ Church and Vice-Chancellor, wrote to Leicester about the preparations on 5 May. Leicester was to alter them as he saw fit, but Cooper proposed that he himself should deliver a sermon in Latin, and Dr Westfaling would give one in English. There would be disputations in Divinity, when the questions would be the two pillars of Papistry: the authority of the Church and the supremacy of Rome. The questions in Natural Philosophy had not then been chosen. There was to be a play or show of *The Destruction of Thebes*, and the contention between Eteocles and Polynices for the governance thereof. However, Leicester's help was desired for some 'apparaiti [*sic*] and things needful'. Cooper hoped that the visitors would stay at least two days, and that Leicester and the Cardinal would lodge in Christ Church — which had a kind of appropriateness, since Wolsey had originally founded that institution as Cardinal College.[51]

Cooper was soon to be promoted. On 2 June 1569 Parker and Grindal wrote to Leicester from Lambeth and recommended him for the Deanery of Gloucester which, they went on, 'is not far distant from Oxford, so as he may very well have due regard to both the charges. We have heard also of some that have made importunate suit of their own persons for the said deanery, of whom we have no good opinion: besides that the

119

example so to sue is not commendable.'[52]

Leicester was also the recipient of a very interesting letter from Thomas Wilson, from the Queen's Majesty's Hospital at St Katherine's, dated 20 July. The prologue to the 'epistle' runs:

> I have known you, and that noble race of your brethren, even from their young years. And with your honour . . . I have had more familiar conference than with the rest: and especially with your honour (I do thank you most humbly therefor) I have had sufficient proof of your careful mind, even in reading not only of the Latin, but also of the Italian good and sound writers, to know and to understand the best used government, and the chief laws that have been made in all ages . . . For I know, and therefore will not fear to say, that you have been next to the Queen's Majesty's most mild and gracious disposition, a great help and mean of this most calm and merciful government . . .[53]

Even allowing for a degree of sycophantic eulogy, this is interesting for the light it throws on Leicester's ability in academic matters, and if he really did have Latin, then those disputations and sermons may not have been so boring for him after all.

But he was, above all, a man of the world, and this gave him the ability to rub shoulders with the great and be regarded by them as an equal. François, Duke of Montmorency, wrote to him from Chantilly on 22 January thanking Leicester for his letter and the enquiries about his health,[54] and Frederic, Elector Palatine, wrote from Heidelberg on 17 April 1569. He had sent his councillor John Junius to England and he, on his return, had told the elector how kind Leicester had been to him. They talked about the troubles of the times, and from this the elector said he had learned how prudent, pious and religious Leicester was:

> And from your position I rejoice the more that you have these virtues, by which many not very secure, but otherwise not bad men, will be helped to promote the kingdom of Christ and to overthrow the bloody design of the Pope. Wherefore I hope that you may show yourself zealous and ready to help these endeavours, and I likewise will help you.[55]

Even the great, however, had to come to more mundane matters on occasion, and on 16 January De La Mothe Fénelon, the French ambassador, wrote to request exemption from duty on wine.[56]

In March and April news came from Henry Killigrew who was

travelling from Hamburg to Heidelberg;[57] on 29 May William Lord Cobham wrote with news from France, and Norreys also continued to correspond from France.[58] His letter of 24 March is perhaps the most interesting, since it shows that he eventually began to suffer from the complaint that afflicted most of Elizabeth's ambassadors at one time or another. He requested that Leicester should use his influence for his recall, or at least a letter from the Queen for his wife's return with her children and family, and that her highness's packets both going and coming might have free passage. Norreys was still there in September, when he requested Leicester, in a letter from Tours, to obtain his recall on grounds of ill health,[59] though he was destined to be there almost a year later. The 'injuries' that Norreys was experiencing seem to have been the direct consequence of the arrest of the Spanish ambassador.[60] The latter was released from prison, however, though he was forced to remove his embassy from Paget Place in the Strand, for in June 1569 Leicester took a lease on the house from the Paget family, and De Spes was forced to move over the river to Southwark, to Winchester House. Leicester then moved along the Strand from Durham House to Paget Place and renamed it Leicester House.

Under its new tenant the house was to become a treasure house, as the inventories show, and the displaced ambassador and bishop had no alternative but to accept. De Spes wrote on 1 July: 'We have agreed that the Earl of Leicester's valuation of it [the lease of Winchester House] shall be accepted, and I will move into it.'[61] The Bishop of Winchester, Robert Horne, had even less to do or say in the matter. He wrote to Leicester from Bishop's Waltham on 28 June to the effect that if the earl must find a house for the Spanish ambassador, then he was content that no rent be paid for his house, despite the fact that he had intended to be in residence himself during the coming winter. If, however, the ambassador had to find himself a house at his own charge, then the price would be 300 crowns until St George's Day next, since the bishop was of the opinion that 'much spoil will be made about the house in that small time'. One is reminded of the Earl of Bedford when the Princess Cecilia and her train descended on his house.

Horne then went on to mention the Queen's proposed progress into Hampshire that summer. Fifty persons had been sick and five had died in the bishop's house at Waltham since 25 March last, and thirteen in the town. Last Saturday one died at the constable's house there, and all the neighbours feared it was of the plague: 'If the spring had been hot, as it hath been very cold, it would have been a kindly plague; at the least it is *febris pestilentialis*. And there is no port along the coast free from it.' He observed that some people thought that the bishop was making more of the matter than was necessary so as to avoid having to spend money; implying that of course this was far from the truth, but in view of the terrifying expenditure involved when the Queen descended on households in the course of her progresses, who could blame him?[62]

There is an interesting story dating from this month of June 1569 about Leicester and Dr William Chaderton, Master of Queens' College, Cambridge, who had been chaplain to the earl. Chaderton consulted Leicester about his desire to marry, which in his position was quite a brave thing to do, since the Queen was notoriously unsympathetic to married clergymen in cathedral closes and college courts. Leicester gave a very guarded reply, and the rather more extreme view of matrimony as found in St Paul's writings to the effect that: '. . . marriage, as it is lawful, so it is convenient for such as cannot otherwise contain'. He hoped, at any rate, that the matter would 'turn to his comfort and consolation'. Chaderton went on to become Bishop of Chester, of which palatinate Leicester was chancellor.[63]

It was not Chaderton's marriage, however, or even Leicester's own marriage that was uppermost in his mind at that moment, but the projected marriage between Mary Queen of Scots and the Duke of Norfolk. At the end of July the Court moved to Richmond, and Norfolk followed a day or two later. Without the moral support of Sussex, who was now in York as Lord President, Norfolk lacked the necessary resolve. He encountered Leicester fishing in the Thames, not far from his house at Kew, and learned from him that the Queen was of the opinion that they intended to proceed with the marriage without even telling her. There had been gossip amongst the women at Court, which Leicester said he had told the Queen was false, but this only meant that they would have to choose their moment to discuss the matter with the Queen even more carefully.

In fact the Queen appeared to be perfectly aware of what was happening, but had decided to give Norfolk the chance to tell her himself what was on his mind, shortly before the Court left Richmond for the summer progress. Norfolk had been into London, to Howard House, and the Queen, who was in the garden, noticed him return. She summoned him and asked him whether he had any news. When he replied in the negative, she retorted: 'No! You come from London and can tell no news of a marriage?' Norfolk's courage failed him, and since Lady Clinton came up at that moment, he went off to find Leicester. The latter was stag hunting near Kingston, but Norfolk waited for him, talking to Throckmorton. When Leicester returned, he still insisted that Norfolk said nothing until he had had a chance to talk to the Queen first. So the matter had still not been broached when the Court set off on progress on 5 August.[64]

While Leicester was stag hunting in England, far away on the Continent a friend of his was doing the same thing. Hans Casimir, second son of the Elector Palatine, had paid a visit to England, and in 1564 had made his bid for the Queen's hand through Sir James Melville, then at the Elector's Court in Leipzig. Or at least he had intended doing so, but Melville had put him off. Casimir might have tried to find himself a better confidant, since in such a matter Melville was hardly likely to put Casimir's interests first. In Leicester, however, he found a loyal friend, and they remained in touch and thought of each other with affection. As Henry Killigrew wrote to Leicester from Leipzig on 11 August 1569: 'Casimir wished you this hunting time when he was at the death of eighty stags in one day, whereof one weighed 700 pounds.'[65]

During this summer of 1569 Norfolk found himself obliged to take part in the royal progress, a thing which he disliked, and usually managed to avoid by retiring to his own estates. In order to keep Leicester to his promise, therefore, he went from the royal palace of Oatlands, near Weybridge in Surrey, to Guildford, to Loseley, the house which Sir William More had just completed the year before. Norfolk spoke to Leicester, and the following morning — probably 12 August — he came upon the Queen at the threshold of the room that was being used as the Privy Chamber. It was a curiously domestic scene, with one of Sir William's children playing a lute and singing, the Queen sitting on the doorstep, and Leicester kneeling by her. As Norfolk later described the incident:

> Her Majesty commanded me to come by, into her chamber. Not long after my Lord of Leicester rises and came to me, leaving her Highness hearing the child, and told me that as I was coming, he was dealing with her Majesty in my behalf; to which I answered, if I had known so much I would not have come up; but I desired to know how he found her Majesty, when he told me, indifferent well, and that her Highness had promised to speak with me at Thornham.[66]

The Court was not due at Thornham — Lord Arundel's house in Kent — until much later in the progress, but in fact Elizabeth gave Norfolk another opportunity at Farnham on 15 August. She invited him to dine

alone with her at her table but he still declined to open his mind to her
— either through his own lack of courage, or because of his reluctance to
upset Leicester's plans, or through a combination of both. The Queen
concluded, not unreasonably, that Norfolk no longer merited trust.
However, the whole of Leicester's role in this matter invites deeper
scrutiny. Did he deliberately set a trap for Norfolk by spinning out the
business as long as possible? If so, the longer he encouraged, or hood-
winked, Norfolk into delaying, the more his own complicity risked
becoming apparent.

The Court went on into Hampshire, and the duke remained with
them all for a few days at Southampton, and then returned to London.
There he gave his consent to a plan that the Earl of Northumberland and
his former enemy Leonard Dacre should, at a given signal, rescue Mary
Queen of Scots from Wingfield in Derbyshire, where she had been taken
from Sheffield. Elizabeth was at Winchester's house at Basing, and
Cecil at The Vyne, near Basingstoke. Pembroke wrote to Norfolk from
Basing, assuring him that Elizabeth would not refuse her permission for
the marriage, and Cecil wrote from The Vyne, telling him to come to
Court quickly, since the Queen had asked for him. It was with reluctance that he set out, and on arrival he did not ask for an audience at
once, but waited for a summons.

Leicester, meanwhile, had retired to Lord Southampton's house at
Titchfield, where he had taken to his bed. Camden maintained he was
'counterfeiting the sick', and it is more than likely that the illness was
diplomatic and that, sensing that the game was almost up as far as
Norfolk was concerned, Leicester wanted to unburden himself to the
Queen. He knew, moreover, that she would come when asked, for she
hated the loss of her friends through death, and willingly visited them
when they were ill. She came to his bedside on 6 September, and he told
her all. The Queen was furious, probably more at the thought that those
around her had been plotting behind her back, than what they were
actually plotting about, for it suddenly opened up hideous visions of
unrest and strife in her realm. And, indeed, from many points of view
this was potentially the most critical point of her reign so far. Norfolk
did not leave the Court at once, but the Queen's confrontation of him
with the facts made him a shunned creature, and he left for London
eventually without taking formal leave of absence.

Elizabeth meanwhile made her own arrangements. Huntingdon was
sent to remove Mary from Wingfield, which was unfortified, and from
the care of Shrewsbury, who was ill, to Tutbury. The ports were closed

and the militia put on the alert, and Elizabeth retired to the safety of Windsor. In the opinion of the Duke of Alva, writing to Philip of Spain on 25 September, Leicester and Cecil were governing the Queen entirely, and did as they pleased. Whether this was true or not, it showed that the current rumours gave out that Leicester had not taken any harm from his involvement with Norfolk. Indeed one must always consider the possibility that Elizabeth actually encouraged him to become involved, so as to act as her spy. She did, after all, give him the nickname of Eyes, and two circles with dots in the centres was the symbol they used in their letters to each other.

The Queen ordered Leicester and Cecil to write to Norfolk, telling him to come to Windsor and submit. Norfolk told Cecil that he was ill, but hoped to be there by 26 September. Instead of remaining in London, however, he went to his seat at Kenninghall in Norfolk, and it was from there that he wrote to Elizabeth to complain that his enemies had found such comfort in her heavy displeasure that he had become 'a common table talk'. His very friends were afraid of his company, and he had become a suspected person. His removal to Kenninghall was, however, seen as a prelude to rebellion — in fact many thought that he was on his way north to join Northumberland and Westmorland — and in realisation of this he sent a message to them to withdraw before it was too late. He himself finally decided to go to Windsor, but was intercepted and taken to the Tower. By the end of November the earls' rebellion was over, too, for the most part. Ironically enough, one of the stated aims in their proclamation at Ripon on 16 November had been to oppose those around the Queen who sought and procured 'the destruction of the nobility'. Through Norfolk's efforts and their own they ensured that this happened with much greater certainty than any of those — whoever they might be — around the Queen could ever have dared hope. The redistribution of their forfeited estates put an end, once and for all, to their feudal hold over the north. Moreover it meant that Mary was kept in much closer custody, and the ill-advised papal bull *Regnans in excelsis*, issued by Pius V the following year, not only came too late to help the rebels, but only served to clarify for Catholics their priority in loyalty to Rome or to Elizabeth.

The Scots problem continued to exercise men's minds for the rest of that year. There is a document in the Pepys Collection dated 29 October 1569, drawn up by Sir Walter Mildmay, Chancellor of the Exchequer, possibly as a minute for the Council, in which he set out the problem as he saw it.[67] In the same collection is a letter from Leicester to Sussex on the same topic,[68] and as the year drew to its close, John Leslie, Bishop of Ross, wrote to Leicester from Kingston on 21 December with the same problem uppermost in his mind.[69] Elizabeth herself was in no doubt but that Mary was the 'Daughter of debate that eke discord doth sow', but for the time being she was prepared to act with tolerance towards her, and in this she was encouraged by Leicester. As for Norfolk, his examination subsequent to his arrest was unable to prove that he was guilty of treason, and in due course he was allowed to return to his own home in London.

Through all the alarums and excursions of the last few months, the same problems had continued to come before Leicester. On one hand there was trouble at Cambridge, and on 31 August Bishop Cox of Ely wrote from the city about a controversy between the Master of St John's College and one Fulke, lately fellow of that college, who was charged with celebrating marriages within the forbidden degrees of relationship as set out in the Thirty-nine Articles of the Church of England. The bishop told Leicester that he had visited the college in an attempt to sort the matter out, but in the meantime a charge of felony had been brought against Fulke by another fellow, Elias Mead, before the Mayor of Cambridge, who in turn had brought it before the Vice-Chancellor. As Visitor of the college the bishop had no authority to deal with felony, and wanted the 'foul matter' referred to some of the 'discreet and wise' of the university.[70] In October it was the turn of Oxford, whose Chancellor Leicester was. Dr Laurence Humphrey and four others wrote to Leicester on the 7th about the Queen's commission for the search for heretical books, vagrant persons and masterless men in the town and university.[71] Whatever the turmoils going on at the heart of the realm, and Leicester's desperate need to keep himself on the right side of the Queen, to many of those on the outside he was very much at the centre of power as ever he had been.

From a completely different point of view, there was the intimate realm of his own family, who had served the Queen well in the rebellion. Huntingdon and brother Ambrose had been especially trusted, and despite the shadows that fell on Leicester himself, he had survived the storm and seemed as firmly in favour as ever. January 1570 found him, then, at Kenilworth. On the 10th of that month he wrote to the Queen: 'From your house. Fearing lest this hard weather forces messengers to be the slower, I have prayed this gentleman to take the more pains, whose desire is as much to see you as my longing is to hear from you, thinking it now very long since I heard.'[72] Warwick ought to have been at Court, but since his involvement in the rebellion he had not yet had time to present himself there, but was at Kenilworth, too: '. . . after a little rest with your 👁👁, he will attend according to his duty.'

By the 16th of January their two sisters, Lady Mary Sidney and Katherine, Countess of Huntingdon, had joined them there. Leicester wrote to the Queen:

> If it lay in the power of so unable creatures to yield you what our will would, you should feel the fruits of our wishes . . . We two here, your poor thralls, your Ursus Major and Minor [a reference to the bears that were their badge], tied to your stake, shall for ever remain in the bond-chain of dutiful servitude . . . So long as you muzzle not your beast, nor suffer the match over hard, spare them not.[73]

On 30 January De Spes observed that Leicester was still there. He had originally suspected that Leicester had gone there so as to pay a visit to Mary Queen of Scots in Derbyshire without drawing attention to himself. However, De Spes now said that this was not so: Leicester had gone so as to superintend the fortifying of Kenilworth, and for this purpose had taken with him an Italian, Giulio Spinelli, who had had experience of engineering in the Netherlands.[74] Leicester was supposed to have said that he greatly feared the possibility of civil war in the country. Be that as it may, by 13 February he had left Kenilworth and was at Teddington with a bad cold. From there he wrote to the Queen and said that he was grateful to her:

> . . . for sending so graciously to know your poor 👁👁 doth; I have hitherto so well found myself after my travel as I trust I am clearly delivered of the shrewd cold that so hardly held me at my departing from you. I have always found exercise with open air my best remedy against those delicate diseases, gotten about your dainty city of London, which place, but for necessity, I am sorry to see you remain about, being persuaded it is a piece of the sacrifice you do for your people's sake.[75]

The papal bull which made its appearance in London in May created severe problems for those Catholics who were truly devoted to their faith, but for many people it clarified and crystallised their feelings about the Queen. The seemingly indefatigable Arthur Golding translated, the following year, Bullinger's confutation of the bull, which he dedicated to Leicester. As Bishop Jewel wrote in his *Answer to the Excommunication*: 'God gave us Queen Elizabeth, and with her, gave us peace, and so long a peace as England hath seldom seen before . . . Thanks be to God, never was it better in wordly peace, in health of body, in abundance of victuals.' But perhaps an even more accurate estimate of the emotional feeling was given by the broadsheet registered at Stationers' Hall the following year, in the form of a dialogue between England and Elizabeth:

> I am thy lover fair
> Hath chosen thee to mine heir,
> And my name is Merrie England.
> Therefore come away,
> And make no more delay,
> Sweet Bessie, give me thy hand!

To which the Queen replied:

> Here is my hand
> My dear lover England,
> I am thine both with mind and heart,
> For ever to endure,
> Thou mayest be sure,
> Until death we two do part.[76]

What room was there for Leicester, then, in this scheme of things? Little, one would have thought; but the rumours continued to fly. In that year one Marsham was sentenced to lose both his ears or pay a fine of £100 for having stated publicly that Leicester had given the Queen two children. On the other hand, the spectre of another foreign competitor for Leicester reappeared in August during the summer progress. The Queen had gone as far as Chenies, the Bedford house in Buckingham-shire, when she developed an ulcer on her shin and was forced to stay there longer than expected. She received the French ambassador there with her feet up, and in *négligé*. It would now appear that she was considering marriage with the Duke of Anjou, brother to the King of France. That month of August De Spes wrote: 'The Queen's own opinion is of little importance and that of Leicester still less, so that Cecil unrestrainedly and arrogantly governs all.'[77]

However, Leicester had things other than thoughts of the Queen's marriage to occupy him. On 4 June 1570, for example, John Hawkins wrote to him about the Spanish Indies fleet that was due to come to the

Azores in the middle of August, with gold, silver and jewels to the value of 20,000,000 ducats, or some £6,000,000 English. Plans were set on foot for its capture. Leicester and his friends were to obtain *Bonaventure* and *Bull* from the Queen, furnished with ordnance, powder and munitions.[78] Then in September Norreys wrote again from Paris,[79] and on 10 October Leicester wrote to Matthew Parker from Windsor about the doings in Norwich Cathedral of the dean, Herbert Astley. This letter was written by Leicester at the Queen's command, and in it he told Parker to remember who appointed him, and so therefore to do what he was told — though in not quite such blunt terms.[80] There was also contact with Mary Queen of Scots, who wrote to Leicester on 29 December, signing herself 'Your right good friend and cousin. Marie R.'[81]

An interesting dedication during the course of 1570 was Thomas Blundeville's translation *A Very Brief and Profitable Treatise . . . counsels and . . . councillors of a prince*, with a bear and ragged staff on the title verso; also Thomas North's translation, through an Italian source, of the *Fables of Bidpai*, published as *The Moral Philosophy of Doni* in North's version. Blundeville's dedication is perhaps easy to dismiss as a piece of traditional flattery, but he nevertheless maintained that in this treatise he was presenting to Leicester, 'as it were in a glass, many of those good virtues and qualities that do reign in you, and ought to reign in every other good counsellor'. At the close of 1570 there were numerous signs to the casual observer that this was no less a tribute than Robert Dudley deserved.

6

More about Marriage

. . . yet is there nothing in the world . . . that I would not give to be in hope
of leaving some children behind me, being now the last of our house . . .

Robert Dudley

At the beginning of 1571 De Spes told the Duke of Alva's secretary,
Zayas, that Leicester had given the Queen a jewel containing a painting,
on which she was shown sitting on a throne with the Queen of Scots in
chains at her feet, and France and Spain being drowned in the sea, 'with
Neptune and the rest of them bowing to this Queen'.[1] New Year was a
time for giving lavish presents to the Queen, and over the years Leicester
gave her many such tokens of his esteem and affection. And yet this
month saw the setting on foot of another foreign marriage project for
Elizabeth, and one in which Leicester was closely involved. In fact the
possibility of a match with the Duke of Anjou, brother to the King of
France, had been mooted as early as 1568, but only began to be seriously
considered in the autumn of 1570, as we saw in the last chapter. In
December the French ambassador, De la Mothe Fénelon, had a long
conversation on the subject with Leicester, who seemed to be favourably
disposed. The Queen then received the ambassador herself, in great
splendour, and the conversation was such that Fénelon felt sanguine
enough to write to the French Queen Mother, Catherine de' Medici, to
the effect that he felt an official proposal might be made.[2]

In early January 1571 Sir Francis Walsingham became the new ambassador in Paris. Through his connections with Throckmorton and his ultra-Protestant views, Walsingham was an almost natural ally for Leicester. While he was there, Leicester asked Walsingham for portraits of Charles IX and the Duke of Anjou to add to his collection of portraits of royal personages, but Walsingham informed him that such portraits were only painted under royal licence, and the penalties for infringement were severe.[3] The month of February found Leicester ill, and away from Court. There is a letter at Longleat from Claudio Corte, written to Leicester from Paris on the 4th of that month, asking for payment of money due to him when he left Leicester's service.[4] Such matters must have been potentially irritating to him when the question of the Queen's marriage was looming so large. As he confided to Walsingham in a letter he wrote on 14 February: 'I perceive her Majesty more bent to marry than heretofore she hath been.'[5] Exactly so, but the trouble was that her bent did not appear to be towards Leicester. Even so, nothing ruffled the surface of their relationship at this point. On the 17th Leicester wrote to the Queen very much in his usual manner: 'Your great favour, thus oft and so far to send, to know how your poor ⚭ doth, is greatly beyond the reach of his thanks, that already for a thousand benefits stands your bondman.' He then went on to mention plans for the progress that summer: 'Nothing is better for your health than exercise, and no one thing has been a greater hindrance thereto than your over-long stay in that corrupt air about the city; but you have so earnestly promised a remedy, as I hope to see you in time this year put it into practice, respecting yourself before others.' The house of Grafton, in Oxfordshire, would be ready for her by the end of May, he wrote; 'Meanwhile, other good places shall see you, which if they could speak, would show how sorry they are that you have been so long from them. Wishing you above all earthly treasures, good health and long life, I take my leave; rejoicing in your postscript, that you have felt no more of your wonted pangs.'[6]

On 25 February the Queen made Cecil Baron Burghley, and Leicester was well enough and back to support him, along with Cobham, on either hand at the ceremony, while Hunsdon carried his mantle. Outwardly all was affability, but inwardly there were mixed feelings and mutual mistrust. Leicester told the French ambassador that Cecil was against any husband for the Queen, which was simply not true. It was quite the other way round. Cecil knew that Leicester disliked the idea of the marriage, and was doubtless doing all that he could to put obstacles in its way. Indeed it may well have been because of Leicester that Elizabeth was so adamant over the question of the duke's religion, which was to prove the stumbling block; though of course Leicester had very good reason to worry, since this certainly seemed potentially the most dangerous threat to his position since the Habsburg incident — certainly as far as foreign rivals were concerned. True, there had been Christopher Hatton at home, but a foreign prince was a very different proposition. Leicester's view was probably aptly summed up in a letter from Sir Henry Neville to Burghley which he wrote in the previous July: 'My Lord of Leicester sings his old song unto his friends, that is, that he had the Queen in very good tune, till you took her aside and dealt with her secretly, and then she was very strange suddenly.'[7] Nevertheless, both Leicester and Burghley knew that they would have to work together in the matter.

In March there was every appearance that things were going ahead. In April 1571 Guido Cavalcanti came as the French Queen Mother's personal agent with a formal offer. Having worked for Elizabeth in the past, he was now ostensibly in the opposing camp. As long ago as 14 November 1564 he had protested in a letter to Leicester from Marseilles that he had in no way cooled in his desire to serve Elizabeth,[8] so his appearance in this new role gave legitimate grounds for questioning whose interests he was serving best. As he landed at Dover he was stopped, and taken up to London, to Burghley's house, before going to the French embassy. Catherine de' Medici had set out four chief conditions, namely that her son and his household should have complete freedom to practise their faith; the day after the wedding he was to be crowned and rule jointly with Elizabeth; he was to have an annual allowance of £60,000 from the Exchequer, and if Elizabeth died without heirs, he was to retain his title and allowance for the rest of his life. The Queen was apparently prepared to let Anjou rule with her as Philip of Spain had done with her sister Mary, and he might even be called king, but she would not agree to a coronation. He might have an allowance, but not for life. On the religious question, however, there was to be little hope of compromise.

According to D'Ewes, the bill for founding the Leycester Hospital at Warwick was read in the Lords in May 1571. One of Leicester's favourite projects, its realisation probably came as some consolation at this difficult time. Leicester endowed it with lands worth £200 a year and obtained possession of the fourteenth-century premises of the dissolved guilds of Holy Trinity and St George, after promising the

Corporation of Warwick that he would make provision for a new burgess hall, school and schoolhouse. Ralph Griffin was the first master of the hospital, and when he was preferred to the Deanery of Lincoln in December 1584, at Leicester's 'earnest suit', Thomas Cartwright was appointed in his place on 21 November 1585.[9]

In May the Duke of Feria wrote that the Queen was simply teasing Spain 'with inventions and fears that she will marry in France'. He went on, 'She will no more marry Anjou than she will marry me'.[10] Someone, at least, had seen through Elizabeth's feint, but the farce was kept alive, and in June Alvise Contarini, Venetian ambassador to France, reported back home that:

> . . . the negotiation for the marriage between the Queen of England and Monsieur d'Anjou still continues. The Court is at Gaillon and the English Ambassador has been granted a long and gracious audience by the Queen Mother who, for the great love which she bears her son, is doing her best to bring the affair to a conclusion; and although there are many reasons to the contrary, and amongst others the disparity of age and the difference of religion, it is nevertheless the opinion of many that the negotiation will be successful.[11]

Contarini might have thought that in June, but by July Walsingham had more or less come to the conclusion that the marriage would never happen. That month Burghley and Leicester wrote to him in France: 'As for the inward intention of her Majesty in this case, we cannot certainly give you to understand more than it pleaseth her to utter. To the matter itself she yieldeth, as to a matter necessary to her estate and realm, otherwise we see no particular forwardness such as is common between persons that are to be married.'[12]

The French made yet another effort, by sending a former ambassador, Paul De Foix, over to England in August, and though he was received warmly, he failed to make Elizabeth relent on the religious question. At his return in September, the Venetian ambassador to France had been told that the scheme had definitely collapsed, but that a 'good understanding' remained between England and France.[13]

In fact all was not quite lost, because the involvement of Norfolk in the Ridolfi plot had just come to light, and England's isolation was made horribly apparent. There is a considerable amount of material in the Hatfield papers about the aftermath of the affair, especially, for example, Pembroke's 'answer' and the examinations of Throckmorton and the Bishop of Ross.[14] Elizabeth then decided that she would, after all, be prepared to allow Anjou to have Mass in his private chapel. This did not cut any ice, however, as Walsingham made clear to Burghley on 8 October: 'the Duke of Anjou utterly refusing the match, all being granted that he desires.'[15] In other words, no matter how many of the French requests Elizabeth agreed to, she risked a brutal rebuff. The matter was to be dragged out even further, as we shall see, but effectively by September 1571 there was no hope of it ever coming to pass.

On 29 September Leicester wrote to the Queen from Warwick: 'Thinking it long since I heard of your good estate, according to the duty of your bounden ⊙⊙, I have sent this bearer to understand the same, meaning not to be long after in coming to give my attendance.' He was down in Warwick on family business, helping his brother Ambrose and, as he explained, 'it had been no small hindrance, both for my brother and myself, if I had not been now here. All that we both have proceeded from your only goodness.' In response to the Queen's enquiry about his health he wrote:

> . . .to satisfy your over-great care of my present estate, though I departed away in some pain, yet in no suspicion at all of what you feared, only it seems, for lack of use, my late exercise wrought some strange accident, through my own negligence, to take more cold than was convenient after such heat. I was well warned by you, but neither fearing nor mistrusting any such cause as followed, I have felt some smart for my carelessness, whereby I am driven to use the commodity of a bath to ease the pain.

In fact, he went on, the pain was really not worth telling the Queen about: '. . . but to satisfy your good pleasure, being more careful of me, poor wretch, than the loss of a thousand such lives are worth.'[16]

The 29th of September is observed in the Book of Common Prayer as the Feast of St Michael and All Angels, and this day was chosen for Leicester's investiture by proxy as a member of the Order of St Michel. The ceremony was to take place in St Mary's Church, Warwick, for with Ambrose Earl of Warwick, and Leicester Constable of Warwick Castle, and his own seat at Kenilworth five miles away, this was very much a fief of the family. Moreover, as we have already seen, Leicester had been granted permission by an Act of Parliament this year to found a hospital at either Kenilworth or Warwick 'for sustentation and relief of needy, poor and impotent people'. Warwick had been decided on, and Leicester was therefore very much a local benefactor.

The Earl and Countess of Warwick were already there, though not resident in the castle but at a Mr Fisher's house known as the Priory. In the Earl of Leicester's party, when it was assembled, were Sir Henry Sidney, Lord Hertford and the Marquess and Marchioness of Northampton, who had been married the previous April. Naturally the bailiff and burgesses of Warwick were eager to make a present to their benefactor when he arrived, but were somewhat at a loss to know what would be most suitable.[17]

In all the debate over the choice of gift and the place of welcome, the actual day was confused, so that instead of finding the streets full of people when he and his grand friends arrived in Warwick on the Thursday, Leicester made his entry into the town as if he were a nonentity. Naturally the word got around very quickly, and the poor townspeople determined to wait on the earl the next morning at eight o'clock. When they arrived at the Priory with their yoke of oxen, Leicester had already left for Kenilworth. They waited patiently all morning, whilst the earl's servants came out and expressed their amazement that the people of Warwick 'would not so much as bid the Earl of Leicester welcome, but hid themselves'. Had it been Bristol or Norwich — neither of which towns had been blessed with a charity from him — he would have been properly received: 'But this town was so stout, it regarded not of his lordship.'

At last, at three o'clock in the afternoon, Leicester and his friends returned, but he was still so furious, and so determined to let his anger be felt, that when the poor bailiff and people attempted to make their presentation: '. . . the said Earl of Leicester passed by them hastily, saying he would not charge the town so much, and would not look towards the said bailiff or his company; but rode still unto the house, and so the said bailiff and his company both disappointed of their intentment and half amazed knew not what to do.' Finally, however, they were allowed into the garden: '. . . where the said earl out of the chamber might see them (but they could not see him) . . .' All of this took place on 28 September, presumably, since it is described in the account as Michaelmas Even, for it was made known that night that Leicester would observe the feast of the order of which he was a companion, and therefore he wished the bailiff and burgesses to wait on him, both to and from the church, by nine o'clock next morning, or soon after.

Even at this juncture Leicester was unwilling to let the people of Warwick forget the injury they had done him. The following morning they made the mistake of keeping him waiting, so that word had to be sent that my lord was ready to come to church, but stayed for the bailiff and his company. They were duly put in their places — in more than one sense — and then the procession set off. Rouge Dragon pursuivant and Clarenceux King at Arms, 'both in coat armours', went before the Earl of Leicester, who walked alone:

> . . . apparelled all in white, his shoes of velvet, his stocks of hose knit silk, his upper stocks of white velvet lined with cloth of silver, his dowlet of silver, his jerkin white velvet drawers with silver, beautified with gold and precious stones, his girdle and scabbard white velvet, his robe white satin embroidered with gold a foot broad very curiously, his cap black velvet with a white feather, his collar of gold beset with precious stones, and his Garter about his leg of St George's Order, a sight worthy the beholding. And yet surely all this costly and curious apparel was not more to be praised, than the comely gesture of the same earl, whose stature being reasonably [*sic*], was furnished with all proportion and lineaments of his body, and parts answerable in all things; so as in the eyes of this writer, he seemed the only goodliest personage male in England, which peradventure might be affected. But surely to all the beholders it was a sight most commendable.

It is in this ceremony at Warwick that the proud and ambitious Leicester is really seen to full advantage, and that one begins to be able to understand what glory meant to him, and why it was important to him. Certainly he took sufficient pride in the Order of St Michel that he had its insignia, along with that of the Garter, added to his arms on his portrait. This was his moment of glory, and in that moment one hopes that he began to feel less bitter about the townsfolk of Warwick. If not, then even his rancour must surely have been assuaged by the sight of the interior of St Mary's Church decked out in splendour for no one else but himself. A cloth of estate was set up in the choir of St Mary's, with the French royal arms over it, under which he sat: 'And over the place where my lord sat was fastened my lord's own arms environed with the Garter, and without the Garter a wreath of gold after the French order, in manner of knots (being scallops' shells).' All the rest of the stalls in the choir were hung with cloth of gold or gilded leather, and the rest with tapestry and arras. 'On the stall before my lord, lay a rich cloth with a fair and costly cushion. On the communion table was laid another fair cloth of Arras; before the table was laid a Turkey carpet whereupon my

lord knelt when he offered, which carpet was spread by two gentlemen.'
As he entered the choir of the church, Leicester made a 'low curtsey to
the French king's arms' — whereupon there followed a sermon. Communion was celebrated from the north end of the altar, as befitted such a
convinced Protestant, though there was an elaborate offertory procession, in the course of which Leicester put one piece of gold in the basin
from either side, bowing first to the French arms, then his own, as he
passed them.

After this curious mixture of vestimentary opulence and Protestant
propriety, Leicester withdrew to the Priory, 'where, very solemnly he
kept the feast with liberal bounty and great cheer. Himself sitting in a
parlour by himself, without any company, kept the state, and was
served with many dishes all covered, and upon the knee, with assay.' In
other words, he appropriated to himself such a state as was usually
reserved for royalty. The account ends with a vivid glimpse of the man
sitting alone, in his splendour, desirous of extending his vicarious regal
role for as long as possible, but being thwarted by that most English of
phenomena, the weather: 'After dinner the said earl remaining in the
house with his said robes on until evening, minded to go again to
evensong, but the weather being foul and very great rain, he could not
go forth according to his intent.'

The poor old Marquess of Northampton had to be carried to the
ceremony in a chair because he was so ill, and he was unable to go with
the party to Kenilworth. In fact he died a few weeks later, leaving a
Swedish bride of only six months — though of far longer attachment.
The Queen herself footed the bill for his costly funeral. The following
year, when Leicester paid another visit to the town in company of the
Queen on 12 August 1572, his royal mistress showed him what it was
like to be truly royal. She not only showed herself at her window in
Warwick Castle, but the people were allowed inside to see her.
Moreover, when presented with a purse containing £20, which she
accepted with the utmost graciousness, she turned to Leicester and said:
'My lord, this is contrary to your promise.' He had obviously told her
what a mean lot the people of Warwick were, and how little she was to
expect from them.[18]

As the summer progress ended and the autumn declined into winter,
Elizabeth took up once more the tangled skein of her dealings with
France. In December 1571 she sent Sir Thomas Smith to France to see
whether the marriage project with the Duke of Anjou might not be
revived. Failing that, she wanted him to begin negotiating for a

friendship treaty. Smith was received by the King of France, after a bad crossing, on 4 January 1572, and two days later by the Queen Mother. Catherine still insisted that the religious issue was the only bar to the marriage. Having said as much, however, when Smith delved further, he realised that Anjou wanted a full, public Mass, and nothing less: 'Why, madame,' retorted Smith, 'then he may require also the four orders of friars, monks, canons, pilgrimages, pardons, oils and cream, relics and all such trumperies. That in no wise can be agreed.'[19]

Very soon the resourceful Queen Mother put another suggestion to Smith. She had another son, Hercule-François, Duke of Alençon. What about him as a husband for Elizabeth? He was only seventeen, undersized, and somewhat disfigured by smallpox, but these were only of secondary importance — or so his mother seemed to think. Even ignoring the fact that Elizabeth felt in some way that she had been treated badly over the matter of Anjou, she was vain enough to want as handsome a man as possible for her consort.

On 14 January the trial of the Duke of Norfolk began in Westminster Hall. On this occasion there was little doubt what the verdict would be. The warrant for his execution was drawn up for Monday 8 February. It was not to be so simple, however, and as Burghley wrote to Walsingham on 11 February:

> I cannot write you what is the inward stay of the Duke of Norfolk's death . . . Suddenly, on Sunday, late in the night, the Queen's Majesty sent for me and entered into a great misliking that the duke should die the next day and . . . she would have a new warrant made that night to the sheriffs, to forbear until they should hear further . . . God's will be fulfilled and aid her Majesty to do herself good.[20]

Burghley's chief complaint in the letter was that the Queen wanted to be merciful, and yet in being so was doing more harm to herself than by acting with justice. When she thought she was making herself beloved, she was in fact doing herself injury. And this turned out to be injury not only in the figurative sense. As the tension continued and February gave way to March, the Queen became ill, and Burghley and Leicester had to sit up with her three nights running. When she recovered and received Fénelon, she told him that for five days the pains had so 'straitened her breath and clutched her breast, she thought she was dying'.

As Norfolk's life hung in the balance, Leicester pressed on, in a somewhat relentless way, with his particular interests, especially at this time with his promotion of the Puritan cause, which makes an odd contrast with the more gentle aspects of Christian love and charity. On 28 January he had written to Edmund Scrambler, Bishop of Peterborough, in favour of Mr Wyborne, preacher at Northampton, where they held a 'weekly exercise by the assembly of the ministers and preachers of all the county about, who are examined of their doctrine and life'. Leicester wanted the bishop to do the same, for the poor men of Northampton had been reformed by Wyborne, and if he was 'defaced', they would be discouraged.[21] Leicester wrote again on 19 February from the Court, saying that although he had no liking to keep Mr Wyborne at Northampton, the bishop was the chief cause of his leaving his book at the university to go there two or three years ago.[22] Leicester's involvement with the Church was not confined to doctrinal matters or questions of preferment, for on 5 April 1572 he himself became Chief Steward of the see of Rochester.[23]

In this year William Malim's translation of Nestore Martinengo's *True Report of all the Successes of Famagosta*, published by Day in London, with the bear and ragged staff on the title verso, was dedicated to Leicester. The dedication is an interesting one, since Leicester's involvement with the Republic, and particularly with those of its citizens in London, was a long and deep one. There has been speculation about its exact nature, but it is hard to see how it could have been political, let alone religious, and the most likely explanation is simply that he had a financial interest. To some extent this is borne out by the fact that in 1575 Leicester used his influence with Elizabeth to obtain a monopoly of the import trade from Venetian territories for Acerbo Velutelli, who also obtained the export monopoly from Venice (*see* p. 114).

Another dedication in 1572 was Thomas Wilson's *Discourse upon Usury* (*see* p. 120). Although the book itself appeared this year, the dedication was actually dated 1569.

The warrant for Norfolk's execution was issued again for 9 April, but again the Queen withdrew it after midnight on the 8th, and Burghley received it at two o'clock in the morning. Naturally this could not go on for ever, and when Parliament met again in May, there were bound to be problems. Nor was the Queen the only person to have her difficulties at the prospect of the coming session of Parliament. Leicester also had to do battle — though on a much smaller scale — with those who usurped what he regarded as his prerogative. In this month of April, 1572, he was in the midst of a struggle with the bailiff, aldermen and burgesses of Denbigh in Wales, of which Leicester was lord of the manor, over his nominee, Henry Dynne, as their representative in Parliament. They defied him, and chose their own man, Richard Candish. Leicester was furious, and insisted that they accept his man, 'not for any great accompt I make of the thing, but for that I would not it should be thought that I have so small regard borne me at your hands, who are bounden to owe me, as your lord, thus much duty as to know mine advice and pleasure.' All the Dudley pride and anger is there. Even if they tried to say that they had chosen Candish before they received his letter, they ought not to have done so before consulting him: 'so have I thought good to signify unto you that I mean not to take it in any wise at your hands.'[24] It was the loss of face as much as anything, and on this occasion he did lose, so that he became particularly vindictive towards the people of Denbigh.

Leicester's devotion to his nearest and dearest, and refusal to brook what he regarded as the merest hint of insubordination from those he considered as bound to his service, is scarcely better illustrated than in his correspondence with Walsingham, still in Paris, during the month of May 1572. On the 26th of that month he wrote about his nephew Philip Sidney, who was eighteen, and about to travel abroad: ' I have thought good to commit him by these my letters, friendly unto you, as unto one I am well assured will have a special care of him during his abode there. He is young and raw, and no doubt shall find those countries and the demeanours of the people somewhat strange unto him.' Of course Leicester adored Philip Sidney, and at this time, one must remember, he had no son of his own.

On the other hand, one of Leicester's pages had run away, and entered the service of the Cardinal de Guise, who declined to send him back. Leicester had already written to Walsingham about him on 23 April, then on 21 May, and now in the same letter of 26 May, one appreciates the marked contrast between his concern for Philip Sidney, and that for the boy:

> As for the boy Clarke, since I cannot obtain him as I desire, I must content me. I wish I had one of my lord cardinal's monks, to see how devoutly he should be kept here . . . The boy hath sought sundry ways to return unto me, as well by letters to his friends, as by supplications to myself, but I mind not to have him so. The cause that I did so earnestly seek him, was to punish him in example of others, which if it will not be, I will leave it for a time, and hope to give you knowledge where he is shortly, trusting you will give order that he may be suddenly apprehended.[25]

One can only hope for the boy's sake that Walsingham did not co-operate in this business. It seems strange that so powerful a grandee as Leicester had now become was still so conscious of his authority and potential affronts to it that he felt obliged to go to such lengths.

Norfolk was finally executed on 2 June 1572. That same month an embassy arrived from France, led by the Duke of Montmorency, both to ratify the Treaty of Blois, which had been agreed on 19 April, and also to make an offer for the Queen's hand on behalf of Alençon. They were entertained lavishly, and Montmorency was given the Garter, but there was little or no real indication that the Queen had any serious intentions towards Alençon. If Leicester appeared to be difficult, he was to receive the hand of a Valois princess in marriage. Clinton, recently elevated to an earldom, was then sent to Paris, from where he wrote to Burghley on 18 June, and to where Leicester wrote about Alençon, in whom he naturally had a certain interest.[26] A new appointment fell to Leicester at this time. On 10 June 1572 he was made High Steward of Great Yarmouth, with a stipend of £4.[27]

In July the French Queen Mother sent over a friend of Alençon, Monsieur de la Mole, whose manner charmed the Queen. She received him at Warwick Castle, where she gave him supper, played on the spinet, and put on a firework display. When he returned to France in August, however, despite the good impression he had made, he had achieved nothing of any importance. That summer progress, and in particular the part of it centred on Warwick, must have been idyllic. During the stay at Warwick the Queen went over to Kenilworth privately, to spend a few days with Leicester there, and then moved on from Warwick, to have her public reception at Kenilworth as the next stage of her progress. A black cloud suddenly darkened the summer sky, however, for it was there, whilst she was out riding, that the news of the St Bartholomew Day massacre was brought to her. She returned to the castle immediately, and Fénelon, who was of the party, was not permitted to see her. It was only four days later, by which time the Court had moved on to Woodstock, that he was granted an audience, on 8 September. The Queen received him coldly, and left him in no doubt as to her feelings.

The progress went on into Gloucestershire, where Leicester involved the Queen in what seemed to be a particularly mean action, and one which she presumably condoned at the very least. Warwick and Leicester were in the midst of a long and bitter lawsuit against Lord Berkeley — a lawsuit that was not settled until 1609. It was over property which, at the death of Edward VI, reverted to Lord Berkeley, but which had originally been claimed by an ancestress of the Dudley family, Joanna Beauchamp. As her eventual heirs, the earls of Warwick and Leicester thus made their claim. Anyone who had the misfortune to cross Leicester, let alone be involved in a lawsuit against him, became little better than an animal in his eyes. He regarded Berkeley Castle as his — or his and his brother's, which was tantamount to the same thing. When the progress was near the castle, therefore, and in view of the fact that Lord Berkeley was away, Leicester induced the Queen to let him take her hunting in the park, despite the fact that this was no part of the intended progress. There was a particular area of the park, known as the Worthy, that Lord Berkeley had made into a game reserve. In one day the royal party killed twenty-seven stags. Lord Berkeley's rage on his return was such that he 'disparked that ground' so that no one should hunt there again, and his remarks were retailed to the Queen, doubtless being somewhat elaborated in the process. To which the Queen merely replied that he had best take care; Leicester might well take the castle as well as the deer, since, after all, she gathered that he had a good claim to it.[28]

This is one of the very few instances that has come down to us when the Queen appears to have gone along completely with Leicester's less pleasant nature, and one assumes that his influence over her at that period must have been especially strong. Moreover, it shows Leicester in the role of the hard-riding, hard-hunting and — to the Queen in particular — glamorous figure for whom she always had a place in her enigmatic affections. Hand in hand with this rather less than gentlemanly behaviour on Leicester's part went an apparently materialistic reaction to the St Bartholomew Day massacre. He was keen to encourage the art of manège — well known in France and Italy, but as yet little practised in England. He therefore wrote to Walsingham in September 1572, asking whether he knew of a rider 'appertaining to any of the late lords that were murdered', and who would now, as a result, be out of work. Leicester was offering £30 a year with meat and drink, 'and his horse found in my stable'. Walsingham replied promptly that Captain Lassety was taking care of the matter, and that he was 'most willing to do your lordship any service'. However, all the riders that Lassety found wanted an annual salary of 300 crowns, 'and the least they can be reduced to is 200 crowns'. The captain tried to make them accept that '150 crowns in England will go further than 300 here, but as yet, no persuasion will serve to make them so to think'. Eventually, in the early part of 1573, when Captain Lassety despaired of finding a French rider who was competent but not exorbitant, he 'hearkened out' an Italian who was willing to come for an acceptable sum: 'If your lordship will have him, then must you send into Italy a bill of credit for so much money as may defray his charge into England.'[29]

Early in the next month — October 1572 — Leicester was sent to Portsmouth about the fortifications there,[30] but not long after the Queen was ill again, this time with a rash, which at first was feared to be a return of smallpox. Smith wrote to Walsingham: 'Now it makes no matter what it was; thanks be to God she is perfectly whole, and no sign thereof left in her face.'[31] She had a relapse, however, the next night — though fortunately it turned out to be of short duration. As Smith wrote to Burghley: 'Her Majesty hath been very sick this last night so that my Lord of Leicester did watch with her all night . . . This morning, thanks be to God, she is very well. It was but a sudden pang.'[32] Leicester had done the Queen this service before, and obviously had skill in nursing her in such circumstances. He wrote to Walsingham about her: 'The fits that she had hath not been above a quarter of an hour, but yet this little in her hath bred strange bruits here at home.'[33] In other words, Walsingham was not to believe that they were anything like as bad as they had been reported.

On 23 November 1572 Sir Henry Killigrew was summoned to a private audience at which only the Queen, Leicester and Burghley were present. Killigrew was to go to Scotland to discuss with Regent Mar whether or not Mary could be executed if she were returned to Scotland. Elizabeth had intervened, it must be remembered, when the Scots had previously attempted to do this by judicial process; now she doubtless regretted that she had done so. Elizabeth wanted to ensure that execution would be carried out within hours of the Scottish Queen crossing the Border. Mar received the proposal favourably, but asked for 3,000 English troops to guarantee that the execution was carried out, and that thereafter Elizabeth should pay the Scots what she was paying for Mary's annual upkeep. Burghley was furious, but before he could do much else, Mar died. This made further progress impossible, but the way in which Elizabeth had behaved while the matter was being discussed was an important pointer to future difficulties when the onus for ordering Mary's execution was to fall on herself.

Burghley wrote to Leicester, who was with the Queen at Windsor, to let him know that the scheme had failed: 'God send her Majesty strength of spirit to preserve God's cause, her own life and the lives of millions of good subjects.'[34] By this he meant that Mary would have to be brought to trial in England. Leicester agreed, but openly conceded that it needed Burghley there to persuade Elizabeth. Whatever Leicester's influence over the Queen, when it came to political matters, Burghley clearly had the edge. For this reason, Leicester went on, he wished that Burghley were there.[35]

In December 1572 the company of players known as Lord Leicester's Men appear in the accounts of the Revels Office. Earlier in the year the City of London had forbidden players to go on tour unless they were under the protection of a nobleman. Leicester's Men had been in existence for some years, and as early as 1561/2 there are mentions of them in the Ancaster MSS. In October 1561 for example they appear in the accounts: 'To my Lord Robert Dudley's players at Grimsthorpe, which offered themselves to play but did not, 10 shillings.' Then in December 1561: 'To two of my Lord Robert Dudley's men which came to play before them upon the drum and the fife, 6 shillings.'[36] There is also record of them at this time in the records of the Corporation of Gloucester.[37] The Earl of Warwick also had 'his' players, and they went to Grimsthorpe in January 1562, for which they received seven shillings and six pence.[38] But naturally such a relatively loose association between players and noblemen whose livery they wore might easily lead to abuses, especially if not closely supervised, and ten years later the Corporation of London obviously felt it necessary to take steps to tighten controls. The letter from Leicester's Men to their protector was therefore chiefly by way of an affirmation of their relationship, and an expression of the hope that it would continue. They prayed that, in consequence of:

> . . . a certain proclamation put out for the reviving of a statute as touching retainers . . . you will now vouchsafe to retain us at this present as your household servants and daily waiters, not that we mean to crave any further stipend or benefit at your lordship's hands, but our liveries as we have had and also your honour's licence to certify that we are your household servants when we shall have occasion to travel amongst our friends, as we do usually once a year and as other noblemen's players do . . .[39]

Six of the company signed the letter, led by James Burbage, father of the actor.

The authorities not only controlled the size and number of these companies but also the substance of their performances, though this last was specifically the business of the Revels Office when the plays were to

144

be performed at Court. In December 1572 we read:

> Perusing and reforming of plays: The expense and charges when my
> Lord of Leicester's Men showed their matter of *Panecia*. Gloves for my
> Lord of Leicester's boys that played at Court: For the carriage of their
> stuff and for the carter's attendance that night. For the hire of a horse
> two days to the Court to furnish my Lord of Leicester's players, the
> frost being so great, no boat could go and come back again: For holly
> and ivy for my Lord of Leicester's servants.

The clerk then added: 'When I came to Mr Peters to receive the money I
could not, without further order of my Lord Treasurer . . . for my boat
hire to and from Westminster to receive the money, one shilling.'[40]

The Christmas entertainments were a particularly good time for
players, and an atmosphere of good will and good humour pervaded the
Court much of the time. It was also a time for flirtations, and the
Christmas of 1572/3 seems to have brought out into the open what had
been relatively carefully hidden for some time. At least if it had not
become apparent at Christmas, it was common knowledge by May
1573. That month Gilbert Talbot wrote from Court to his father the
Earl of Shrewsbury, giving substance to what had been suspected in
other quarters for some time, namely that Leicester had by no means led
a celibate existence since the death of his wife, nor had he been devoted
to the Queen entirely. Not, of course, that the Queen herself, in her
heart of hearts, can have imagined that this was so, though she may well
have wished that it was. As long as it was not put before her very eyes,
however, she could ignore it. Talbot's letter ran as follows:

> There are two sisters now in the Court that are very far in love with
> him [Leicester], as they have been long; my Lady Sheffield and
> Frances Howard. They, of like striving who shall love him better, are
> at great wars together, and the Queen thinketh not well of them and
> not the better of him; by this means there are spies set over him.[41]

Douglas, Lady Sheffield, was indeed in a difficult situation. If her
sister was genuinely competing with her, and Leicester was responding
to her flirtation— even if only to distract attention from his real interest
in Douglas — then there was little she could do. Her liaison with
Leicester had begun, if gossip is to be believed, almost five years before,
in 1568, during a royal visit to Belvoir Castle, the home of the Earl of
Rutland. Both Leicester and Douglas's husband John, second Earl of
Sheffield, were present. Douglas, daughter of Lord William Howard,

great-uncle to the Queen, was only twenty-four or five, and seems to have rapidly fallen a victim to Leicester's charms. In the words of Holles, writing a history of the family some ninety years later — and from the Sheffield family's point of view — Leicester 'found her an easy purchase'.[42] The enamoured lady foolishly carried one of Leicester's love-letters with her on her return home, and promptly lost it. She asked her sister-in-law, who denied any knowledge of the letter's existence, but who had in fact found it on the great staircase of the house, and when she realised what it revealed, kept it to show her brother when he returned.

When Lord Sheffield discovered that the man who, as Chancellor of the University of Oxford, had two years previously bestowed the degree of Master of Arts *honoris causa* on him, had then cuckolded him, he 'parted beds that night' with his wife, and the next day set out for London to institute divorce proceedings. Before he could do so, however, he became ill and died rather suddenly, of a disease known, somewhat ironically, as the Leicester cold, thus giving plenty of ammunition to those who wished to blacken Leicester's character by putting it about that he had arranged for Sheffield's demise. *Leicester's Commonwealth*, for example, put it as 'an extreme rheum in his head (as it was given out), but as others say, with an artificial catarrh that stopped his breath'.[43] There is no evidence that Leicester did any such thing, and indeed there was no motive for him to do so, since his subsequent behaviour revealed that he had no intention of marrying Douglas Sheffield, even when she was legally available to do so. When the period of mourning was ended, Lady Sheffield returned to Court, and apparently received several offers of marriage, which she resolutely declined. Her liaison with Leicester must have been a very well kept secret, for it continued. In later years Douglas maintained that she had been contracted to Leicester in a house in Cannon Row, Westminster, in 1571. Certainly before the end of 1573 she became pregnant, and on 7 August 1574 gave birth to a son by Leicester. There was also a rumour that she had earlier produced a daughter who had died in infancy.[44]

Unfortunately the evidence for all this was not produced until 1603, when the illegitimate son was attempting to prove his claim to the earldoms of Leicester and Warwick, proceedings in the Star Chamber that were contested by Leicester's widow, Lettice Knollys.[45] Douglas maintained that she was, after the contracting in the house in Cannon Row:

. . . solemnly wedded to him, in a chamber at Esher in Surrey, by a

lawful minister, according to the form of matrimony by law established in the Church of England, in the presence of Sir Edward
Horsey, Knight, that gave her in marriage; as also of Robert Sheffield, Esq., and his wife, Dr Julio [Giulio Borgherini, Leicester's
physician], Henry Frodsham, Gent., with five other persons, whose
names are there specified: and that the ring, wherewith they were so
married, was set with five pointed diamonds, and a table diamond,
which had been given to him the said earl by the then Earl of
Pembroke's grandfather, upon condition that he should not bestow it
upon any but whom he did make his wife. And moreover, that the
Duke of Norfolk was the principal mover of the said marriage [dating
it before June 1572, or even September 1571, when he was sent back
to the Tower]; but that the said earl, pretending a fear of the Queen's
indignation, in case it should come to her knowledge, made her vow
not to reveal it till he gave leave; whereupon all her servants were
commanded secrecy therein.[46]

The trouble was that by 1603 none of these witnesses was available, nor
was the clergyman; in fact no one could remember his name, and indeed
there was no trace of any licence having been procured in ecclesiastical
records. This does not in itself mean that no such ceremony took place,
for a man posing as a clergyman might easily have produced a forged
document. There is also, however, another important piece of evidence
in the shape of a draft of a letter in Leicester's own hand to a woman who,
from internal evidence, was a widow and with whom he had had a
liaison of some long standing. He reminded her that she had agreed to
be his mistress, fully accepting that she could never be his wife:

> I have, as you well know, long both loved and liked you and found
> always that faithful and earnest affection at your hand again that
> bound me greatly to you. This good will of mine, whatsoever you
> have thought, hath not changed from that it was at the beginning
> towards you. And I trust, after your widowhood began, upon the first
> occasion of my coming to you, I did plainly and truly open unto you
> in what sort my good will should and might alway remain to you, and
> showing you such reasons as then I had for the performance of mine
> intent, as well as ever since. It seemed that you had fully resolved
> with yourself to dispose yourself accordingly, without any further
> expectation or hope of other dealing.[47]

However, during the course of the last year (up to the time the letter was
written) she had begun to press him 'in a further degree than was our

condition'. He drew her attention to the fact that they had discussed the matter again, and that after 'a great strangeness' they had made it up. But this had not lasted, and so he had decided to sort the matter out once and for all.

Leicester's reason for not marrying the lady in question was very cogent, he maintained, because by failing to do so, he was the cause: 'almost of the ruin of mine own house . . . my brother you see long married and not like to have children it resteth so now in myself'. Ambrose had in fact had a son, John, by his first wife, but he predeceased his mother. So, as much as Leicester might want to marry, and indeed felt it his duty to his family to do so and produce an heir, yet he felt he could not do so for fear of losing the favour of the Queen:

> If I should marry, I am sure never to have favour of them [i.e. the Queen] that I had rather yet never have wife than lose them, yet is there nothing in the world next that favour that I would not give to be in hope of leaving some children behind me, being now the last of our house. But yet the cause being as it is I must content myself, and cannot but show my full determination to you that you may assuredly know my mind and resolution as it is.

From this letter it would seem that there was no kind of marriage contract, nor was there likely to have been, between Leicester and the recipient of it. If that lady was Douglas Sheffield, and the evidence seems to suggest that it was, then either she was mistaken in claiming that there had been some sort of contract in 1575, or else the letter was written before that date. Assuming that it was Lady Sheffield, then it must certainly have been written before the end of 1573, when her pregnancy became known. This last fact may have changed Leicester's mind, and induced him to go through some sort of ceremony during that winter, but then that does not accord with another claim that they were married two days before the birth of the child, which would have made it as late as 5 August 1574. Either way, Leicester certainly did not want public recognition of the liaison because of the Queen, though he later accepted the responsibility for his illegitimate son to some degree.

When the boy was born, Leicester's servant Will Clewer was sent to his master with the news. At this time — August 1574 — Leicester was with the Queen on progress in Gloucestershire. Clewer was supposed to have brought back a letter to Lady Sheffield from Leicester, signed 'Your very loving husband', though Mrs Erisa, who attended Lady Sheffield during her lying-in, was in doubt about this. As the Dugdale version runs:

. . . within two days after the birth of the said Sir Robert Dudley (who afterwards was born at Sheen, and there christened by a minister sent from Sir Henry Lee, having to his godfathers the Earl of War-wick with the same Sir Henry, and godmother the Lady Dacres of the South[by their deputies]) the said Lady Douglas received a letter from the earl (which one Mrs Erisa, but then Lady Parker, read) wherein his lordship did thank God for the birth of his said son, who might be their comfort and staff of their old age (as are the words of the said letter) and subscribed, Your loving husband, Rob. Leicester. As also, that the said lady was after this served in her chamber as a countess, until he commanded the contrary, for fear the marriage should be disclosed.[48]

Douglas's attempt to assert her position as a countess is understandable, though highly ill-advised at the Court, as she must have known very well. She was in a difficult situation, by any standards, with very little to use as a weapon against Leicester that would not harm them both. Moreover, she does not seem to have had the force of personality to stand up to him, even if there was occasion to do so. Such was his power and influence at the time, very few people could have contemplated opposit-ion to him. In the early part of 1574 he seemed especially high on the crest of a wave. On 25 February, for example, he was made High Steward of the manors of the Dean and Chapter of Norwich, with a stipend of £10,[49] and on 23 April he was the Queen's Lieutenant for the Garter ceremonies on St George's Day.[50] He acquired another wardship, the Old Palace at Maidstone, and lands in some twenty counties.[51] A survey of the 'wardrobe stuffs' alone at Longleat for the period from 7 March 1571 to 3 March 1574 shows the magnificence of his houses,[52] and the dedications continued. Arthur Golding produced yet another translation, this time of Calvin's sermons on the Book of Job; Lewis Evans dedicated a *Short Dictionary . . .*, and there was Blundeville's *The True Order and method of writing and reading histories*. The dedication to this last is interesting for what it reveals of the Tudor concept of history and its utility:

. . . knowing your honour amongst other good delights, to delight most in reading of histories, the true image and portraiture of man's life and that not as many do, to pass away the time, but to gather thereof such judgement and knowledge as you thereby be the more able, as well to direct your private actions, as to give counsel like a most prudent counsellor in public causes, be it matters of war, or peace . . .[53]

How far this could ever be applied honestly to Leicester is, of course, questionable. Certainly there was a considerable difference between his public and private personae, of which the Douglas Sheffield business was only one example.

There was, moreover, to be more of this matter before long, caused largely by the revival of another old flirtation of Leicester's, namely with Lettice Knollys, whose husband Walter Devereux, Viscount Hereford, had been created Earl of Essex in 1572. This time, however, things were to go much further. In 1573 Essex was sent to Ireland, in an attempt to colonise Ulster. In 1575 he was recalled early in the year to explain himself to the Privy Council. At this interview it appeared that the Earl of Leicester wanted all the previous deficiencies to be overlooked, and for Essex to be sent back to Ulster immediately. Leicester's brother-in-law, Sir Henry Sidney, had had three terms of office as Lord Deputy in Ireland, and was a personal friend of Essex. He wrote to the Council, but Leicester's immediate concern was stronger than family ties for once. A letter from Edward Waterhouse to Sir Henry Sidney, dated 21 March 1575, puts the matter in detail:

> It seemeth that your letters to the lords were not agreeable to the Earl of Leicester's mind, whereby he took occasion of . . . somewhat of offence against you, as though your lordship had not made it apparent enough to her Majesty, or the lords, that you earnestly wished the earl's return . . . But your lordship did much better, and far more agreeably to my Lord of Essex' mind, who understanding of my Lord of Leicester's conceit, did forthwith satisfy his lordship of your most friendly and effectual dealing.[54]

Camden maintained that Essex threatened Leicester this year for his behaviour towards his wife, and that by way of retaliation Leicester got him sent back to Ireland 'with the empty title of Earl Marshal'. This only happened some months later, however. For the time being Leicester continued to be as attentive as ever to the Queen. That same month of March 1575 he accompanied her to Dr Dee's house at Mortlake on the Thames near Richmond, as the latter recorded in his *Compendious Rehearsal:*

> The Queen with her most honourable Privy Council and other her lords, ladies and nobility came riding across the fields from Richmond . . . Her Majesty being taken down from her horse by the Earl of Leicester, Master of the Horse, at the church wall of Mortlake, did

see some of the properties of that glass, to her Majesty's great contentment and delight.[55]

The glass was supposed to have been brought to him by an angel, and to have possessed magical qualities. He was obliged to bring it out for the Queen to see because his wife was but four hours buried and the Queen therefore declined to enter his house.

When not actually with the Queen, Leicester was occupied with his usual wide variety of concerns. Building was one in particular in the spring of 1575, and in May it was the construction of a banqueting house in the grounds of Leicester House in London, on the river bank. The building was only two storeys high, the ground floor being divided into a lower room and a gardener's room, and the upper floor being the state room. Some of the stone for the building was acquired through Burghley, in thanks for which Leicester wrote:

> I have to thank your lordship very heartily . . . that your lordship is pleased to help me that I may have some stone toward the making of a little banquet house in my garden . . . the pleasure will be great you do me and I will be ready to the best of my power to requite. And so, committing your lordship to the Almighty, the 17 of May, your lordship's very friend: R. Leicester.[56]

There was not only building in London, however. At Kenilworth Leicester was preparing such a reception for the Queen as he had never ventured on before, and it seems as if this was destined to be his last bid for her hand.

7

The Pleasures of Kenilworth

I stand on the top of the hill, where I know the smallest slip seemeth a fall.

Robert Dudley

A letter from Henry Killigrew to the Earl of Leicester, probably dating from the month of May 1575, gives some idea of what the latter had on foot to delight the Queen that summer:

> The man that desired me to present this enclosed unto your lordship would gladly know your pleasure therein for it will ask two months' work. If therefore you like his device, it may please you to take order with Mr Dudley or some other for the furnishing of him with money. By his account the charges will draw to £50, which sum he desires not to have in his own hands, but that he may receive it, by £4 or £5 at a time, and would gladly also that some by your lordship's appointment may see how he doth employ the same. The man is honest and I think will serve your turn very well and far better in deed than in words. The £7 which he had of me is employed about a fountain which he mindeth to present unto the Queen's Majesty — a singular piece of work, whereof the like was never seen in these parts. I beseech your lordship to let him know your pleasure by my brother or some other, for that I think to go over myself this journey with my Lord of Hunsdon, if he obtain leave for me as I think he will.[1]

The 'enclosed' was a document in Italian, setting forth a programme as follows:

> The first evening in the meadow: Serpents of fire. Eight or ten pots of wonderful and pleasing things. Also birds to fly about in the air scattering fire. Two dogs and cats which will fight in fireworks.
>
> The second evening in the courtyard of the palace: A fountain throwing wine, water and fire seven or eight hours continuously. This will be worth seeing for its marvellous fireworks. Three wheels of wonderful scented fire and of different colours.
>
> The third evening in the river: A dragon as big as an ox, which will fly twice or thrice as high as the tower of St Paul's, and at that height, burn away, and suddenly will issue from its whole body dogs, cats and birds which will scatter fire on all sides.
>
> There will be many other things in these fireworks impossible to describe in writing. I will do it all at my best according to the money sent me for expenses.[2]

It may well have been the expense in the end that decided Leicester against this particular programme, since it does not correspond to any of the accounts of the entertainment when it took place. Even so, it reveals the extent to which the earl was prepared to go to ensure that the Queen's stay with him at Kenilworth would be a memorable one.

Also in the Pepys Collection is a 'Remembrance for the Progress'. Three alternative routes are given from Windsor to Kenilworth, with their respective mileage. The first goes via Chenies (the Bedford house in Buckinghamshire), Rycote, Oxford, Woodstock, Banbury, Coventry and Warwick. The second goes via Bisham, Ewelme, Bicester or Buck[ingham?], Banbury, and then as the first one. The third via Missenden, Aylesbury, Buck[ingham], Daventry, Coventry, and then as above. Carriage was to be appointed for all the nobility, and all office for the Queen and her house. No 'herdward, shoemaker or artificer' was to have carts, but their carriage with horses. Letters were to be sent to the sheriffs of Oxford and Warwick to levy 300 quarters of wheat in each shire, besides the privy bakehouse, or they were to say whether they could serve baked bread. Letters were also to be sent to the commissioners of the peace of both shires, or other gentlemen, to know how the Queen might be served of 'beeves, muttons, veals and lambs, herons, shovelards, bitterns or any kind of fowl or freshwater fish, rabbits, etc.', and also what might be served by the day at Woodstock, Coventry, Warwick and Kenilworth, and the price set for the same for her stay.

One sees from the memorandum what very complicated logistics were involved in moving the Queen and her Court about the countryside on her progresses. All sorts of details had to be thought of, and eventualities provided for. The brewing of Oxford and Coventry would serve for Woodstock, Warwick and Kenilworth, and also bought bread if need be. A staple was to be held for the poulterers for a month at Oxford and Coventry. A salt store was also to be laid, though the document leaves the location blank, and wood was to be had 'of the Queen's own about her grace'. Standing houses were to be laid in, as well as local rushes for putting on the floors, and an adequate supply of charcoal. Orders were to be given to the sheriffs of the shire at the said standing house by letters for the laying in of 'hay, litter, oats, horse-bread and such like'. Wines of all sorts were to come from London and be laid in the appointed places for the journey. If the ale of the country did not please the Queen, then it must come from London, or else a brewer was to brew the same in the towns near. Ale and beer was to be brewed at Oxford, and to serve within twenty miles of the city.[3]

Of course Leicester had much experience of this sort of arrangement in his capacity as Master of the Horse, and years of practice, so that he knew what things were likely to be overlooked, and where problems might well arise. Even so, the arrangements had to be made, and they might well vary from year to year and from place to place, so that he could never be sure that it would all happen automatically, once his pattern had been established. However, this year of 1575, and this visit to Kenilworth, was to be specially important, and Leicester was all the more concerned that nothing should mar it.

Dugdale notes:

> Here, in July, 1575, having completed all things for her reception, did he entertain the Queen, for the space of seventeen days, with excessive cost, and variety of delightful shows, as may be seen at large in a special discourse thereof then printed, and entitled, *The Princely Pleasures of Kenilworth Castle*.[4]

On Saturday 9 July, the same day as Elizabeth came to Kenilworth, Leicester was made Chief Steward of his friend Lord North's manors in Middlesex,[5] which had a niceness in its timing, since Leicester was to help Lord North out when it was his turn to entertain the Queen on progress, and North was to be his confidant in his matrimonial ventures. The Queen was to reach Kenilworth via Grafton, in Oxfordshire, where she had a house, and at Stockston Leicester gave her 'a glorious entertainment here, in her passage towards Kenilworth Castle, erecting a tent of extraordinary largeness for that purpose, and pins belonging whereto amounted to seven cart-load, by which the magnificence thereof may be guessed at'.[6] Because Leicester had 'made her Majesty great cheer at dinner, and pleasant hunting by the way after . . . it was eight o'clock in the evening ere her highness came to Killingworth.' The clocks were stopped for the duration of the visit and the two sundials made to point always to two o'clock.[7] It was to be perpetual summer afternoon in this halcyon enchantment.

Reaching Kenilworth itself, the Queen was greeted by one of the ten sybils wearing a pall or cloak of white silk. She recited some verses written by William Hunnis, Master of Queen Elizabeth's Chapel. Hunnis dedicated his *A Hive Full of Honey* to Leicester in 1578, and three years later the latter intervened on Hunnis's part to protect his child actors. The sybil told how the Queen brought gladness into every place she visited, especially to this place, which had so long wished for the visit, and then prophesied prosperity, health and felicity, which the Queen benignly accepted. Entering the Tiltyard, the Queen was confronted by a porter 'big of limb and stern of countenance' — though also dressed in silk — wielding a club and keys of quantity according. His speech was apparently rough and full of passion, in a meter suitable for the purpose, written by one Master Badger of Oxford, Master of Arts, and Bedel in the same university. When he came near, however, the porter confessed that he found himself 'pierced at the presence of a personage so evidently expressing an heroical sovereignty over all the whole estates and high degrees there besides, calmed his astonishment, proclaims open gates and free passage to all, yields up his club, his keys, his office, and all, and on his knees humbly prays pardon of his ignorance and impatience.' To this the Queen, naturally, graciously granted her pardon, which was a sign for the trumpeters on the gate to begin their tune of welcome. The six trumpeters were in fact dummies eight feet tall, with false trumpets five feet long, dressed in silk, but with men with real trumpets behind them. As the Queen rode under the gate they passed to the inside, so that she had music all the while, and then she was greeted in the Base Court by the Lady of the Lake, with two nymphs waiting on her, all dressed in silk. The Lady of the Lake was on a raft or movable island, which floated from the pool to land, lit with blazing torches. Her verse was penned by George Ferrers, sometime Lord of Misrule in the Court, and after telling how she had kept the lake since King Arthur's day, she now thought it her duty to offer up the same to the Queen. The Queen thanked this personage, too, though was inspired to add: 'We had thought indeed the lake had been ours, and do you call it yours now? Well, we will herein commune more with you hereafter.'

This pageant was concluded with 'a delectable harmony of hautbois, shawms, cornetts, and such other loud music', which played as the Queen proceeded to the main gate, to the right of Henry VIII's lodgings and the left of the keep, to which access was gained by a bridge thrown across the dry moat by Leicester. According to Laneham, the bridge was twenty feet wide and seventy feet long, gravelled for treading, and railed on either side with seven posts at intervals of twelve feet, with well-proportioned turned pillars between them. Each of these pairs of posts was to be the occasion for a display of liberality.

On the first posts were square wire cages, three feet long and two feet wide and high, containing bitterns, curlews, shovellers and herons, 'godwits, and such like dainty birds', which were the presents of Sylvanus, god of fowl. Next were two large silvered bowls, filled with apples, pears, cherries, filberts, walnuts — still on their branches — with oranges, pomegranates, lemons and pippins, the gift of Pomona, goddess of fruits. A similar pair of bowls graced the third set of posts, full of ears of wheat, barley, oats, beans and peas, the gift of Ceres. The fourth set of posts progressed to drink. On the left hand was a silvered bowl containing bunches of red and white grapes with their foliage, and on the right hand was a pair of great white silver livery pots for wine, with two full glasses of good capacity in front of them, one containing white wine, the other claret. They were, in Laneham's words; 'so fresh of colour, and of look so lovely, smiling to the eyes of many, that by my faith me thought by their leering they could have found in their hearts (as the evening was hot) to have kissed them sweetly, and thought it no sin.' These were, of course, the presents of Bacchus, god of wine.

The fifth pair of posts carried trays strewn with fresh grass, on which were (conger) eels, burt or bret, or young turbot, mullet, fresh herring, oysters, salmon, crayfish or crab, and other such fish from Neptune, god of the sea. The sixth pair of posts was more pointed in its significance. They bore silver ragged staffs from the Dudley arms, and were effectively trophies, with bows, arrows, spears, a shield, helmet, gorget, corselets, swords, targets, and similar items, from Mars the god of war. Laneham commented, perhaps somewhat naively, that the tines of the ragged staffs seemed perfect for carrying armour, but also because they — and therefore by extension their possessor — might take upon

156

themselves the protection of the Queen's person in that place. By way of contrast, the last pair of posts carried four-foot branches of bay adorned with lutes, viols, shawms, cornetts, flutes, recorders and harps, presents from Phoebus, god of music — 'to rejoice the mind, but also of physic for health to the body'.

As the Queen passed into the castle proper, there was a huge royal coat-of-arms surmounting a black board ten feet square, bordered with wreaths of ivy, and bearing in white letters a Latin poem written by Mr Paten, mentioning the succession of gods and their gifts, but every time there was a reference to the Queen, the letters were in gold. Since the evening was drawing on it was not easy to read by torchlight, so a poet, dressed in a long blue garment over crimson, all silk, and wearing a garland of bay, was duly appointed to read the said verse. Then as the Queen passed into the inner court, flutes were playing, as befitted the last gifts from Phoebus.

At this point the Queen dismounted and went up to her chamber. There was to be no let-up yet, however, for at that moment a great peal of guns sounded, with fireworks, just to show that Jupiter himself was no further behind with his welcome than the other gods had been .The noise and flames were said to have been seen and heard twenty miles away.

On Sunday 10 July the morning was spent fittingly at the parish church with divine service and preaching, though the latter could be a touchy business in the presence of the Queen. After that the afternoon was spent with music and dancing, much to Laneham's satisfaction. Later that same evening, however, Jupiter was to bestir himself again, and though at first he merely fired a warning piece or two, soon he warmed up to his main display: '. . . with blaze of burning darts, flying to and fro, leams [beams] of stars coruscant, streams and hail of fiery sparks, lightnings of wildfire on water and land, flight and shot of thunderbolts: all with such countenance, terror and vehemency, that the heavens thundered, the waters surged, the earth shook' — all of which went on until after midnight.

Monday was hot, so the Queen remained indoors until five o'clock in the evening, when she went out to the Chase to hunt the hart. One was started, chase was given and the hounds hotly pursued, so the animal took to the water. What with the baying of the hounds and the swiftness of the deer, the running of the footmen, the galloping of the horses, the sounding of the horns and the calling of the huntsmen reverberating through the woods, across the valley, and off the surface of the water,

Laneham conveys directly what the chase held for the Elizabethans, moved as they were, in his words, by a 'pastime delectable in so high a degree, as for any person to pleasure by most senses at once, in mine opinion there can be none any way comparable to this'.

The deer was killed, but that was not the end of the evening's events by any means. As the Queen returned by torchlight, a wildman emerged from the woods bearing an oaktree pulled up by the roots, and himself covered in moss and ivy. He told how he had asked all his familiars and companions — the fauns, satyrs, nymphs, dryads and hamadryads — who these people might be, but only Echo was able to help him. At this point Echo entered into dialogue with the wildman, in verse devised, penned and pronounced by George Gascoigne. What followed was almost the cause of a disaster. To signify his submission, the wildman broke his tree in two, and threw the top from him. In his zeal the discarded part almost landed on the Queen's horse's head, which caused the animal to start, much to the wildman's dismay. The Queen was quick to set everyone at ease, however, and said: 'No hurt, no hurt!'

Tuesday was given up to music and dancing, but towards the end of the day the Queen went on foot into the Chase over the bridge, and into a barge on the pool, from which point she heard a recital of music. A pleasant way indeed of spending a summer night, and a very English one, too. By way of contrast, Wednesday was more energetic, with hunting once more. The deer again took to the water, but was captured there, and the waterman held him up by the head to know the Queen's pleasure. She commanded him to lose his ears for a ransom, but spared his life.

On Thursday ban-dogs were produced in the outer court, and thirteen bears in the inner court. Whoever made up the panel or jury, observed Laneham, had made sure that there were enough bears for an inquest and one for a challenge. The foreman seemed to be 'a wight of great wisdom and gravity', but then it was not a matter for a jury, but to 'answer to an ancient quarrel between them and the ban-dogs'. The Elizabethans enjoyed bear-baiting, and it was considered Puritanical by many people to be against it. Later that night there were pyrotechnics again, but these were new to Laneham, insofar as they flew about, went high up into the sky, and burnt in water, which by his standards was contrary to their nature. To increase the noise and excitement there was gunfire, too, for the space of some two hours. Meanwhile, indoors, a remarkable Italian tumbler was performing before the Queen.

On Friday and Saturday there were no outdoor entertainments, because the weather was wet and windy. This was welcome, however, for it 'very seasonably tempered' the drought and the heat that had been created by the prolonged fine weather previously, and which had persisted during the whole of the Queen's stay up to this point. On Sunday the good weather returned, there was worship in the parish church, with a 'fruitful' sermon, and since 17 July was St Kenelm's day, and in honour of God and Kenilworth, a rustic bride-ale or wedding was appointed to take place. The procession assembled in the Tiltyard, from where it was to pass into the great court of the castle, where a quintain was set up. It would then leave by the north gate and return to the town. The 'lusty lads and bold bachelors of the parish' went first, with the groom, then morris dancers, three maids carrying cakes, followed by a cupbearer — who had his work cut out to prevent the flies from consuming the contents of the cup— and lastly the bride, supported by two ancient parishioners, and followed by a dozen bridesmaids. The running at the quintain and the rustic tournament that then took place were enough, said Laneham, to have made a man merry even if he had been told that his wife was dying.

Then came men from Coventry, who asked permission to perform their Hock Tuesday play before the Queen. Puritanical elements in the city had had the play banned, but if the Queen expressed a wish to see it, then who could prevent them? This caused a considerable counter-attraction to the wedding, much to the annoyance of the bride, who was determined at all costs to dance before the Queen. In the event the Queen did not see much of the play, so requested a repeat performance the following Tuesday, and was so pleased then that she gave the men a couple of bucks and five marks. Not surprisingly, they expressed the wish that she would come often to Kenilworth.

To return to the Sunday evening, however, there had been plans for a play in any case, and though it lasted all of two hours, on top of the day's events, it was judged to have been so well presented that it seemed very short. Afterwards there was a 'most delicious and . . . ambrosial banquet'. Laneham did not know what was the most worthy of wonder, the daintiness, shape or cost, or else the variety and number of the dishes— some 300 of them, according to him— of which the Queen ate 'smally or nothing'. A masque was to have accompanied the feast, but because of the lateness of the hour it was not presented, despite the vast sum spent on it.

Monday 18 July was hot, so the Queen did not venture forth until five o'clock to the hunt. It was as she was returning that she was greeted by the water pageant that is thought to have found its way into Shakespeare's *A Midsummer Night's Dream* as Oberon's vision. Laneham describes a swimming mermaid eighteen feet long, though it does not seem to have been a mermaid so much as a merman or Triton, armed with a trumpet made out of a wrinkled whelk. When the Queen reached the bridge he spoke his piece, and the Lady of the Lake came with her nymphs, floating on her island again. She in turn introduced Arion, with his old friend the dolphin, some twenty-four feet long. Arion began a 'delectable ditty of a song, well apted to a melodious noise, compounded of six several instruments all covert, casting sound from the dolphin's belly within'. Laneham found it all very splendid, though another source relates that when it came to the singing, Harry Goldingham, who represented Arion, found his voice hoarse and unpleasant. He therefore tore off his disguise and swore that he was ' "none of Arion; not he! but eene honest Harry Goldingham," — which blunt discovery pleased the Queen better than if it had gone through in the right way. Yet he could order his voice to an instrument exceeding well.'[8] We shall soon see how this interlude came to figure so importantly as a piece of evidence in determining what was happening at Kenilworth beneath the outward jollification. For the time being, however, we shall follow the course of events. That same day, 18 July, five new knights were created, namely Burghley's son Thomas; Henry Cobham, brother of Lord Cobham; Thomas Stanhope; Arthur Basset and Thomas Tresham. The Queen also touched, and was said to have cured, nine people with the 'painful and dangerous disease' called the King's Evil.

On Tuesday 19 July the Coventry men came as arranged, and then on the next day something seems to have gone wrong. The Queen was to have gone to Wedgenall (Wedgnock Park), some three miles from the castle, to sup. A pavilion was got ready, and other provision made, but the order was countermanded. Laneham said that it was because of the weather being 'not so clearly disposed'. He then went on to say that if the Queen had gone, there was yet another spectacle arranged, this time a 'device of goddesses and nymphs'. What is more significant by far is the fact, added almost as an afterthought by Laneham: '. . . this day also was there such earnest talk and appointment of removing, that I gave over my noting, and harkened after my horse'. In the event the Queen stayed on, but what had happened to cause this sudden upset? We must turn to the passage from *A Midsummer Night's Dream* already referred to. Oberon is talking to Puck:

Oberon: My gentle Puck, come hither. Thou rememb'rest
            Since once I sat upon a promontory
            And heard a mermaid, on a dolphin's back
            Uttering such dulcet and harmonious breath
            That the rude sea grew civil at her song,
            And certain stars shot madly from their spheres
            To hear the sea-maid's music?
Puck: I remember.
Oberon: That very time I saw — but thou couldst not —
            Flying between the cold moon and the earth
            Cupid all armed. A certain aim he took
            At a fair vestal thronèd by the west,
            And loosed his loveshaft smartly from his bow
            As it should pierce a hundred thousand hearts;
            But I might see young Cupid's fiery shaft
            Quenched in the chaste beams of the wat'ry moon,
            And the imperial votaress passed on
            In maiden meditation, fancy free.
            Yet marked I where the bolt of Cupid fell:
            It fell upon a little western flower,
            Before, milk white; now purple with love's wound:
            And maidens call it 'love in idleness'. . .[9]

Halpin maintained that Shakespeare had inside information through his family on his mother's side, and indeed it was widely held that Shakespeare was recalling one of Leicester's less glorious moments.[10] Edward Arden, who had been High Sheriff of Warwickshire immediately before the time of the Queen's visit, was eventually put to death on a charge of high treason. Leicester had taken part in the prosecution. As Camden, in his *Annals* of 1583 put it: 'This woeful end of this gentleman, who was drawn in by the cunning of the priest [a Roman, his son-in-law, Master Somerville, had made an attempt on the Queen's life], and cast by his evidence, was generally imputed to Leicester's malice.'[11] We turn to Dugdale to continue the story:

> . . . for which he was prosecuted with so great vigour and violence by the Earl of Leicester's means, whom he had irritated in some particulars (as I have credibly heard) partly in disdaining to wear his livery, which many of this county of his rank thought, in those days, no small honour to them, but chiefly for galling him by certain harsh

expressions, touching his private access to the Countess of Essex, before she was his wife; that through the testimony of one Hall, a priest, he was found guilty of the fact, and lost his life at Smithfield.[12]

Presumably it was through Arden that Shakespeare had his inside information about the Kenilworth visit: 'I saw — but thou couldst not', as Oberon says to Puck, and Arden knew that Leicester was aiming for Elizabeth's hand, even though ultimately he lighted on Lettice Knollys. It was a piece of considerable irony, then, that — according to Laneham — Venus had charged her son, Cupid: '. . . that he shot not a shaft in the Court all the while her Highness remained at Kenilworth'.[13]

By a comparison with the dramatis personae of John Lyly's *Endimion*, published in 1591, Halpin makes a very credible interpretation of Oberon's speech to Puck, bearing in mind that *A Midsummer Night's Dream* was probably written some four or five years after Lyly's play. The eponymous hero of Lyly's drama is none other than Leicester, who is in love with Cynthia — Queen Elizabeth. But Endimion is beloved of two other ladies, namely Tellus (in love with his 'person') — who is sometimes taken to be Mary Queen of Scots, but would more probably seem to be Douglas Sheffield — subsequently married to Corsites (Sir Edward Stafford, the marriage having taken place in 1579). The other lady was Floscula (meaning 'little flower'), who was in love with Endimion's 'virtues', and no other than Lettice Knollys. Her appearance in Oberon's speech, then, as a 'little western flower', is all the more appropriate. Other characters are Eumenides, taken to be the Earl of Sussex (or possibly Sir Philip Sidney), and Semele, either Frances Sidney, his second wife, daughter of Sir William Sidney and foundress of Sidney Sussex College, Cambridge, or — if one accepts Sir Philip Sidney — then perhaps Lady Rich. Two other characters in the play are Dipsas, 'a mischief-making old crone', and Geron (Greek for 'old man') her husband, which seem admirably suited for Bess of Hardwick and her fourth husband the Earl of Shrewsbury.

According to Halpin's interpretation, then, this would make a paraphrase of Oberon's speech run something like this: Wavering in his passion between Cynthia (Elizabeth) and Tellus (Douglas Sheffield), Endimion (Leicester), was either 'alarmed' at the progress of Alençon, or 'all-armed' in the magnificence of his preparations at Kenilworth for storming the heart of his royal mistress. He made a pre-determined and well-directed effort for the hand of Elizabeth, Virgin Queen of England.

Presumptuously he made love to her—rash under all the circumstances
— as if he fancied that neither she nor any woman in the world could
resist his suit. But it was evident to me (and to the rest of the initiated)
that the ardent Leicester's desperate venture was lost in the pride,
prudery, and jealousy of power which invariably swayed the tide of
Elizabeth's passions, and the Virgin Queen finally departed from
Kenilworth Castle unshackled with a matrimonial engagement, and as
heart-whole as ever.

And yet, continues Oberon, curious to observe the collateral issues of
this amorous preparation, I watched (whatever others may have done)
and discovered the person on whom Leicester's irregular passion was
secretly fixed. It was fixed upon Lettice, at that time wife of Walter,
Earl of Essex, and an Englishwoman of rank inferior to the object of
Leicester's great ambition. Previous to this unhappy attachment, Lettice
was not only pure and innocent in conduct, but also unblemished in
reputation, but after it she became not only deeply inflamed with a
criminal passion, and still more deeply (perhaps) stained with a husband's
blood, but the subject also of shame and obloquy. Those,
however, who pity her weakness, and compassionate her misery, still
offer a feeble apology for her conduct by calling it the result of her
husband's voluntary absence, of the waste of affections naturally tender
and fond, and of the idleness of a heart that might have been faithful if
busy with honest duties, and filled with domestic loves. You cannot
mistake, after all I have said — go — fetch me that flower.

But this is to anticipate somewhat. Possibly there was some indiscretion
at Kenilworth between Leicester and Lettice, and perhaps the Queen
got wind of it. Certainly something went wrong on the twelfth day of
the visit, for according to Laneham the Queen would not attend at
Wedgenall, nor see the show provided later. Gascoigne also had his
views on the matter: 'There was nothing but weeping and wailing,
crying and howling, dole and desperation, mourning and moan . . . the
which sudden change I plainly perceived to be, for that they understood
above that your Majesty would shortly (and too suddenly) depart out of
this country.' He concluded with a request on behalf of his master
Deep-desire (Leicester) that her Majesty would 'either be a suitor for him
unto the heavenly powers or else but only give her gracious consent that
he may be restored to his pristine estate'.[14] It seems at best to have
been extraordinarily tactless of Leicester, in the midst of his great bid for
Elizabeth's hand, to have been paying court to Lettice Knollys — if this
is indeed what happened — and no wonder the boat was rocked.

At all events the Queen remained at Kenilworth for another week, until Wednesday 27 July, making nineteen days in all for her stay. Laneham tells us virtually nothing more, however, apart from pointing out the significance of the number seven in relation to the Queen's name (which he believed meant 'seventh of my heaven' in Hebrew), that she had come in the seventh month, to be greeted by seven gods and their seven gifts. Laneham also drops in the fact that in the space of three days seventy-two tuns of ale and beer were consumed, or as he put it, 'piped up quite'. Forty tuns were found locally — from sundry friends — until new supplies could be brought in.

There was a farewell, devised and spoken for him and Kenilworth by Gascoigne as Sylvanus, as the Queen set on to Middleton, Lichfield and Worcester. It was from the last place that Laneham wrote his letter, dated 20 August 1575. However, when the party arrived at Chartley, in Staffordshire, Lettice acted as hostess on her own, because her husband was in Ireland. One can well imagine what the atmosphere must have been like. In December that year De Guaras, the Spanish commissioner, wrote to Zayas, Alva's secretary, in the following terms:

> As the thing is publicly talked about in the streets there is no objection to my writing openly about the great enmity which exists between the Earl of Leicester and the Earl of Essex, in consequence, it is said, of the fact that whilst Essex was in Ireland his wife had two children by Leicester. She is the daughter of Sir Francis Knollys, a near relative of the Queen, and a member of the Council, and great discord is expected in consequence.[15]

On 17 November Leicester had been made Steward of the See of London, with an annual stipend of £10,[16] and on 5 December that year he received an annuity of £100 from Taunton and the See of Winchester. As a New Year's present for 1576, Leicester gave the Queen a cross of gold, in which were five large emeralds, and from which three pearls were hung. Early in that year, more was added to Leicester's list of appointments when he was made High Steward of the See of Norwich, with a stipend of £10,[17] in March. This year he also invested £50 in Frobisher's voyage to find a North-west passage to Cathay, which was, in the circumstances, wisely kept to such a modest sum.

In July Leicester was advised by his physician to take spa waters, and so he went to Buxton, in Derbyshire, which was on the property of the Earl of Shrewsbury, who had built a special bathhouse there at St Ann's Spring. There was also a row of houses where those taking the waters might lodge. Leicester was to visit Buxton for three successive years.

On his return the following month, however, he found himself involved in considerable controversy with the Puritan Thomas Wood. The latter was not in orders, but had been at Le Havre with the Earl of Warwick in 1562, and on his return to England had been the first to bring Leicester news of his brother's wounded leg. By now Wood was farming in Leicestershire, an area very much enjoying the protection of Leicester's brother-in-law, the Puritan Earl of Huntingdon. Despite not being ordained, Wood took part in a weekly meeting, known as a prophesying, which involved interpretation of the Bible, and was regarded as 'a most fruitful and comfortable exercise'. At least the Puritans thought so, but the Queen in particular looked upon them with deep suspicion, since Puritanism in its most extreme form attacked the episcopacy, and indeed almost anything in the Church for which no direct warrant might be found in Holy Scripture, and since the Established Church was necessary to support the monarchy, anything that attacked the Elizabethan Church settlement might ultimately be interpreted as an attack on Elizabeth herself — or at least her position and authority.

Archbishop Parker had been obliged to forbid the propheysings in 1574, but they continued to flourish, and a notorious case occurred at Southam in Warwickshire in 1576. In the Queen's view it was Leicester's responsibility to do something about it. In the Privy Council, Leicester and other members of the Council were concerned to do a deal with the Southam Puritans, as much in their own interests as in a concern for the upholding of law and order, since if they were allowed to continue unchecked in their activities, then the full force of the law would be brought against them, and they would be completely suppressed. Leicester took no active part, however, maintaining that he knew nothing about the Southam meetings to influence his opinion either way. When Wood heard about the Council's actions, however, he assumed that Leicester was personally responsible, and wrote to him in no uncertain terms, including for good measure, '. . . other bruits, very dishonourable and ungodly', about Leicester's behaviour which he would not commit to paper. Evidently he had wished to speak to Leicester about them at Kenilworth the year before, had there been an opportunity. Luckily there had not been, for the matter may well have concerned rumours about Lady Sheffield and/or Lady Essex, and that would have been far from the appropriate moment.

Rather than send his letter direct to Leicester, however, Wood enclosed it in a letter to the Earl of Warwick, so that Ambrose might read it before passing it on to his brother. Wood was well aware that it was 'plain, and peradventure may be thought too plain', but with the bigoted conviction of all those who esteem the salvation of souls — especially other people's — above all else, Wood was not to be put off. Ambrose replied on 16 August:

> I have received your letter wherein it sheweth you are greatly grieved with slanderous reports the which are come to you of my brother. If they were as true as they be reported, there is none hath so much cause to be grieved therewithal as myself, but since there is no man knoweth his doings better than I myself, I must therefore declare my knowledge without any brotherly affection, but even as the truth shall lead me . . . I cannot a little marvel that either you or any other will so lightly condemn him upon every slight report, who hath done so great good amongst you as he hath done. It is well known that if he had not been, a great sort the which hath their mouths opened at this day had not been suffered neither to preach nor yet to teach, and peradventure it had not been done without some danger of displeasure to himself and with more difficulty than is fit should be known. Therefore I think it to be very hard dealing towards him who hath deserved so well at their hands as he hath done, to be so hardly rewarded. But the best is that God the which hath made him an instrument for His Church heretofore will continue or rather increase His zeal in him to the end, whatsoever it shall please his enemies either to think or say . . .[18]

This is the sort of letter that one might have expected from Ambrose the Good, as he became known, and from one so devoted to his brother. It is loyal and discreet, merely hinting at what Robert might have done in private on the Puritans' behalf. Robert's reply, dated 19 August, runs to over three thousand words, and takes Wood, and the Puritans in general, to task:

> There is no man I know in this realm, of one calling or other, that hath showed a better mind to the furthering of true religion than I have done, even from the first day of her Majesty's reign to this . . . I have manifest wrong to be thus charged, to be a slider or a faller from the Gospel or I cannot tell what . . . I am no hypocrite nor Pharisee; my doings are plain, and chiefly in the causes of religion. I take Almighty God to my record I never altered my mind or thought from

my youth touching my religion, and you know I was ever from my cradle brought up in it.

It was true that Leicester had intervened on their behalf in the vestments controversy, and he had used his influence in the matter of ecclesiastical patronage and academic appointments, but on the other hand he had also offered on two occasions to hand England over to Spain in return for help to win the Queen's hand, and people's memories were not so short that they had entirely forgotten the Duke of Northumberland's abject declaration on the scaffold that, despite his attempt to exclude Mary Tudor from the succession, he had nevertheless ever been a Catholic. When it came to his personal life, Leicester was equally determined:

> I will not justify myself for being a sinner and flesh and blood as others be. And beside, I stand on the top of the hill, where I know the smallest slip seemeth a fall. But I will not excuse myself; I may fall many ways and have more witnesses thereof than many others who perhaps be no saints neither, yet their faults less noted though some ways greater than mine. I never saw or knew in my life more envy stirring, and less charity used, every man glad to hear the worst, to think the worst, or to believe the worst of his neighbour, which be very uncomfortable fruits of our profession.[19]

It is difficult to determine what Leicester's real religious convictions were. Outright Presbyterianism can hardly have been reconcilable with his interests, apart from the fact that it would have been regarded with horror by the Queen, and therefore highly dangerous. There is no evidence, in any case, that he was in any way sympathetic to it, and even the more extreme aspects of Puritanism generally failed to appeal to him. In particular the zealous carping and factious, uncharitable elements so prevalent amongst extreme Puritans annoyed him. As he said in his letter to Wood, 'he that would be counted most a saint I pray God be found a plain true Christian.'

Having said that, however, it is nevertheless true that he supported several fairly radical Puritans, both preachers and magistrates, and there must have been a very good reason for this. It has been suggested that he saw in them a safeguard against the danger of Catholic subversion, and that his religious policy was concomitant with his state policy, formulated under Walsingham's influence,[20] and indeed this may have been true later in the reign, but it is harder to advance as an explanation for his earlier attachment to the Puritan cause. In all fairness to Leicester, however, one ought to point out that if the Puritans turned their attacks from the Bishop of Rome to the bishops of the Church of England, then he regarded them in a different light. This could only be expected, from what has already been said about the relationship between the Elizabethan monarchy and the Elizabethan Church. Moreover, Leicester cannot be put above the charge of financial considerations in his patronage of the Puritans, and Thomas Nashe, in his *Piers Penniless, his Supplication to the Devil*, dated 1592, represents Leicester as a bear scheming to fatten himself on the honey of the Church.

The translation of Edmund Grindal from the See of London to that of Canterbury in 1576 was doubtless pleasing to Leicester, since he approved of Grindal's brand of churchmanship, but it was scarcely calculated to please the Queen, for when she told Grindal to suppress the propheysings, he declared that he could not, in all conscience, do so. The following year he was suspended. It is interesting to see how hatred of Leicester could make people come to strange or even absurd conclusions. Leicester's physician Dr Julio had, in 1573, married a woman who already had a husband, and Julio had been summoned before the Bishop of London; however, the case was postponed and it was not until 1576, by which time Grindal was Archbishop of Canterbury, that he took the case in hand and made a decision, which went against Julio. Despite the fact that Leicester saw eye to eye with Grindal, especially for his Puritan sympathies, it was widely rumoured that Leicester had brought about Grindal's disgrace because of the Julio affair. Camden adds the quaint, but somewhat irrelevant comment at this point: 'And to his [Grindal's] care (if I may mention so small a matter) are the Englishmen beholden for tamarisk, which, having found it by experience to be exceeding good to ease the hard distemper of the spleen, he first of all brought into England.'[21]

What was much stronger meat for gossips at this time, however, was the death in Dublin, in September 1576, of the Earl of Essex. In the opinion of many he was the latest in the succession of sudden deaths that had begun with Amye Robsart and continued with Lord Sheffield. There was a post-mortem, and although no trace of poison was found, rumour had already spread its own venom. As Camden said, it was all the more easily credited 'because Leicester so quickly afterwards abandoned Douglas Sheffield by whom he had a son (whether she was his wife or paramour I will not say)'. Either way, with the death of Lettice Knollys' husband, she was now free to marry someone else, and Leicester seems to have decided that he was to be that someone else— or possibly Lettice decided for him. There seems little doubt that they had a close relationship by this time, and that Douglas Sheffield must be bought off, despite the fact that she had borne him a son. As Camden put it:

> . . . he endeavoured to persuade the said Lady Douglas to disclaim the marriage above mentioned, offering her no less than £700 *per ann*. in the close arbour of the Queen's garden at Greenwich, in the presence of Sir John Hubaud and George Digby, in case she would so do; and, upon her refusal, terrifying her with protestations, that he would never come at her, and that she should never have penny of him.
>
> It seems that the said Lady Douglas had then the custody of her son; for I find it deposed, that the earl tendered her £1,000 to deliver him unto Sir Edw. Horsey, Captain of the Isle of Wight, to be conveyed into the said isle, there to be brought up by him, which she refused. And there wants not strong suspicion, that, being doubtful lest the life of the same Lady Douglas might minister discourse of this foul play, he designed to dispatch her out of this world: for certain it is, that she had some ill potions given her, so that with the loss of her hair and nails, she hardly escaped death; which being discerned, to secure herself from the like attempts for the future, she contracted marriage with Sir Edw. Stafford Kt (a person of great honour and parts, and sometime employed as an ambassador into France) whereof, afterwards, most sadly repenting, she said, that she had thereby done the greatest wrong that could be to herself and son.[22]

This is to anticipate somewhat, however, for this did not take place until November 1579, after Lettice Knollys' marriage with the Earl of Leicester had been made public, to the extent that the Queen at last knew what several others had known for some time, but had been too frightened to acquaint her with.

In February 1577 Sir Henry and Lady Mary Sidney lost their elder daughter Ambrosia, named in honour of her uncle the Earl of Warwick, and in offering her sympathy to the parents, the Queen suggested that they might like to send their younger daughter Mary, who was only fourteen, to Court. Within less than a year she was contracted to the Earl of Pembroke, aged forty-two, and she was only fifteen when she became his third wife. Sir Henry Sidney believed the match to be the result of the influence of his brother-in-law Leicester, as he wrote: '. . . which great honour to me, my mean lineage and kin, I attribute to my match in your noble house.' [23]

Marriage was also to claim Leicester's attention in another quarter, and though not involving his immediate family as the previous one did, it was a pointer to the future when he should have a legitimate son of his own. There is a letter at Longleat from Bess of Hardwick, thanking Leicester for his efforts to find a match for her 'daughter Lennox', in other words Elizabeth Cavendish, widow of Charles Stuart, Earl of Lennox, who died in 1577. The letter is dated 18 May, from Sheffield, but there is no year. It seems very likely that it was this year, however, since Bess went to Court the next month in connection with the inheritance. It was Arbella, the daughter of this widowed lady, who was subsequently mooted as a bride for Leicester's son.[24]

In June 1577 Leicester went once again to Buxton, with his brother Ambrose, and the Earl of Pembroke joined them shortly afterwards. As Leicester wrote to Burghley on 13 June: 'We observe our physician's orders diligently and obediently, and to say truth there is no pain or penance in it but great pleasure both in drinking and bathing in the water.' However, there was also a word of warning to Burghley. If he decided to come too, then he ought to bring as few servants as possible, for the accommodation was far from extensive, and there were problems with the sanitation system. 'The house is so little a few fills it, and hard then to keep sweet.' Nevertheless he acknowledged: 'My Lord and Lady Shrewsbury have dealt nobly with us every way.'[25] The Queen herself wrote on 25 June to thank the Shrewsburys for their kindness to Leicester: '. . . not as done unto him but to our own self, reputing him as another our self; and, therefore, ye may assure yourselves that we, taking upon us the debt not as his but our own, will take care accordingly to discharge the same.'[26] Not all the letter was in this vein, however, for the Queen jokingly went on in mock serious terms, to detail his diet, which was not to contain more than two ounces of meat a day and the twentieth part of a pint (i.e. a fluid ounce) of wine at dinner. He might have, however, 'as much of St Ann's sacred water as he listeth to drink'. For festal days he might have: 'the shoulder of a wren, and for his supper a leg of the same, beside his ordinary ounces'. Warwick was to have the same rations, except that because he was the stouter of the two, he had better not have the additional leg: '. . . for that light supper agreeth best with the rules of physic'.

This summer the Queen went on progress to Norwich, the prospect of a match with Alençon was revived, and Leicester was understandably nervous. By August he was back in the south, and in his residence of

Wanstead, the White House. He had bought this the previous year,
when it was still known as Naked Naw Hall, and then set about
transforming it into a residence worthy of the owner of Kenilworth and
Leicester House. From the rural peace and quiet of his bed at Wanstead
on a Friday morning he wrote to Walsingham: 'I am loth to trouble you
with the whole discourse that passed last night between her Majesty and
me upon the discussion of your letter.'[27] Walsingham wanted the
Queen to give help to the Huguenots by engaging Duke Casimir to
bring a mercenary army to their aid. The Queen, according to Leicester,
regretted that she had not agreed to this, and now wanted to do so, but
where was she to find the money needed? As far as Leicester could see,
there were only two alternatives. Either the Queen would have to
borrow in Hamburg or Frankfurt, or she would have to call in money she
had already lent to the Netherlands. He was of the opinion that she
would agree to either suggestion, but had a preference for the latter.[28]

The Netherlands question was destined to involve Leicester for the
next ten years — almost for the rest of his life, in fact — and lead him
into one of the most ill-judged ventures of his career, and one which
brought from the Queen one of her most stinging rebukes. In 1577,
however, Leicester can hardly have imagined all of this, though it is
clear that he was already seen as one of those who supported the
Netherlandish cause, as we see from a letter written by him to William
Davison, English agent in Antwerp, dated 28 September 1577:

> Many thanks for all you have done and daily do for me . . . I am glad
> to find your service so agreeable, not only to those there, but her
> Majesty here conceiving so good an opinion of you that you have cause
> to rejoice . . . I know not how this letter hang together, being
> written at hasty fit. I leave [it] to your discretion to understand, and
> commit you to the Lord.[29]

The whole problem of giving support to the Netherlands against the
Spanish would have been a difficult one for any English sovereign to
undertake at this juncture, but given the Queen's habitual reluctance to
make up her mind about any important matter, then those who wished
to influence her had a hard task indeed on their hands. In the first place
the cost of such aid would be extremely difficult for Elizabeth to bear,
and overt assistance could well bring the whole weight of the military
might of Spain against England. Against these two considerations,
however, had to be set the possible alternative, which was that if the
Dutch capitulated totally to Spain, then England would be next in line

of attack. In order to keep that resistance alive, the Queen lent money, and in 1579 was to increase it to the enormous sum of £50,000. Nevertheless, William of Orange felt that he needed still more money. He also wanted the moral and practical support of an English presence on Dutch soil, and felt that Leicester was the person most likely to persuade the Queen to take the necessary steps.

In October 1577 Davison wrote to Leicester that the Prince of Orange very much wanted him to go over and help them with the benefit of his influence and advice, but at the same time he did not want to take Leicester away from the Court, for he knew that he would best advance Dutch interests there. Prince William would like him to go there for even a short time, however, 'and to bring with you some such qualified person, as in case you should be revoked, might be fit to take charge'.[30] In Davison's opinion, the Earl of Warwick or Philip Sidney — both of whom would be acceptable to the Prince of Orange — might be the chosen substitute: '. . . but he [the prince] would have all referred to your own direction.'[31] One sees from this what enormous prestige and reputation Leicester enjoyed abroad — so much so, in fact, that he was seriously able to consider, late in 1577, making a bid for the hand of the now widowed Princess Cecilia of Sweden. Queen Elizabeth herself supported him in his bid, moreover, though she could have hardly guessed then at his degree of involvement with Douglas Sheffield or Lettice Knollys. The princess consulted the King of Sweden — her brother Karl, who had succeeded Eric — and he replied in January 1578 that after all she had experienced in England, it was strange that she should seriously contemplate returning there.[32] This seems to have settled the matter for her, and the princess declined. But if 1578 opened with the failure of one marriage prospect for Leicester, it was to close with the surety of another, though from a very different quarter.

That year Duke Casimir came to England, hoping to persuade the Queen to help him bring military aid to the Dutch, and in February 1578 Leicester took his old friend to Oxford on a visit. The Queen may well have been glad of even a temporary respite from the continual pressure being brought to bear by the two men for her to intervene in the Netherlands. By March Leicester had come to the conclusion that she was not going to send military aid, at least, to the Dutch.[33]

In May Leicester gave a houseparty at Wanstead for the Queen. We have a detailed description of the way in which it was appointed in the Harleian Roll in the British Museum.[34] On this occasion a play by Philip Sidney, entitled *The Lady of May* was performed, which may have helped to some extent to bring Sidney back into favour, for the Queen was slightly alarmed by his militant Protestantism. In this he found an ally in Walsingham, but the Queen saw it as a potentially serious threat to her careful and somewhat fragile foreign policy. It may have been this year that the Queen gave Leicester the gittern bearing both their coats-of-arms that is now in the British Museum.

Also in May 1578, Gilbert Talbot wrote to his father that Lord Leicester was threatening to make another expedition to Buxton that summer— though we may assume that this was intended in a humorous vein. This visit to Buxton was mentioned on 3 June by the new Spanish ambassador, Bernardino de Mendoza. Accredited in March, 1578, he was the first such for six years, since De Spes had been expelled when his involvement in the Ridolfi Plot was discovered. Mendoza put a very different construction upon the visit, however, which one can only attribute to his lack of familiarity with English affairs:

> They say the Earl of Leicester will leave this week for Buxton near Derby, ostensibly to take the baths there, the place being only twelve miles from where the Queen of Scotland is; great suspicion is engendered here about his going, as Walsingham, who is his familiar spirit, will be away at the same time, and the abandonment of business by both of them at once seems to prove that the matter they have in hand must be one of great importance. All the Councillors are extremely jealous and distrustful as the design, whatever it is, is kept closely between the Queen and Leicester. Some of them even say she is the person who is being deceived.[35]

Walsingham was in fact about to go to the Netherlands with Lord Cobham, to see about negotiations with the Duke of Alençon.

There was sufficient activity for Mendoza to persist in his suspicions, however, for on 13 June the Countess of Shrewsbury was in London, and saw the Queen. The former had met Leicester on his way north, and whilst he was away she was put up in Leicester House in London. As it happened the Queen was deeply worried about something, but it was nothing at all to do with the Queen of Scotland. Something had made her anxious and depressed. Sir Christopher Hatton wrote to Leicester about it at Buxton on 18 June 1578:

> Since your lordship's departure, the Queen is found in continual great melancholy: the cause whereof I can but guess at . . . She dreameth of marriage that might seem injurious to her . . . I defend that no man

can tie himself to such inconvenience as not to marry . . . except by mutual consent on both parts . . . My lord, I am not the man that should thus suddenly marry, for God knoweth I never meant it . . . I think you shall hear more of this matter, I fear it will be found some evil practice.[36]

Had someone hinted at something to the Queen, or was it merely her own instinct that had made her feel that something was in the wind? Outwardly there was no trace of panic or alarm on Leicester's part. On 24 June he wrote to Walsingham from Buxton: 'I find great good in this bath already for the swelling you felt in my leg, not by drinking but by going into the bath . . . I would fain write to Lord Cobham, but I am pulled away from this, being forbidden to write much, as this day I have to her Majesty and others.'[37] Then on 9 July he wrote to Hatton: 'I hope now, ere long, to be with you, to enjoy that blessed sight which I have been so long kept from. A few of these days seem many years, and I think I shall feel a worse grief ere I seek so far a remedy again. I thank God, I have found hitherto great ease by this bath.'

'That blessed sight' was, of course, the Queen, and Leicester heard from Hatton that in his absence she had spent some time at Wanstead. Had he known in advance, 'St Ann should have had a short farewell'. As it was, he was thinking of returning in any case. In particular he wanted to hear Walsingham's news, but there was the general feeling of being out on the periphery, and: 'the late hot weather is now here returned again'.[38]

Leicester left Buxton soon after this, and joined the Court on the summer progress. On 27 July they reached Audley End, and the Vice-Chancellor and heads of houses of Cambridge University came out to welcome the Queen there. It was during the course of this visit that a young scholar from Pembroke College, a protégé of Leicester by the name of Edmund Spenser, was presented to the Queen — a meeting that was to have far-reaching results. Leicester had met Spenser through Gabriel Harvey, who wrote a special Latin poem, *Gratulationum Valdinensium*, to celebrate the visit. The title took its name from that of Lord de Walden, the owner of Audley House. The first section of the poem is dedicated to the Queen, the second to Leicester, the third to Burghley, and the fourth to the Earl of Oxford, Sir Christopher Hatton and Philip Sidney. Harvey's references, in the Leicester section, to the possibility of a royal marriage are seen — with the benefit of hindsight — to have been especially unsuitable. For Spenser, however, it seemed

174

the opening of a door to the future.

By this time the number of works dedicated to Leicester had grown considerably, and he had added to his estates lands in Merioneth and Caernarvon this year, as well as being made Chancellor of these two counties and Anglesey.[39]

The progress went on into Suffolk and Norfolk, and it was while the Queen was at Long Melford Hall in Suffolk, in August, that she received the Duke of Alençon's ambassador De Bocqueville. Leicester wrote to Walsingham that month:

> It may be I do not give you light enough on our doings as much as you would wish; but I assure you, you have as much as I can learn . . . For the matter now in hand of her marriage, no man can tell what to say, as yet she has imparted with no man, at least not with me, nor for aught I can learn with any other. Avoid her Majesty's suspicion that you doubt of Monsieur's love to her . . . Though I promise you I think she has little enough herself to it. In much haste, her Majesty ready to horseback.[40]

After reaching Norwich the progress turned back towards London, and on 1 September reached Lord North's house at Kirtling in Cambridgeshire. North was a friend of Leicester, who sent his own cooks and players to help entertain the royal guest.[41] Even for a comparatively short stay the preparations were immense, and when the Queen set out on Wednesday 3 September, Lord North must have been relieved. It was not only the strain of the royal presence, however, but the terrifying secret to which he must have been party by then. Shortly after this Leicester withdrew from the progress to go to Wanstead, where he arrived on Monday 8 September. Two days later he wrote from there to Walsingham. Though the Queen did not know it, by the time she arrived there her 'sweet Robin', her almost constant companion, was once more a well and truly married man.

8

A French Match?

I have no more to offer again but that which is already my bond and duty: the body and life . . .

Robert Dudley to Queen Elizabeth

In a deposition made subsequently, Lord North said that Lord Leicester, with whom he had been 'very conversant . . . by the space of this ten or twelve years last past', had confided in him that 'there was nothing in this life which he more desired than to be joined in marriage with some godly gentlewoman, with whom he might lead his life to the glory of God, the comfort of his soul, and to the faithful service of her Majesty, for whose sake he had hitherto forborne marriage, which long held him doubtful.' Leicester told North that the lady he had in mind was the Countess of Essex, and the Lord North 'comforted his lordship therein and heartened him thereunto'.[1] On Saturday 20 September 1578, when the Queen was at 'Stover's House in the forest', Leicester invited North to go to Wanstead with him for the night, and when they arrived, the earls of Warwick and Pembroke were already there, together with Sir Francis Knollys and his daughter the Countess of Essex. After supper Leicester told Lord North that 'he intended to be married next morning, by the leave of God, and therefore prayed this deponent [Lord North] to rise somewhat betimes for the purpose'.

The next morning North found Leicester 'walking in a little gallery, looking towards the garden', whereupon the latter gave North a key, 'praying him to go down, and bring up thither, by the privy way, Mr Tindall, a chaplain of his lordship's'. This he did; the rest of the party arrived, and Mr Tindall performed the marriage ceremony. There was yet another witness, according to Lord North's account: '. . . Mr Richard Knollys, brother to the countess, [whom he saw] stand in the door which came out of the earl's chamber, with his body half in the gallery, and half out, who, together with the persons before-mentioned, both saw and heard the solemnization of the said marriage.' The Knollys family were certainly taking no chances.

Some three years later Tindall, too, made a deposition, dated 18 February 1581, which is now at Longleat together with a certificate by one Edward Barker, BD, dated 4 March 1592.[2] Tindall's deposition corroborates Lord North's substantially, but gives two additional facts: that the bride's father was evidently anxious that all the witnesses' names should be given, despite the fact that the ceremony was performed 'with the free consent' of both parties; and that the bride wore a loose gown. This could have been a négligée of some sort, since it was between seven and eight in the morning on a Sunday, but also — and what is much more likely — that it was a pregnancy garment, for if Lord Denbigh was about six when he died in July 1584, he must have been born later that year of 1578, or early in 1579. Unfortunately his tomb inscription at Warwick does not help us, for to have given the date of birth would doubtless have drawn attention to its proximity to the date of his parents' wedding.

The wedding took place on Sunday 21 September, then, and on 23 September the Queen arrived at Wanstead on the last stage of her progress before reaching London. Far from being a case of 'the funeral baked meats did coldly furnish forth the marriage tables', it was almost completely the reverse, and had Elizabeth but known, the marriage tables had in fact coldly furnished forth the funeral — of her relationship with Robert Dudley, such as it was. At all events, she could have used Horatio's words in all sincerity à propos her visit to Wanstead, and said to Hamlet: 'Indeed, my lord, it followed hard upon.' In any case the baked meats were of excellent quality, and of sufficient lavishness to fill the company with due admiration and send one and all rejoicing on their way back to London. One can only imagine the fragility of Leicester's peace of mind, and the anxiety with which he faced the future.

Of course there was no reason at all why Leicester should not have married Lettice Knollys— in theory, that is, and assuming that he was not already married to Douglas Sheffield, of course. But then that was nothing more than theory, because in practice things were very different, as the hapless maids-of-honour had discovered to their cost when they had contracted marriage without the Queen's approval, which they dared not seek in any case, knowing what a fury it would provoke. In Leicester's case, however, the reasons which, from his own point of view, argued against matrimony, and which he had set out in his letter to Douglas Sheffield, were still as valid now as they had been then, and one can only assume that Sir Francis Knollys was more successful in protecting his daughter, who was in any case a strong enough personality, than Douglas Sheffield had ever been in protecting herself. In other words, Leicester was probably forced into the marriage, and the alacrity with which his widow remarried after his death, and with the much younger Christopher Blount, with whom she was presumably already in love, if not having a liaison, would seem to suggest that it was not an especially happy one for her either, despite the glowing words on their combined tomb at Warwick, or the sentiments expressed in Leicester's will.

There is a rather strange letter from Leicester to Burghley, written within a week of this wedding, about a committee for the overseeing of the Mint, of which Leicester was a member and Burghley chairman. Burghley had issued orders to the Mint but neglected to have them signed by all members of the committee. Leicester's letter reveals an almost paranoic attitude on his part:

> I had more cause to think unkindness, to be in your lordship's company all this summer as I was, and so often talked of these Mint matters, and would not acquaint me with your resolution, being joined as I was in commission . . . Either must I think it was for want of desire to confer with me, or some weak opinion of my insufficiency to judge further in this cause . . . and yet, to none is my care and good will for the service of her Majesty better known than to your lordship . . . if I have not both long since and of late perceived your opinion better settled in others than in me, I could little perceive anything . . . What opinion you have indeed of me, I have, for these considerations alleged, somewhat in doubt, though I promise you I know no cause in the world myself that I have given you, other than good . . . And surely, my lord, where I profess, I will be found both a faithful and a just, honest friend.[3]

No doubt Leicester felt that he might, at any time now, need as much support and sympathy as he would be able to muster, though for the time being to the world at large nothing had altered. Although the Queen twice put off the French ambassador because of a pain that she was supposed to have in her cheek, the Spanish ambassador heard that she had been out dining with the Earl of Leicester.

When it came to the New Year's gifts for 1579, Leicester was especially lavish in his choice for Elizabeth. He gave her, for example, a 'very fair jewel of gold, being a clock fully furnished with small diamonds pointed, and a pendant of gold, diamonds and rubies, very small; and upon each side a lozenge diamond, and an apple of gold enamelled green and russet'. His brother the Earl of Warwick gave the Queen a huge topaz, set in enamelled gold, with eight pendant pearls, and Warwick's wife gave her a black velvet cap with thirteen gold buttons — a ruby or diamond in each one of them — a knot of small pearl with a Garter and a bird on it, and a pearl pendant. From the lady known still as the Countess of Essex, but now technically the Countess of Leicester, the Queen received a 'great chain of amber garnished [but only 'slightly'] with gold and small pearl'.[4]

Though Leicester did not know it at the time, however, trouble was already close at hand in the shape of the confidential agent and friend of the Duke of Alençon, Jehan de Simier, who arrived on 5 January. The French wooing ambassador was admirably suited for his task, and so captivated the Queen that he soon became one of the privileged few to earn a royal nickname, in this case Monkey, as a pun on his name. The accredited French ambassador, De Mauvissière, reported that: 'She is gayer and more beautiful than she has been these fifteen years. Not a woman or a physician who knows her but says there is no lady in the realm more fit for bearing children than she is.'[5] Walsingham was not happy about the prospect of the marriage. As he wrote to Davison in the Low Countries: 'The negotiation of Monsieur here takes greater foot than was at first looked for . . . her Majesty thinks this the best means to provide for her safety . . . though otherwise not greatly to her liking.'[6]

Naturally Leicester himself was not pleased with the idea either, though at first he had other things on his mind.

On 22 January his old friend Duke John Casimir came to spend three weeks in England, and Leicester was busy entertaining him. He took him to Oxford, for example, and on 12 February Leicester wrote to Davison: 'Cousin Davison, the cause that of late I have not written to you is for that since Duke Casimir is come hither, I have been almost always in his company, or otherwise so busied in her Majesty's affairs that I assure you I have had no leisure to write.'[7] Of course this was very much the sort of face that Leicester liked to present to people, but in this case it was accurate, and indeed Mendoza bore this out.[8] He also tells us that the King of France had written to Leicester to assure him that he would not lose in any way when the marriage between Elizabeth and Alençon took place, since he would still be a trusted guide and friend.

Simier had brought 12,000 crowns' worth of jewels to hand out at Court, of which Leicester himself must have received a good share, but he was contemplating a far greater outlay on personal appearances. Davison wrote to him on 27 March to remind him that he had asked for prices of the velvets and satins woven in the Low Countries: 'I sent you a rate of the prices . . . and I have since been expecting your answer.'[9] On 25 April Leicester gave his answer: 'I wish you to take up for me 4,000 crowns' worth of crimson and black velvet, and satins, and silks of other colours, and if there be any cloth of gold of tissue, or of gold, or such other pretty stuff ', would Davison reserve it for him, 'to the value of £300, or £400, or whatever the charge shall be'.[10]

Naturally there were those, especially of the feminine sex, who felt, in ignorance of any knowledge of his marriage, that Leicester was being rather shabbily treated, and one of her ladies dared to formulate this thought to the Queen herself, which simply earned the retort: 'Dost you think me so unlike myself and unmindful of my royal majesty that I would prefer my servant whom I myself have raised, before the greatest prince of Christendom, in the honour of a husband?'[11] To Sir Amyas Paulet, ambassador in Paris, she wrote about Simier: 'He has shown himself faithful to his master, [is] sage and discreet beyond his years in the conduct of the case . . .', and she added: '. . . we wish we had such a servant of whom we could make such good use,'[12] — which is hardly a fair comment in view of the several skilled and devoted servants on whose time, loyalty and patience she could call at any time, and indeed had done so throughout her reign. Such praise of Simier was like a red rag to a bull as far as Leicester was concerned, and according to Camden he accused the Frenchman of using 'love potions and other unlawful arts' to gain the Queen's affection.

Much of this was simply the garnish on top of the dish, however, and while it was being whipped up, the much more serious business of the composition of the dish itself was being debated. As Gilbert Talbot wrote to his father on 4 April, the Council had been sitting in continu-

Lettice Knollys became Dudley's third wife and bore him his only legitimate son. In this portrait (*c.* 1585), attributed to George Gower, the embroidery of her dress incorporates the Dudley ragged staff, as well as roses from her family coat-of-arms.

This portrait by an unknown artist, painted *c.* 1575-80, has a distinctively more naive quality than the one attributed to van der Muelen, but even so shows clearly how in the interval Dudley had become more fleshy and begun to age.

Lady Mary Sidney, Robert Dudley's sister and the mother of Sir Philip Sidney. She disfigured herself for life when she nursed the Queen during a bout of smallpox and caught the disease, so consequently retired from Court.

Hollar's engraving of the Noble Imp's tomb — in the Beauchamp Chapel of St Mary's Church, Warwick — from Dugdale's *Antiquities of Warwickshire* (1656). He died in 1584, but his age was deliberately left vague in view of the secrecy that had surrounded his parents' marriage. His death put an end to hopes of an alliance with Arbella Stuart, Dudley's last attempt to win the crown for his family.

Sir Philip Sidney, painted by an unknown artist. He was a great favourite of his uncle and, after the death of Dudley's son, became his heir. His untimely death was a deep blow to Dudley.

The central and largest of three armorial tapestries commissioned by Dudley in the Low Countries, and destined to adorn the Queen's bedroom at Kenilworth. It is at present undergoing restoration; the flanking tapestries are in Glasgow.

A medieval gittern bearing the arms of Dudley and of the Queen on the silver plate attached to it. It was already ancient when it was given by the Queen to Dudley, possibly at Wanstead.

An anonymous artist's impression of Elizabeth receiving Dutch ambassadors. Dudley is second from the left in the background, and the unlikely lady in black is meant to be Mary Queen of Scots.

Marcus Gheeraerts the Elder probably painted this portrait of Elizabeth in the early 1580s. She is shown in the garden of Dudley's house at Wanstead, where she was a frequent visitor.

A suit of armour made for Robert Dudley, and now in the Tower of London. In addition to ragged staffs, it is decorated with the collars of the orders of both the Garter and St Michel, of which Dudley was extremely proud.

Elizabeth was very fond of dancing in her more active years, and this painting is traditionally held to show her indulging in the pastime with Robert Dudley, though others see a distinctly French influence.

Little remains of Rycot now, but this view captures something of the atmosphere of the house where Dudley and Elizabeth spent many happy hours, and from where Robert wrote what was to be his last letter to the Queen.

ous session for the past five days, from eight in the morning until dinner time.[13]

Simier, on behalf of his royal master, was looking for a coronation immediately after the marriage, an income of £60,000 per annum and the right to make various appointments. Then of course there was the inevitable question of religion. To try and swing round opinion, Simier worked hard not only to charm the Queen herself, but the Council as well, and on 14 May Mendoza reported that he had given 'two grand banquets this week to the Council'.[14] In the end, however, his master would have to come to England himself, and with this in view Simier tried to persuade the Queen to sign the passport necessary for the visit. Next month he heard that Leicester had been doing his best to dissuade the Queen, and when Simier finally obtained her signature in July, Leicester went off to Wanstead in a rage, though he announced publicly that he was ill. Elizabeth went to see him there, and spent two days with him, partly to be sure that he was not really seriously ill, but also, presumably, to try to console him and get him to accept that it had been necessary for her to do something that she knew would anger and hurt him, and which he had in any case made quite plain that he disapproved of.

Not long after this, however, one of the Queen's guard fired on Simier whilst he was in the grounds of Greenwich. This was the second such incident, and although there was no evidence that Leicester was behind it, Simier was only more convinced than ever that Leicester would have to be taught a lesson, and a fairly drastic one at that. He had found out about his marriage with Lettice Knollys, and that August he decided to break the news to Elizabeth. As Camden wrote, the Queen:

> . . . grew into such a chafe, that she commanded Leicester to keep himself within the Tower of Greenwich, and thought to have committed him to the Tower of London, which his enemies much desired. But Sussex, though his greatest and heaviest adversary, who wholly bent himself to set forward the marriage with Anjou, dissuaded her . . . he held opinion that no man was to be molested for lawful marriage, which amongst all men hath ever been honest and honoured.[15]

Leicester was incarcerated in a tower built by Humphrey of Gloucester, called Mireflore by Henry VIII because Ann Boleyn lodged there. To draw away attention from his sudden disappearance, Leicester gave out that he had taken physic, so no one could see him. So Fulke Greville said in his life of Sir Philip Sidney: 'Like a wise man (under colour of taking physic) voluntarily [he] became a prisoner in his own chamber.'[16] After a few days he was allowed to retire to Wanstead.

Leicester had not only deceived and betrayed the Queen with that 'she-wolf' Lettice Knollys, but he had consistently opposed her own marriage when he was secretly married all the time himself. It was simply no good pointing out in his own defence that he had longed to marry the Queen whenever she had seen fit, and had remained technically a widower for some eighteen years in order to do so. That would not have cut any ice with the Queen at all. If anyone undertook to devote himself or herself to her cause, then total loyalty was required, with all its inconveniences and sacrifices. In all the events of her troubled life, certainly since those dark and dangerous years of the reign of Mary Tudor, that friendship, that association, call it what we will, had been there for Elizabeth to rely on, take for granted, even spurn at times, but never had she doubted for one moment that it existed. No matter how irrational this may seem to the independent observer, in the context of such a relationship the most terrible thing that can happen is the discovery of a secret or a lie. Elizabeth must have realised that Leicester had had his affairs — she may well have known about Douglas Sheffield — but she thought that he appreciated her situation, and therefore trusted in him to understand and make allowances. The sudden shock of learning of his marriage at second hand would in any case have infuriated her, but the realisation that it had been kept from her deliberately must have made the very ground shake under her feet.

Of course having walked into the trap that he had, to a large extent, made for himself with Lettice Knollys, it was inevitable that when the Queen found out there would be a horrible scene, which their relationship might not be able to survive, and this was always a calculated risk with Leicester, as one saw in the letter to Douglas Sheffield. In the immediate aftermath of the affair Lettice was of course forbidden to appear at Court, and Lady Mary Sidney was so distressed that she withdrew to Penshurst. And yet Leicester himself was not officially exiled. When Hatton, as Vice-Chamberlain, issued summonses to the Privy Council, Leicester replied that he was 'most unfit at this time to make repair to that place, where so many eyes are witnesses of my open and great disgraces delivered from her Majesty's mouth. Wherefore, if by silence it may be passed over (my calling for being but in general sort), I pray you let it be so.'[17]

To Burghley Leicester was to write in similar terms on 12 November

1579, saying how unkind the Queen had been after twenty years of faithful service:

> And as I carried myself almost more than a bondman many a year together, so long as one drop of comfort was left of any hope, as you yourself, my lord, doth well know, so being acquitted and delivered of that hope, and, by both open and private protestations and declarations discharged, methinks it is more than hard to take such an occasion to bear so great displeasure for.[18]

And yet, looked at from a purely mercenary point of view, 1579 was not so bad a year for Leicester. He was given two wardships and the lease of Woodgrave Manor in Essex,[19] and he was still seen outwardly as a person of power and patronage. On 24 April, for example, Gabriel Harvey the poet wrote to him from Trinity Hall, Cambridge, asking Leicester's 'favourable and gracious means . . . for the procuring of Doctor Byddle's prebend at Lichfield', maintaining that 'this little body of mine carrieth a great mind towards my good lord'.[20] This was also a year of dedications. Leonard Digges dedicated his *An Arithmetical Military Treatise named Stratioticos*, which was completed by his son Thomas, who was muster-general to Leicester. Other dedications of this year were a translation from Mornay by John Field of *A Treatise of the Church*; Edward Hake's *News out of Paul's Churchyard*; John Harmar's translation of Calvin's sermons on the Ten Commandments, and possibly Spenser's *Virgil's Gnat* (though not published until 1591), and Thomas Palfreyman's *Certain Selected Prayers*.

Alençon landed at Gravesend on 15 August and arrived at Greenwich early on the 17th. Despite his physical disadvantages, he managed to delight the Queen, and he, too, soon had his sobriquet: Frog. If the name is the common pejorative *appellation contrôlée* in English for a Frenchman, it ought also to be borne in mind that the Romans used frogs as charms for lovers, and they were symbols of constancy and mutual desire. There was an air of unreality, since the visit was supposed to be a secret, and the Queen assured Mendoza that when she heard the Countess of Derby and Lady Russell talking about the duke, she had ordered them to remain in their quarters until he had left.[21] He remained for twelve days in all, though since the visit was supposed to be secret, there is not much information about it. We know, however, that there was a ball on Sunday 23 August at Greenwich, at which the Queen danced, waving and smiling the while at the duke, who was barely concealed behind the arras.[22] He returned abruptly on 27 August when his favourite Bussy d'Ambois was killed (by the man whose wife he had seduced) in a duel, but before he left he gave the Queen an enormous diamond ring supposedly worth 10,000 crowns, that Catherine de' Medici had chosen for his bride, and Leicester came in for jewels worth 3,000 crowns.[23]

Leicester cannot have been more relieved to see the back of the Frog, and indeed Mendoza had reported shortly before the abrupt end of the visit on 25 August: 'Leicester . . . is in great grief.' There had been a dinner that night at the Earl of Pembroke's house at Baynard's Castle, at which Leicester and Sir Henry Sidney were present, with other members of the Dudley faction. As Mendoza went on: '. . . some of them afterwards remarked that Parliament would have something to say as to whether the Queen married or not. The people in general seem to threaten revolution about it.'[24] The last comment was wishful thinking on Mendoza's part, for it is extremely difficult to see who could have roused the people to such a demonstration of disloyalty. Even so, there was deep unrest and alarm at the possibility of the French marriage, regardless of the particular chagrin of the Dudley faction. Leicester's nephew Philip Sidney wrote to the Queen on behalf of her Protestant subjects — 'your chief, if not your sole strength'. She would alienate these people if she were to marry a Frenchman and a Roman Catholic, a man whom the people knew to be the son of 'a Jezebel of our age'.[25] Sidney addressed his letter to the Queen privately, and so escaped anything more severe than a scolding, but the Puritan John Stubbs, who published his pamphlet *The Discovery of a Gaping Gulf whereunto England is like to be swallowed by another French marriage* that summer, was ordered to have his right hand cut off. With his left hand he was able to remove his hat and shout 'God save the Queen', before falling down in a dead faint.

In early October the Queen summoned the Council to discuss the proposed marriage, and on 6 October Burghley drew up a minute in his own hand entitled 'Cause of misliking of the marriage'.[26] Burghley himself, it ought to be pointed out, was still in favour of it. However, the message that the Council as a body disapproved of it was conveyed to the Queen the following morning, and naturally she was annoyed at their decision. At any rate she seemed to be, for she even resorted to tears at one point, and it may well have been that she had convinced herself that this was the right course of action— which was never an easy thing for her to do — and therefore to be thwarted by someone else was especially frustrating. On the other hand, since the decision had been made for her by her Council, she could play the role of star-crossed lover to the full. All the time Simier was waiting for a decision, and on 9 November the Council was closeted for several hours, according to Mendoza. The following day Elizabeth told the Council that she would marry, and that they were to make the necessary arrangements. Even Mendoza knew, however, that all this had to be taken with a large pinch of salt, and a messenger sent to Alençon was apparently stopped only at Dover, and recalled. Simier himself left on 24 November, and although the Queen continued to talk to Mendoza about it the following month, by January 1580 she was much less enthusiastic. Leicester had been back at Court when the Council was engaged in its deliberations the previous October, as was Walsingham, and once more the religious problem had made its appearance. This may have been the decisive factor yet again, for Elizabeth then wrote to the Duke of Alençon to say that they ought to abandon the idea of marriage, and simply remain friends. He returned after this, and it was not until February 1582 that the Queen was finally rid of him, and ironically it was Leicester who escorted him on the last part of his journey. But all this was yet to come. In November 1579 no one could be quite sure what the outcome of it all would be, least of all the Earl of Leicester.

On 29 November that year Douglas Sheffield, in the aftermath of the disclosure of Leicester's marriage to Lettice Knollys, married Sir Edward Stafford, English ambassador to Paris. Her child Robert by Leicester was now five years old, and in his father's care, so there was no reason for her to hold out hopes that anything might be salvaged from their old liaison. Besides, there was now an heir in the shape of Lord Denbigh, the Noble Impe, and any hold she might have had was thereby removed.

On 5 December 1579 Spenser's first important work, *The Shepheards Calender*, was published whilst he was on the Continent on Leicester's business. This consists of twelve verse conversations between shepherds, and in the March eclogue there is a reference to Lettice Knollys that must have enraged Leicester:

> Then shall we sporten in delight
> And learn with Lettice to wax light,
> That scornfully looks askance.

Instead of the brilliant future that he had envisaged for himself on his return in April 1580, Spenser was sent to Ireland in July that year as secretary to the Lord Deputy, Lord Grey de Wilton, and it may well be this to which Spenser referred in his poem *Virgil's Gnat*, which was dedicated to Leicester, but only published after his death in 1591:

> Wronged, yet not daring to express my pain
> To you, great lord, the causer of my care,
> In cloudy years my case I thus complain
> Unto yourself that only privy are . . .

For the next nineteen years Spenser was to stay in Ireland, with only brief visits to England, and left it only a month or so before his death.

On 15 June 1580, Leicester was made Keeper of the New Forest,[27] and in this year, too, the inventory of Leicester House was made that constitutes volume V of the Dudley papers at Longleat. There were, amongst many other things: '. . . the portraitures of the Queen's Majesty and my lord cast in alabaster', and: '. . . robes of Creation . . . of Parliament . . . of the Garter . . . of St Michel . . .'[28] There is also mention of two globes given by Leicester's steward Thomas Fowler. This year William Chauncie dedicated his *The Rooting out of the Romish supremacy*, though a more famous dedication was John Stow's *Chronicles*.

In September there was correspondence over lands in Anglesey, which Leicester disputed with Sir Richard Bulkeley. As Ranger of Snowdon Forest, Leicester had tried to extend the limits of the forest in such a way as to benefit himself, and Sir Richard, having known the Queen since childhood, refused to stand by and let this happen. The major confrontation did not come until much later, when Leicester was involved in the Netherlands campaign, but letters in the Sidney-De Lisle archives date from 1580.[29]

That same month, Drake completed his voyage round the world. Both Leicester and the Queen had invested in it, and the following April the latter went to dinner on board the *Golden Hind*, which had been laid up at Deptford. It was on this occasion that Drake was knighted. By this time Leicester was well and truly back at the heart of Court life, even if his relationship with the Queen had undergone a certain modification. One must also remember that even at the height of the royal disfavour, he had never actually been deprived of any of his offices or appointments. As Master of the Horse, for example, he went on supplying the royal household with animals, and we find a typical situation, with which he must have dealt often, on 5 April 1581, when the commissioners of musters for Chester told him that it was not possible for the city's gentlemen to provide the number of horses he had asked for. As Chancellor of the Palatinate of Chester, the Master of the Horse had a special interest there — though there were other districts and towns and cities where his interest was equally strong.

In May John Brown wrote to him from the Low Countries to announce that he was soon to bring over, as a present to the Queen from his colonel:

> . . . six Hungarian horses for her Majesty, which horses I hope your lordship will like well, for they are well suited as I ever saw for her Majesty's coach. Their colours are all light grey and their manes and tails all dyed into orange-tawney, according unto the manner of their country; they are horses of light shape, good of travel, and very young.[30]

The very same horses were seen in October 1584 drawing the Queen's coach as she went to open Parliament. Their bridles on that occasion were studded with pearls, and they had diamond pendants on their foreheads.[31]

The men around the Queen vied to offer her the best possible, give her the most sumptuous gifts, and provide her with the most magnificent banquets, as at Deptford on board the *Golden Hind*. It was said that such a dinner had not been seen since the days of her father. Drake also gave the Queen a silver casket, and a frog made out of diamonds,[32] for the Duke of Alençon was still very much in view, and his new agent, Marchaumont, was of the party on this occasion. Curiously, Leicester was in the latter's confidence, and Mendoza reported that when Alençon came to England unexpectedly that June, to negotiate over the heads of the French officials who had been there since the end of April, 'Marchaumont sent to Leicester a jet ring, which was to be the signal of his arrival. Leicester and Walsingham could not believe it, for there was no reason which demanded his coming.'[33]

Leicester's intimacy with Marchaumont was not matched by a similar rapport with the negotiating team. Shortly before the secretary, Claude Pinart, was due to leave, Leicester suggested that they might continue to correspond privately, but Pinart replied that it was not the custom for a person in his office at the French Court to do such a thing, and that if Leicester had anything to communicate, he should do so through the correct channel of the French ambassador.[34] Alençon was only in London for two days, incognito, but in that time he managed to do immense harm. He let Elizabeth understand that his brother the King of France was not prepared to give him support for involvement in the Low Countries, and that he would therefore rely on England to do so. This was of no small importance to Elizabeth.

Of the six commissioners whom Elizabeth had appointed to treat about the marriage, Bedford and Burghley were more or less neutral, whereas Hatton, Walsingham and Leicester were against it, and only Sussex was for it. Given to a natural tendency to quarrel in any case, it was almost inevitable that the last two named would fall out, and that July so violent an altercation arose in the Queen's presence that it reached Dr Dee at Mortlake, and he recorded the fact in his diary: 'The Earl of Leicester fell foully out with the Earl of Sussex, the Lord Chamberlain, calling each other traitor, whereupon both were commanded to keep their chambers at Greenwich where the Court was.'[35] In the absence of Burghley, Walsingham thought the event of sufficient note to write and inform him of it: 'The Queen ordered each to keep his chamber and will commit them in case they shall not yield to stand to her order.'

On 23 July a former protégé of Leicester's, Edmund Campion, was captured in Berkshire at a country house, having been in England since May, as part of a Jesuit mission. He was taken to the Tower, but after forty-eight hours was removed at night to a different place, which turned out to be Leicester House. In a small room there he was confronted by the Earl of Bedford and two secretaries, along with a man and a woman, who turned out to be no other than Leicester and the Queen herself. The Queen was prepared to go to this extreme in order to save Campion, and prevent the inevitable martyrdom if he persisted in his belief. Even this attempt failed to shake his resolve, however, and so he went to his death. On his return to the Tower, a message was sent to the Governor, Sir Owen Hopton, and it was noticed that when it came to execution, he was not taken down and quartered whilst still alive, but was allowed to remain hanging until dead. One can only speculate that Leicester might have given this consideration to his former protégé. His father-in-law, Sir Francis Knollys, and Lord Hunsdon were in charge that day, and such an act would not have been beyond the bounds of possibility.[36]

Certainly the Catholic threat was a sensitive issue at this time, and it made its effects felt in various ways. As Chancellor of Oxford University, Leicester made sure in 1581 that the oath of supremacy and assent to the Thirty-nine Articles was required of every undergraduate over the age of sixteen, and tutors were to find out crypto-Catholics. This effectively closed the university to all but Anglicans, though it was not being carried out with sufficient rigour for Leicester's taste, and he complained the following year to the Vice-Chancellor and dons.

Leicester's lands were again surveyed on 1 September 1581,[37] and a whole volume is devoted to this at Longleat, and on 8 August he was made High Steward of Abingdon with an annuity of five marks.[38] Edward Grant dedicated his edition of Crespin's *Lexicon* to him, with a Leicester badge on the title verso, and Ubaldini presented a copy of his *Vita di Carlo Magno Imperadore* to Leicester in this year, with an inscription in his own hand. Other dedications included John Field's *A Caveat for Parsons Howlet*, and Meredith Hanmer's *The Great Brag and Challenge of M. Champion a Jesuit*, as well as *The Jesuits Banner*, these last two being dedicated to the Privy Council in general with Leicester as one of their number.

That August the Duke of Alençon forced Parma to raise the siege of Cambrai, so that he was free to come to England once more, and he arrived there on 31 October. The round of entertainments began anew, and on 22 November it seemed as if the Queen had really decided to commit herself once and for all. According to Mendoza's account the Queen and Alençon were walking together in the gallery at Whitehall, with Leicester and Walsingham present:

> . . . the French Ambassador entered and said that he wished to write to his master, from whom he has received orders to hear from the Queen's own lips her intention with regard to marrying his brother. She replied, 'You may write this to the King: that the Duke of Alençon shall be my husband', and at the same moment she turned to Alençon and kissed him on the mouth, drawing a ring from her own hand and giving it to him as a pledge. Alençon gave her a ring of his in return, and shortly afterwards the Queen summoned the ladies and gentlemen from the presence chamber to the gallery, repeating to them in a loud voice, in Alençon's presence, what she had previously said.[39]

Burghley was delighted, but Hatton was in tears, and Leicester was so worried that he even went so far as to ask the Queen whether she was still a virgin — presumably indicating that he had never possessed her totally. Sussex and Leicester quarrelled again in the Council, but they all might as well have saved their emotions, for the Queen had simply been putting on one of her better performances. Possibly Alençon knew it, too. He lingered on at Court into the next year, but on 1 February 1582 he finally set out, with £10,000 down and a further £50,000 promised. The Queen accompanied him as far as Canterbury, and Leicester and Hunsdon and others — including Philip Sidney — went with him to Antwerp. In the previous year, when the news reached that city, William of Orange had the bells rung. Now Leicester carried secret instructions from the Queen that he was to keep Alençon there and ensure that he did not return to England. Ironically Sussex was at the same time encouraging Alençon to keep Leicester there, also. Either way, both men were to turn out to be more of a hindrance than a help to the Dutch in their struggles. Leicester's involvement we shall see in due course. Alençon died of a fever in June 1584, to be mourned deeply by Elizabeth, who wrote to his mother, Catherine de' Medici: 'Your sorrow cannot exceed mine, although you were his mother. You have another son, but I can find no other condition than death, which I hope will soon enable me to rejoin him.'

There is at Longleat a will of Leicester's dated 30 January 1582. It bears a seal of arms, namely a signet showing a bear and ragged staff surrounded by the Garter and surmounted by an earl's coronet.[40] There was, of course, a second one which he made at Middelburg in Zeeland on 1 August 1587, but it is interesting that Leicester should have been moved to make this earlier one in 1582. Foreign travel was always a hazardous venture, of course, even in the most favourable conditions, as John Donne, probably writing some ten or twelve years later, recalled:

> . . . dar'st thou lay
> thee in ships wooden sepulchres, a prey
> to leaders rage, to storms, to shot, to dearth?

Possibly Elizabeth really did have some feelings for Alençon, and her grief expressed to Catherine de' Medici genuinely sprang from regret that someone with whom she would have been quite happy to remain on terms of close friendship, had to be sacrificed to the higher interests of the welfare of the nation. For despite the cost to the Queen in terms of money, and possibly from a moral point of view also, the affair was something of a diplomatic triumph. Mendoza — whose reports have to be treated with a certain amount of reserve, despite his vast spy network — said that Alençon blamed Simier for the failure of the negotiations in the first place, because when Simier had exposed Leicester's marriage with Lettice Knollys to the Queen, he had made an enemy of Leicester for Alençon, and thus deprived him of the services of the very person he most needed for the success of his wooing. Simier, of course, had imagined the opposite. In fact he was supposed to have told the Queen that everyone was amazed that the earl still enjoyed her favour. Mendoza said that she had told Simier, by way of reply, that she could not put

Leicester down because he had used the power she had given him to put his relatives or friends into all the most powerful posts in the kingdom — which Mendoza believed to be true. Therefore, he went on, until the Queen could get back some of these positions, she could not get rid of Leicester.

This shows how little Mendoza really understood the nature of Elizabeth's patronage, or indeed of the way in which the legality of the rights of the people might be upheld in the face of the behaviour of a grandee such as Leicester. One only has to look at the incident of the attempt by Leicester to increase the extent of Snowdon Forest, or the squabble with the burgesses of Denbigh to see the truth of this. If, on the other hand, a disproportionately large number of Dudley relatives held high office, the Queen could take away those offices whenever it pleased her to do so. What was more true, and this appears to have eluded Mendoza, was that Leicester had a long memory, and a long arm, and was capable of persecuting, with all the force of the law at his elbow, anyone who particularly annoyed him.

In the early part of this year, on 27 January 1582, a Catholic, Dr William Tresham, wrote to the Earl of Sussex from Paris to explain why it was that he had left Court suddenly, without informing Sussex, 'and contrary to my duty'. He went on:

> I beseech you, whilst perusing these lines, to suffer your judgment to cease as a Councillor of the State and to weigh my cause as a private man . . . If I had seen any means left to preserve myself from the persecution of the Earl of Leicester, whose favour has been lost without defect of mine, and for recovery whereof I have used such humility as has never been used at Court even to princes . . . as appears by my letter to her Majesty, which I beseech you may be read in her hearing, wherein is manifested the just occasion that has forced me to this desperate act . . . No dishonest act or lewd practices, either against Prince or country, or your honour, have moved me thereto, but only the extreme fear of the cruelty of the Earl of Leicester.[41]

On his return from the Low Countries Leicester gave a supper party for various members of his family. Mendoza was informed that during the course of conversation Leicester said that a man who had tried to assassinate the Prince of Orange had been seen leaving the Spanish embassy in London a month before, and that Leicester would try and get the Queen to expel Mendoza. The latter reported Lady Warwick as saying that she had never seen anything in his behaviour to complain of. Mendoza had in fact bribed Sir James Croft, the Comptroller of the Household, for information — though by November 1582 he was lamenting that Croft, too, was a victim of Leicester's ruthlessness, and was too frightened to tell Mendoza anything.[42]

One sees another side of Leicester's character, however, in a letter of condolence that he wrote to the Earl of Shrewsbury this autumn of 1582 on the death of one of his sons. It was a somewhat cold tone for such a letter, but when compared with what was often written on these occasions, it has a directness that is perhaps rather surprising: '. . . Be thankful to Him for all His doings, my good Lord, and take all in that part which you ought; be you wholly His and seek His kingdom first, for it passeth all wordly kingdoms.'[43]

Or again, in writing to Hatton about a visit to Rycote that September, a visit to which the Norreys family had greatly looked forward. Virtually at the last moment Hatton and Leicester had dissuaded the Queen from making the journey in the wet weather, to the great disappointment of the hosts, since Leicester went on alone. When he arrived at ten o'clock at night, Lady Norreys scolded him but, as he wrote to Hatton:

> I was fain to stand to it . . . and would not for anything, for the little proof I had of this day's journey that her Majesty had been in it . . . if it had not been so late, I think I should have sought another lodging, my welcome awhile was so ill . . . but I dealt plainly with her [Lady Norreys] that I knew she would have been sorry afterwards to have had her Majesty come at this time of year to this place.

Leicester had to get both Hatton and the Queen to do their part in pacifying Lady Norreys, and he for his part would promise that if the Queen decided to stay at Oatlands, Lady Norreys should go there and have his official apartments as Master of the Horse: 'They had put the house here in very good order,' he went on to tell Hatton, 'to receive her Majesty, and a hearty, noble couple are they as ever I saw towards her Highness. I rest here this Sabbath day to make peace for us both; what remains, you shall do . . .'[44]

As a New Year present in 1583, Leicester gave the Queen a necklace of twenty letters and a cipher in the middle, each piece set with diamonds, with two pearls between each letter and a diamond hanging from each letter. It seemed as if nothing had ever happened — perhaps — to ruffle the waters of their relationship, and yet early in March it was being said among Catholics on the Continent that Leicester and the Countess of Shrewsbury were plotting to marry little Lord Denbigh to Arbella Stuart. Nor was this all. He was reputed to have offered the hand of his step-daughter Dorothy Devereux in marriage to the young King James of Scotland. Such a line-up of alliances was almost worthy of his father's scheming brain.[45]

One marriage that actually took place in this month of March 1583 was the one between the now Sir Philip Sidney and Walsingham's daughter Frances. The Queen was annoyed that, in her opinion, it had been done in secret, and she hated secret marriages. From Leicester's point of view, however, it only served to make closer his bond with Walsingham, since Philip Sidney was his nephew. To those of his family and close circle, Leicester was a loyal and generous potentate. William Tresham did not appreciate this when he wrote again, this time to Hatton, probably in April 1583. In the circumstances it was highly inappropriate to mention Leicester to Hatton in such a way:

> How may it be thought that even you would have rejected me, your devoted poor friend, for the sole pleasure of the Earl of Leicester . . . knowing as you do . . . that he affecteth you only to serve his own turn? Take heed of him in time! . . . all the harm I wish you is that you will with the eyes of wisdom look into him thoroughly, and there you shall find that he knoweth only to gain friends and hath not the good regard and grace to keep them.[46]

In May Hatton was with the Court at Theobalds, Lord Burghley's house in Hertfordshire, along with Leicester and Hunsdon and others, but in early June he was to receive a very similar warning as the one received from Tresham. Sussex died on 9 June, and as Hatton watched at his bedside at Bermondsey, with a remarkable *coup de théâtre* Sussex uttered a last warning against Leicester: 'Beware of the gypsy, he will be too hard for you all. You know not the beast as well as I do.'[47] Sussex had good cause to say those words with feeling, for superficially the public face of Leicester was more confident than ever. This year he took Albertus Alasco of Poland to Oxford, a visit that was treated as being little short of a royal visitation. Camden described Alasco as:

> . . . a learned man, of a good feature of body, with a long beard, and very comely and decent apparel: who being graciously welcomed by her [Elizabeth], and entertained by the nobility with great respect and feasting, as also by the University of Oxford with learned

divertisements and several comedies, after months stay here, withdrew himself secretly, being run far in debt.[48]

During 1582 and 1583 no less than eleven works were dedicated to Leicester, either exclusively, or together with Burghley or other members of the Privy Council. One of these, *A Tragical History of the troubles and civil wars of the Low Countries*, translated by Thomas Stocker, is especially interesting in view of Leicester's involvement with affairs there. And the acquisition of goods and their concomitant inventories continued, as for example the 1583 inventory of Leicester House at Longleat,[49] and those of Kenilworth, Grafton and Leicester House for 1583 in the De Lisle-Sidney papers. This latter is particularly grand, having as frontispiece a full-coloured blazon of Leicester's arms surrounded by both the Garter and the chain of the Order of St Michel inside a border of flowers. Moreover the title page has an initial letter in blue with 'dexter a lion rampant, vert, langed and armed gules', wearing a ducal coronet, and sinister a bear and ragged staff.[50]

In September De Mauvissière, the French ambassador, reported to King Henry III that Leicester had invited him to dine at Leicester House, with his countess, and gave the following report: 'He has especially invited me to dine with him and his wife, who has much influence over him, and whom he introduces only to those to whom he wishes to show a particular mark of attention.'[51] In other words Lettice kept very much in the background as far as official life was concerned in London. De Mauvissière reported that same party to Mary Queen of Scots, though naturally from a different point of view, since Mary was anxious to know how Leicester viewed her position, especially since the Throckmorton Plot was being hatched at this time. De Mauvissière told Mary:

> I dined today with the Earl of Leicester and his lady, to whom he is much attached. They both received me very kindly and . . . expressed a wish that the countess and my wife might be on intimate terms. After dinner the earl walked out with me, and vowed that he had never been your Majesty's enemy, but had now lost his influence with Elizabeth, the King of France, and your Majesty. As to the Earl of Huntingdon, he [Leicester] would be the first to combat him [his own brother-in-law!], and in the event of the death of his Queen, he, with all his relations and friends, would willingly render some important service; he told me I might acquaint your Majesty with this, but was on no account to let anyone else hear of it, as it would ruin the whole affair . . .[52]

De Mauvissière went on to repeat that Leicester wished to serve her, but while saying: 'if Leicester does not dissemble greatly' — a huge qualification, as is the earlier one: 'in the event of the death of his Queen'. As for the thought that Mary Queen of Scots should cultivate the woman so recently termed 'she-wolf' and 'whore' by the Queen of England, one quickly begins to see that the whole letter was hardly worth the effort involved in its writing. But at a time when intrigue was a way of life, and Mary in particular clutched at any straw, one appreciates its *raison d'être*. Moreover, the Throckmorton Plot, linked as it was with the Enterprise of England planned by the dukes of Guise and Mayenne, was one of the more frightening and potentially most serious threats for Elizabeth. Leicester must have felt that he had covered himself adequately in case the matter was ever made public, and indeed should anything have happened to Elizabeth, Mary might well have become queen. This was not necessarily treason, but simply a realistic appraisal of the situation — though naturally Elizabeth would not have concurred in that view.

As it happened, the relationship between Leicester and the Queen was as tender as ever. In October 1583 he was ill, possibly with malaria, since from his letter to her at this time it is evident that it had troubled him previously, and the Queen had suggested remedies before.[53]

The next month, November 1583, saw the discovery of the Throckmorton Plot, and one of the consequences was the expulsion of Mendoza for his complicity. There was to be no Spanish ambassador for the rest of the reign. Naturally the discovery of the plot merely increased sympathy for Elizabeth among her loyal subjects, in directly inverse proportion to which, sympathy for Mary Queen of Scots decreased. De Mauvissière wrote to Henri III how that on 19 December, as he accompanied Elizabeth from Hampton Court to Whitehall, people knelt by the way in the winter mud to beg her to take care of herself, asking for blessings on her, and punishment for her enemies.[54]

But the baleful influence of Mary Queen of Scots was to continue, and in ever increasing circles, so that more and more people were brought within its shadow. She exacerbated an already difficult situation between the Earl of Shrewsbury and his wife by her very existence — though in the case of the latter that was no very difficult thing to do. What was worse, however, was the way in which almost anything was grist for Mary's mill. In March 1584 she wrote to De Mauvissière:

I wish you could say to her [Elizabeth] privately (if possible obtaining

195

her promise neither to communicate it to anyone, nor to make any further inquiry), that nothing has so alienated the countess [of Shrewsbury] from me as the vain hope which she has conceived of placing the Crown of England upon the head of her little [grand] daughter Arbella, and this by marrying her to a son of the Earl of Leicester . . . But for the notion of raising one of her family to the rank of queen, she would never have so turned away from me.[55]

In return De Mauvissière had his own little complaint to make about Leicester:

Leicester has told Elizabeth that I went about and endeavoured to gain her counsellors, and everyone in the kingdom for you; but that he considered nothing except the intentions and service of his Queen. By this and all other means at his command he has sought to regain her good will, and is now in higher favour than he was four years ago. In a word, he cannot be much depended upon . . .

Monsieur Bodin, who is a learned man, an astrologer and mathematician . . . wrote to me only two days ago . . . that you would soon see the end of your troubles.[56]

Monsieur Bodin was all too accurate, though in a way that he had no possible conception of. In less than three years — in February 1587 — Mary would be dead.

On 23 April that year Leicester was Elizabeth's Lieutenant for the St George's Day Garter ceremony,[57] and a week or so later, De Mauvissière's claim that Leicester had not dealt fairly with him found an echo in a letter from Sir Edward Stafford — husband to the cast-off Douglas — which he wrote from Paris to Burghley on 1 May 1584:

I have written to my Lord of Leicester, but more because it was your advice than for anything else; for at my going away, he sent for me and assured me he would be as good a friend to me as any I left behind, and yet I have found the contrary. I am but a poor gentleman, but I love plain dealing.[58]

On 26 May Leicester visited Shrewsbury, and in June he again went to Buxton to take the waters. As soon as he had left, De Mauvissière reiterated the request that he had already made to Burghley, on behalf of Mary Queen of Scots, that he would seek permission for her to go there as soon as Leicester had departed. Leicester's Shrewsbury visit might well be taken as a 'typical' visit of its kind, for from the dedication of the sermon preached before him on that occasion, we learn of his:

. . . thankful accepting of many welcomes, your cheerful hearing of many orations, your circumspect view of the situation and buildings of the town, your grave conference with the magistrates in the government thereof: your comfortable going into the free grammar school, to experience the towardliness of the youth there, your Christian presence in the church at the sermon, your painful travail in arbitrating controversies, your large gifts unto Master Bailiff's officers, your liberal rewards unto the schoolmasters, your charitable alms unto the poor, all the which virtues did then shine in you, as in a most clear mirror of true nobility.[59]

Of course Philip Sidney went to school at Shrewsbury, which obviously commended the place considerably in Leicester's eyes.

On his return journey from Derbyshire Leicester went to visit his sister, the Countess of Huntingdon. The visit of such a potentate called for the mayor and other town dignitaries to make an appropriate offering — in this case a hogshead of claret and two fat oxen. Leicester and its folk fared better than Warwick. Leicester the earl accepted the gifts, and in return gave money to be distributed among the various charities of the town. There were also six bucks, the fruits of his hunting, which he left with his sister, also for the corporation. Even so, the place Leicester was not Shrewsbury, and 'His honour stayed but one night in Leicester and was gone of the Friday morning by five of the clock.'[60]

The next month, July 1584, the Earl and Countess of Leicester arrived unannounced at Burghley's house Theobalds, in its owner's absence. They were nevertheless received with due hospitality, and Leicester wrote to inform Burghley on 31 July, and thank him. He also thanked him for what he had done on behalf of the Countess of Leicester: '. . . that it pleased you so friendly and honourably to deal in behalf of my poor wife. For truly, my lord, she is hardly dealt with; God only must help it with her Majesty.' Leicester promised that Burghley would 'find us most thankful, to the uttermost of our powers'.[61] We know well enough why Elizabeth disliked Lettice Knollys, and we may well appreciate that the Queen's persistent refusal to yield seemed hard to some people. Even so, Lettice hardly helped herself, and although other sources, such as the De Mauvissière letter already quoted, indicate a degree of discretion, there is also evidence — even if somewhat exaggerated — that she was quite capable of flaunting her magnificence. One sees it in the Longleat portrait, where her richly embroidered dress incorporates both the ragged staff of the Dudleys and the roses from her father's arms, and one reads it in the following account: 'She . . . rides through Cheapside drawn by four milk-white steeds, with four footmen in black velvet jackets, and silver bears on their backs and breasts, two knights and thirty gentlemen before her, and coaches of gentlewomen, pages and servants behind, so that it might be supposed to be the queen or some foreign prince or ambassador.'[62]

As ever, the minutiae of day-to-day life had to be seen to, even when the Leicesters were living on this scale. There is a letter from Leicester to Burghley dated 8 July 1584 dealing with duties on cloth — an important source of revenue — and the lunacy of the Countess of Warwick — not Ambrose's wife, but the widow of his elder brother John.[63] In that year two more of Calvin's sermons, translated by Home and Munday, were dedicated to Leicester, and it is interesting to see what other works were dedicated to him at this time. For example, on 15 December 1584 Meredith Hanmer put the following dedication to the second edition of his translation of *The Ancient Ecclesiastical Histories*: 'Wherefore (my good lord) seeing that as Plato saith running wits are delighted with poetry, as Aristotle writeth, effeminate persons are ravished with music, and as Socrates telleth us histories agree best with staid heads: I present unto your honour these histories agreeing very well with your disposition, and being the fruits of my travail and study.' Among the books — all in Italian — mentioned in the Leicester House inventory this year are Boethius' *De Consolatione*; Nova Silva; Tullius' (Cicero *De Officiis*) *Offices*; Xenophon's *Cyclopedia*, and (in Latin) Seneca's *Tragedies*.[64] This was also the year in which Raleigh gave him a 'laver, the body of a strange shell of a fish, supported by a mannikin, and surmounted by Neptune'. At this point it seemed that no matter what storms had assailed the Dudleys in the past, the structure was unharmed, and indeed more splendid than ever before.

This magnificent edifice was severely shaken, however, if not seriously endangered, when a calamity overtook the Leicesters on Sunday 19 July. On that day their only son, Lord Denbigh, died at Wanstead. In that one blow went all Leicester's hopes of perpetuating the male line of Dudley. The tombstone inscription in Warwick runs:

> Here resteth the body of the noble imp Robert of Dudley, Baron of Denbigh, son of Robert Earl of Leicester, nephew and heir unto Ambrose Earl of Warwick, brethren, both sons of the mighty prince John, late Duke of Northumberland . . . here interred; a child of great parentage, but of far greater hope and towardness, taken from this transitory unto everlasting life, in his tender age, at Wanstead in

Essex on Sunday the 19th of July in the year of our Lord God 1584
. . .

Bears, ragged staffs and cinquefoils decorate the simple tomb, on which
an effigy of the child reposes, wearing a circlet, his head resting on a
cushion, his rich damask robe patterned with cinquefoils and ragged
staffs, and at his feet a bear which looks away, somewhat quizzically,
perhaps, keeping watch over its young master, head forever raised,
slightly alert. On the other side of the town, in Warwick Castle, is the
tiny suit of armour made for the boy, one thigh piece longer than the
other, implying that he was slightly deformed. It has been suggested
that he suffered from infantile hemiplegia, and epileptic attacks are
often associated with such an occurrence. This was what probably gave
rise to the statement in *Leicester's Commonwealth*, published that year, to
the effect that his father had had him poisoned, and that he suffered
from 'such a stange calamity as the falling-sickness, in his infancy'.[65]
Also, a subsequent addition to this work reproduced as quotation from
the Book of Proverbs: 'The children of adulterers shall be consumed and
the seed of a wicked bed shall be rooted out'.

Three days later Leicester received a letter from Hatton, written from
the Court:

> My singular good lord, your excellent good wisdom, made perfect in
> the school of our eternal God, will . . . I trust, subdue these kind and
> natural afflictions which now oppress your own loving heart . . . I
> have told her Majesty of this unfortunate and untimely cause which
> constrained your sudden journey to London, whereof I assure your
> lordship I find her very sorry, and wisheth your comfort even from the
> bottom of her heart.[66]

The Court had been at Nonsuch in Surrey, and it seems as if Leicester
may well have been summoned to Wanstead when the boy's illness
became grave, and probably reached the house in time, from a letter he
wrote to Davison, at this time ambassador in Scotland: 'Cousin Davison, I have this 2nd of August received your letter of the 27th of July. It
found me from the Court, whence I have been absent these fifteen days
to comfort my sorrowful wife for the loss of my only little son, whom
God has lately taken from us.'[67]

Another death took place this month, on 10 July, this time the
assassination of William of Orange, and in the wake of its shock, a loyal
Bond of Association was drawn up in England, stating that if anyone
murdered the Queen, those who signed the bond would pursue the

murderer to the death, as well as the person in whose interests the murder had been committed, and at the same time declare the heirs incapable of succession. Camden stated that the bond was Leicester's idea, but whether that is true or not, the idea soon caught on, and so many people signed that, when the documents were brought to Hampton Court for the Queen to see, they filled a whole trunk. It was intended next to have the bond made an Act of Parliament, but as touched as Elizabeth was by this spontaneous act of loyalty, she was reluctant to see its provisions made law, especially that in connection with the death of the person in whose interest the murder had been committed. Furthermore, the clause to do with succession might effectively exclude King James from the throne of England without his having had anything to do with the murder in question. In a revised form it was eventually made into a bill, however, and whether or not Leicester devised the original bond, the Queen certainly showed her appreciation for him when the scurrilous work known as *Leicester's Commonwealth* made its appearance in the autumn of 1584.

There is a letter from Sir Francis Walsingham to Leicester, dated 29 September 1584, in which Walsingham acquaints Leicester with the details: 'My very good lord: Yesterday I received from the Lord Mayor enclosed in a letter a printed libel against your lordship, the most malicious-written thing that ever was penned since the beginning of the world.' The author of this work, according to Walsingham, was Morgan, the Queen of Scots' agent in France, with the help of various English Catholics there, amongst whom was William Tresham, already encountered. As Walsingham continued: 'About three years past I had notice given unto me in secret sort of such an intention, with a meaning to reach higher [i.e. the Queen herself?]. There is no good, no honest man (and though he were your lordship's mortal enemy) that doth not condemn this treacherous manner of dealing.'[68] The full title of the work was: *The Copy of a Letter written by a Master of Arts of Cambridge to his friend in London, concerning some talk passed of late between two worshipful and grave men about the present state, and some proceedings of the Earl of Leicester and his friends in England*. It only received its title of *Leicester's Commonwealth* for the 1641 reprint. In view of the fact that the book was thought to be the work of Campion's associate, Parsons, and the first edition had a green cover and green-stained edges to the pages, it was also known as *Father Parsons' greencoat*.

There is much in the work that is patently false and malicious. At the same time, there is a strong strand of detail that would seem to have come only from sources near to Leicester himself. Moreover the fact that it had such a success would seem to indicate that it was very much what people wanted to hear about him. Of course Leicester had done much to make himself hated by a great many people, and when Hatton said, in the letter of condolence for the death of Lord Denbigh, that Leicester's bereavement drew sympathy from 'millions, who on my soul, do love you no less than children or brethren', the reception of *Leicester's Commonwealth* gave those words a very hollow ring.

There were many condemnations of the book, in many forms.[69] Sir Philip Sidney, in a work already quoted (*see* p. 10), the Privy Council, and even the Queen herself, rose to Leicester's defence, but still it continued to go the rounds. On 14 January 1585 Charles Paget wrote to Mary Queen of Scots: 'Leicester (who of late hath said to a friend of his, that he will persecute you to the uttermost, for that he supposeth your Majesty to be privy to the setting-forth of the book against him).'[70] On 16 February King James issued a repudiation of it from Holyrood House, in which it was described as 'a libel devised and set out by some seditious person of purpose to obscure with lewd lies the honour and reputation of our trusty cousin the Earl of Leicester'. Its appearance hit the Staffords in France specially hard, and in March Sir Edward wrote to Walsingham to warn him that a French translation was in existence. Stafford had not told his wife since the English edition had been sufficient to make her ill, through 'the melancholy of the fear of misconception'.[71]

As far as Leicester himself was concerned, there seemed little outward anxiety, certainly not where the Queen was involved; an inventory of Wanstead dated 24 February 1585, for example, mentions hangings 'in the Queen's bedchamber'[72] — indicating that she still stayed there — and we find him writing to her from Kenilworth on 2 April about his heart, which was 'bounden to remain more desirous than able to serve you'. Then he went on: 'I take my leave, trusting shortly to attend at Court. From your old lodging in the Castle of Kenilworth, where you are daily prayed for and most often wished to be.'[73] According to Mendoza, now ambassador in Paris, in May Elizabeth proposed relieving Leicester of the Mastership of the Horse, and making him Lord Steward instead, but he refused to give up the office he had held since the start of her reign.[74] There were strong sentimental reasons, therefore, and there were political ones, too. There was also the threat of the rise of Raleigh, and on 1 June Mendoza reported that Leicester and he were on bad terms. He also touched on the matter of the *Common-*

wealth: 'The ambassador here, Stafford, has, by the Queen's orders, been bringing great pressure to bear on the king to prohibit the sale of certain books which have been translated into French about the lives of the Queen and the Earl of Leicester, and to order the arrest of the translator, who is an Englishman.'[75]

On 20 June 1585 the Queen in Council sent a letter to the magistrates of Cheshire: 'Her Highness not only knoweth to assured certainty the books and libels against the said earl to be most malicious, false and scandalous, and such as none but an incarnate devil himself could dream to be true'; and there is a similar letter to the City of London six days later.

A curious light is thrown on the position of Christopher Blount at this time, looking forward to the way in which he was to supplant Leicester in his wife's affection, and indeed may even have already done so. In July 1585 Thomas Morgan, who was thought by Walsingham to be the author of the *Commonwealth*, wrote to Mary Queen of Scots from Paris to the effect that: 'Because Leicester is a great tryant in the realm, where Catholics are so plagued', the Blount family were all forced 'to their great charges', to live as Leicester's minions, thus hoping to buy their ease. A letter from the same place of origin and in the same month, but from Charles Paget this time, told Mary that Christopher Blount had offered to serve her. As Gentleman of the Horse to Leicester he was in a very good position to be of use to her. Paget advised Mary to use him for some comparatively unimportant task first, and then suddenly put him to greater use.

In the shifting sands of those times, options had to be kept open, and Leicester himself was not above it. On 25 July 1585 he wrote to Sir John Maitland, King James's secretary, whom he had never met, to ingratiate himself in that quarter:

> Sir, I do seldom use to seek acquaintance of strangers, and yet, by some good inspiration I suppose, I am moved to be thus bold with you though altogether unknown to you, to show my earnest desire that some such familiar offices of friendship may pass between us, as men that do serve two princes so near in blood and so dear in friendship as my mistress and your master be. . . . And therefore for my own part . . . I cannot like to live a stranger with such a person but to offer any kindness or acquaintance I may devise . . .[76]

Of course Leicester very conveniently managed to overlook the fact that, far from being 'so dear in friendship' with James, Elizabeth had actually called him 'that false Scots urchin', when she heard of his treachery over the Regent Morton. False he may have been, but if anything happened to Elizabeth, he might very well turn out to be Leicester's new master, and Leicester was determined to make sure that he was still there if anything altered at the seat of power. As it happened, fate had something very different in store for him.

Before turning to this next stage in his career, this is a convenient point at which to conclude his relations with Oxford University. One of his last acts as Chancellor was the official establishment of the University Press, and in 1585 John Case's *Speculum* . . . , printed by Joseph Barnes, was dedicated to Leicester. Other dedications of this year were Robert Greene's *Planetomachia*, and William Gager's *Meleager* (though not published until 1592 in Oxford), which was performed before Leicester in a revival — its second performance — when he visited the university that year of 1585 with Pembroke, Philip Sidney and others. The scene was soon to shift, however, and the delights of Oxford were exchanged for the battlefields of the Low Countries.

9

Disaster in the Low Countries

. . . one that hath always received an extraordinary portion of our favour above all our subjects, even from the beginning of our reign . . .

Queen Elizabeth to Robert Dudley

Elizabeth had already been offered the sovereignty of Holland by Prince William of Orange, and after his assassination it was offered again by the States. At the end of June 1585, when she received the Dutch commission, she told them why she could not do so, for she would risk war with Spain. As Burghley put it to the commissioners: '. . . we have told you over and over again that her Majesty will never think of accepting the sovereignty. She will assist you in money and men, and must be repaid to the last farthing when the war is over; and, until that period, must have solid pledges in the shape of a town in each province.'[1] This was Elizabeth's position, and one to which she intended to stick as long as possible. There were, of course, people in England who wished it were otherwise, and John Strype, in his *Life and Acts of John Whitgift, DD*, even went so far as to maintain that Leicester, for one, actively sought to force English intervention, in his own interests:

> A weighty motion was made this summer, about the month of July, to the Archbishop by the Earl of Leicester; namely, to declare what his judgement was for the Queen's assistance of the inhabitants of the

Netherlands, so grievously now oppressed by Philip, King of Spain:
. . . this great affair had been already concluded upon at Court by the
great men about the Queen; though she herself was very tender of
entering into this open breach with Spain. The lofty earl expected
this mighty addition to the rest of his honours and titles to lead and
govern her forces in those countries for their relief. But now, that the
Queen might be fully fixed and determined, and that he might go
with the greater glory and hope of success, he wanted the Archbishop's approbation of the lawfulness and expediency of this counsel, to be opened by him to the Queen . . . [2]

That was Strype's view, and doubtless it was held by others at the time.
When we look at what Leicester himself wrote, however, and in such a
context that we may assume it to have been a genuine sentiment — at
least at that particular moment, for when the Dudleys scented a kill they
soon threw discretion to the winds — then he would seem to have
thought otherwise. In August 1585 he was at Cornbury in Oxfordshire,
and had an exchange of letters with Burghley, who was equally subject
to being the target for jealous attacks, and had heard that Leicester had
been responsible for some of them. He therefore wrote to complain.
They must have been especially bad at this time, however, for Burghley
wrote at the same time, on 14 August 1585, to his steward William
Herle:

> By your letter of the 11th, I perceive that you have heard the vile,
> false, and devilish exclamations and execrations [made] me by such as
> I know not, and therefore I can less judge what to think of them, in
> their degrees of the malice, and the causes thereof . . . They that say
> that in a rash and malicious mockery, that England has become
> *regnum Cecilianum*, may please their own cankered humour with such
> a device, but if my actions be considered, if there be any cause given
> by me of such a nickname, there may be found out in many others
> juster causes to attribute other names than mine . . . My house of
> Burghley is of my mother's inheritance, who liveth and is the owner
> of it, and I but the farmer . . .

On the charge of his fees as Treasurer, Burghley retorted that they were
only the same as for the last 'four hundred years, whereas the Chancellor
and other hath been doubly augmented within these few years, and
these I do affirm that my fees of my treasurership doth not answer to my
charge of my stable, I mean not my table; and in my household, I do

seldom feed less than one hundred persons.'[3]

In his earlier letter of 11 August to Leicester, towards the end he wrote:

> Knowing in the sight of God mine own innocence of any unhonest action towards your lordship . . . I will quiet my heart [or hurt?] and arm myself against the wrong with patience. But I am sure no man of my sort has abbiden more injuries this way in hearing evil when I have done well . . . And if the place I hold might be bestowed by her Majesty upon another without condemnation of me for mine honesty, I vow to Almighty God I would be most glad.[4]

In his reply Leicester professed the same belief, asserting: 'For my own part, I will answer faithfully and truthfully for myself, I do more desire my liberty, with her Majesty's favour, than any office in England.'[5] Perhaps they were both fooling themselves, as they tacitly revealed by the qualifications they both made in their letters: Burghley's 'if . . .' and Leicester's 'with her Majesty's favour'— for both knew in their heart of hearts that the Queen would not show her favour in either case to agree to their requests. But for a moment, in the late summer of 1585, at peace deep in the Oxfordshire countryside, perhaps Leicester really felt that the time had come to seek a little ease. He was probably fifty-two by now, but prematurely aged if we are to accept the portrait at Parham as an accurate representation of his appearance at this time. The Queen's suggestion that he relinquish his cherished office of Master of the Horse for that of Lord Steward earlier that year may not have been such an unthinkable proposition after all, for although from the point of view of administrative business there was probably little to choose between the two, the office of Steward might have been less physically demanding, and it is typical that the Queen should have taken this into consideration. But he had been Master of the Horse all the reign, and he was not prepared to give it up yet.

However, events overtook such considerations, as they are often wont to do, when Antwerp fell to the Spanish. As Gilbert Talbot wrote to his father on 26 August:

> Her Majesty was greatly troubled . . . And my Lord Treasurer who was at Theobalds somewhat ill of the gout was sent for. And so my Lord Leicester to return to the Court. And it is thought that her Majesty shall be forced of very necessity to send some great person with great forces presently for the defence of Holland and Zeeland, or else they will, out of hand, follow Antwerp.[6]

It was said that the Dutch themselves had asked for Leicester as commander of the expedition, and for Sir Philip Sidney as Governor of Flushing. All the desires for peace and retirement expressed from Cornbury evaporated as Leicester made for London. On 28 August he wrote to Walsingham from Stoneleigh, Mr Leigh's house in Warwickshire, saying that he was ready to take up the command, but he had had a fall from his horse and was as yet unable to pull on his boots. He wished he had a hundred thousand lives so that he might spend them all in the service of the Queen.[7]

On 2 September 1585 Elizabeth agreed to have five thousand foot and one thousand horse in the field — initially it had been four thousand and four hundred respectively, with seven hundred men for garrison duty — and to provide £125,000 a year for their payment.[8] By way of guarantee she was to have Brill and Flushing. Leicester, it must be remembered, had seen no active service since 1557, when he had fought in France for the very man he was now, ultimately, fighting against. Even so, with such experienced soldiers as Sir John Norreys and Sir Roger Williams under him, Burghley's eldest son Sir Thomas Cecil as Governor of Brill, and Sir Philip Sidney as Governor of Flushing, and his stepson Robert Devereux, Earl of Essex, as General of Horse, there was no lack of talent. At one point, when Sidney thought that his appointment was in doubt, he went to Plymouth to try and join Drake's expedition to the New World, but Drake warned Elizabeth, who summoned Sidney back.

Leicester was at last ready to leave towards the end of September 1585, but the Queen's habitual fears and anxieties had been given added point by the fact that the Countess of Leicester arrived in London from Kenilworth to take up residence at Leicester House, and from there who could tell where she might go. As Walsingham wrote, on 5 September, to Davison in the Low Countries: 'I see not her Majesty disposed to use the service of the Earl of Leicester. There is great offence taken in the carrying down of his lady.'[9] Leicester himself at this time was much with the Queen, and experiencing the full force of her doubts and fears. As he wrote to Walsingham:

Mr Secretary, I find her Majesty very desirous to stay me. She makes the cause only the doubtfulness of her own self, by reason of her oft disease taking her of late, and this last night worst of all. She used very pitiful words to me of her fear that she shall not live, and would not have me from her . . . pray you send my wife word in the morning that I cannot come before Thursday to London.[10]

Almost a week later things had still not improved, as we see from another letter Leicester wrote to Walsingham: 'I have this night, at 1 o'clock, received your letter, which doth signify that her Majesty's pleasure is, I should stay my preparations till I do speak with her.' On the Queen's order Leicester had sent out two hundred letters to his friends and servants, telling them to be ready to go with him. As he pointed out: 'I am sure there be one hundred of these already delivered, and the rest will be before I can revoke them.' He had also been to the Tower for armour and steel saddles, and had 'two or three vessels to carry away presently certain provisions'. The envoys from the Low Countries had also been with him to beg him to hurry, and he ended: 'Scribbled in my bed this Monday morning at almost 2 o'clock.'[11] This was a formal letter, however, which might be read by one of Walsingham's household, for with it was a personal letter:

> This is one of the strangest dealings in the world . . . For my part, I am weary of life and all. I pray you let me hear with speed. I will go this morning to Wanstead to see some horses I have there . . . and if the matter alter, I can have no heart to come at Court and look upon any man, for it will be thought some misliking in me doth stay the matter. Send Philip [Sidney] to me, and God keep you, and if you can possible [sic], learn out the cause of this change.[12]

The same day (27 September) Walsingham replied that the Queen had removed her objections, and that everything might now proceed. He added, indicating to what degree Leicester had committed himself financially to this venture: 'If your lordship's requests shall minister matter of charge, though it be for the public service, the impediment will be found in her Majesty . . .'[13]

Thomas Cecil and Philip Sidney left to take up their appointments, at Brill and Flushing respectively, on 16 November. Leicester himself was counting on setting out in the first week of December. On 5 December he wrote to Burghley while on the way to Harwich. Elizabeth's wavering had had an unsettling effect on him, and he was fully aware that he was setting himself at a disadvantage by removing himself from the centre of power. He appealed, therefore, to Burghley to look after his interests in his absence. As for the Queen, Leicester only hoped that 'she will fortify and maintain her own action to the full performance of what she hath agreed on . . . In some haste this 5th of December, on my way to the sea-side.'[14]

From Colchester Leicester went to Manningtree, and then down-river to Harwich, on 8 December. He determined to land at Brill, even though the admiral, William Burroughs, told him that Flushing was far more suitable with such a large fleet. Moreover, Burroughs had only one pilot with him, whom he had engaged to take the fleet into Flushing. Leicester was highly offended at this, and told the admiral that he ought to have enough pilots on hand 'for all the fleet, for any place it should please his lordship to appoint to go unto'.[15] This was hardly an auspicious start to the venture, let alone a good augury for the conduct of the campaign as a whole. As many pilots as could be found were called together, and they were all of the same opinion. By noon Leicester had changed his mind, and the fleet set out for Flushing. There were, however, ships with horses and supplies still in the Thames, so Leicester wanted Burroughs to send a pinnace to them with a message to let them know of the change of destination. The admiral explained that by the time the pinnace got there, in view of the contrary wind and tide, the ships would be already out to sea. The Thames contingent therefore went to Brill in any case.

Leicester landed at Flushing on 10 December with almost one hundred ships. He was received by his nephew, Sir Philip Sidney, and the local inhabitants had prepared a warm welcome. There were fireworks, salvoes from cannon, peals of bells, triumphal arches and allegorical tableaux in Rotterdam, Delft, the Hague and Amsterdam, and a series of twelve etchings was made to record the same, entitled *Delineatio Pompae Triumphalis qua Robertus Dudlaeus comes Leicestrensis Hagae comitis fuit receptus*. All this went to Leicester's head, and in Delft he was heard to say — according to some reports — that in the persons of Lady Jane Grey and Lord Guildford Dudley, his family had been unfairly deprived of the crown of England.[16] To Walsingham, however, he wrote that there were so many shouts of 'God save Queen Elizabeth' in the streets that one might almost think oneself with her as she passed along Cheapside.[17] As for the Queen herself, she was all too aware of what might go wrong, not only if Leicester mismanaged things, but also in the eyes of the rest of the world. In an attempt to justify her action she issued a proclamation, mainly to cut the ground from under the feet of Spain in case King Philip was looking for any justification for reprisals against England. Although, indeed, he would hardly have waited for such a justification once he had decided to launch the Armada, as he did three years later.

Whatever he lacked in experience and charismatic leadership, Leicester attempted to make up for by being efficient, and early the next year he drew up his *Laws and Ordinances* for his troops. In the preamble he gave his reason for doing so:

> . . . seeing that martial discipline above all things (proper to men of war) is by us at this time most to be followed, as well for the advancement of God's glory, as honourably to govern this army in good order: And lest the evil inclined (pleading simplicity) should cover any wicked fact by ignorance: Therefore these martial Ordinances and Laws following are established and published.[18]

Basically, the regulations set forth are very sensible, if somewhat heavily weighted on the side of a standard of religious observance that even the most exemplary army in those days would be highly unlikely to keep. Obviously there had to be a marked contrast between Leicester's army's behaviour and that of the cruel and rapacious Spaniards.

Had Leicester been prepared to take a leaf out of his Queen's book, and bide his time in a display of busy inactivity and let others do the necessary work, a very different story might have been told. True, he probably would not have returned to England with any military glory, but he would have had the distinction of being the person chosen to hold one of the highest positions of trust possible at that time. Elizabeth was in any case prepared to negotiate for peace with Parma over the heads of the Dutch, so he could have remained a noble and distinguished figurehead. Unfortunately the Dudley pride and vanity were still there, as strong as ever, and when the Dutch offered him the position of Supreme Governor of the United Provinces on New Year's Day 1586, he decided to accept it. His installation took place on 25 January (by the Julian Calendar — that is 4 February) and Davison was the person chosen to take the news to England. He did not leave until 5 February, however, and because of bad weather his journey took ten days. By the time he reached Greenwich, therefore, he arrived not as a messenger, but as the recipient of the fullness of the Queen's wrath. She had in fact prepared a letter for Leicester on 10 February, before Davison arrived, and he was so ineffectual in his presentation that it was not altered. It began with no form of address:

> How contemptuously we conceive ourself to have been used by you, you shall by this bearer [Sir Thomas Heneage] understand . . . We could never have imagined, had we not seen it fall out in experience, that a man raised up by ourself, and extraordinarily favoured by us above any other subject of this land, would have in so contemptible a

sort broken our commandment, in a cause that so greatly toucheth us in honour.

He was, in short, to 'obey and fulfil whatsoever the bearer hereof shall direct you to do in our name: whereof fail you not, as you will answer the contrary at your uttermost peril.'[19] The Queen's command was, in fact, that on the same spot that he had accepted the title, Leicester was to renounce it, but when Burghley heard of this he advised that it was not wise, for as much as he too deplored Leicester's action, he nevertheless felt that to force him to make a public renunciation would only make matters worse. The Queen refused to listen at first. Apart from her fury at Leicester's presumption as a Dudley, his action had made nonsense of all her protestations that she did not seek power in the Low Countries, but simply wanted to give aid. Burghley got his way in the end, but only by threatening to resign.

It was most unfortunate that at the same time news got about that Lettice was planning to go out to the Low Countries herself, and take up her duties as wife of the Supreme Governor. Despite the fact that she had been forbidden to go by the Queen when the idea was first mooted, it was now said in a letter to Leicester that: 'It was told her Majesty that my lady was prepared presently to come over to your excellency, with such a train of ladies and gentlewomen and such rich coaches, litters and sidesaddles, as her Majesty had none such, and that there should be a court of ladies, as should far pass her Majesty's Court here.'[20] The Queen put her foot down firmly, but Lettice still entertained the idea, and as late as 24 March Sir Philip Sidney wrote to the effect that he wished that 'some way might be taken to stay my lady in England'.[21]

Ambrose Dudley was most alarmed, and on 6 March wrote to his brother Robert to let him know what he felt about the whole business, and how things then stood:

> Well, our mistress' extreme rage doth increase rather than any way diminish, and giveth out great threatening words against you, therefore make the best assurance you can for yourself, and trust not her oath, for that her malice is great and unquenchable, in the wisest of their opinions here, and, as for other friendship, as far as I can learn, is as doubtful as the other; wherefore, my good brother, repose your whole trust in God.[22]

Ambrose's approach shows just how blinded the other members of the family were to Robert's glory. At the same time, it shows a remarkable confidence in the support of the Deity. Robert himself, at this juncture, was abject in his approach to the Queen, somewhat in the vein that his father chose to use in his extremity. He only wanted to return to England, he said, and his duties as Master of the Horse. Perhaps there he would be some use in rubbing the heels of the Queen's horses, for patently he was of no use where he was. Whilst Ambrose's letter was on its way to him, he was drawing up a long document, dated 10 March, in which he laid the blame for his having accepted the title in the first place fairly and squarely on the shoulders of Davison:

> It hath not grieved me a little, that, by your means, I have fallen into her Majesty's so deep displeasure, but that you, also, have so care-lessly discharged your part, in the due declaration of all things as they stood in truth. Knowing most assuredly, that, if you had delivered to her Majesty indeed the truth of my dealing, her Highness could never have conceived, as I perceive she doth . . . Therefore I conclude, charging you with your conscience how you do deal now with me; seeing you chiefly brought me into it . . . I did very unwillingly come to the matter . . . except your embassages have better success, I shall have no great cause to commend them.[23]

Davison annotated this document with appropriate comments — 'Denied'; 'The contrary appears'; 'Absolutely denied'; 'Hereof let the world judge' — but on 28 February, before he received it, he had written to Leicester, giving news of his countess: 'Tomorrow I hope, God willing, to do my duty towards her. I found her greatly troubled with the tempestuous news she received from Court.' That was when he had seen her ten days before. Now, however, she was better: 'when she understood how I have proceeded with her Majesty'.[24]

As with so many of the Queen's rages, and especially when her favourites were involved, the storm soon passed away as if it had never existed — even in such a business as this — and on 29 March Raleigh appended a postscript to a letter to Leicester: 'The Queen is in very terms with you, and, thanks be to God, well pacified, and you are again her "sweet Robin".'[25] Coming from Raleigh that can hardly have given Leicester very much satisfaction. In the circumstances, however, such news was welcome from virtually any quarter. The Queen's was no total capitulation, and on 1 April 1586, having had some time for reflection, she wrote to him from Greenwich a pained, but dignified and con-sidered view of the matter which, while remaining firm, was none the less basically affectionate in tone for such a formal document. The overall impression one forms is that a crisis had occurred and, irrespective of who was responsible, personal considerations must be forgotten and the best remedy sought and applied. Even then, the Queen made it quite clear to whom he owed his position, and could not prevent herself from referring to the odious Lettice:

> By the Queen: Right trusty and right well beloved cousin and counsellor, we greet you well. It is always thought, in the opinion of the world, a hard bargain when both parties are losers, and so doth fall out in the case between us two. You, as we hear, are greatly grieved, in respect of the great displeasure you find we have conceived against you, and we no less grieved, that a subject of ours, of that quality that you are, a creature of our own, and one that hath always received an extraordinary portion of our favour above all our subjects, even from the beginning of our reign, should deal so carelessly, we will not say contemptuously, as to give the world just cause to think, that we are held in contempt by him that ought to respect and reverence us, from whom we could never have looked to receive any such measure, which, we do assure you, hath wrought as great grief in us as any one thing that ever happened to us . . . But for that your grieved and wounded mind hath more need of comfort than reproof, whom we are persuaded, though the act in respect of the contempt can no way be excused, had no other meaning and intent than to advance our service; we think meet to forbear to dwell upon a matter wherein we ourselves do find so little comfort, assuring you that whosoever professeth to love you best taketh not more comfort of your well doing, or discomfort of your evil doing, than ourself.[26]

It was presumably to Lettice that the Queen referred in this last sentence. From a purely practical point of view, Leicester was to consult with Sir Thomas Heneage and other competent persons as to whether it would be possible to renounce the title of Supreme Governor and revert to the one she had given him, of Lieutenant-General of her forces, but still retain the authority that the first title carried with it. This could really only be decided on the spot, so if it was found necessary for him to retain the title, then 'we can be content, if necessity shall so require, to tolerate the same for a time.'[27]

This change of atmosphere encouraged Leicester to launch out into more regal show. St George's Day 1586 was observed with due solemnity at Utrecht: 'Then came my lord most princelike, invested in his robes of the order [the Garter], guarded by the principal burghers of the town, which offered themselves to that service, besides his own guard, which was a fifty halbardiers in scarlet cloaks, guarded with purple and white velvet.'[28] Stow had all this from William Segar, Portcullis, who was there.

Walsingham saw that the Queen was not interested in having an all-out war, and that it would be better to negotiate for peace — a view shared by Burghley — and in the circumstances Leicester would be the man to take charge: 'I cannot but wish your lordship to be a principal dealer therein, as well in respect of your own honour as that I hope it will be performed with both honourable and profitable conditions . . . whereas I doubt, if it pass into others' hands, it will not be so carefully dealt in.'[29] With the turning of the tide, Leicester seemed to regain some of his former confidence, and on 23 May Lord North wrote to Walsingham of him: 'My Lord of Leicester did so notably advise and direct the making of the trenches, a thing I did not look for, I confess; and to view this place he did put himself in danger of musket shot too much.'[30]

Another thing that occupied Leicester's attention was the pay of his men, and their general conditions. Burghley wrote to warn him on 31 May: 'My lord, until the state of the Queen's army by musterbook and her monthly charges may appear more clear, here will be no further means for any more money.' Leicester failed signally to sort out his finances, however, and instead concerned himself with the generally demoralised state of his army. He deplored the manners and the morals of the younger generation: he had told Walsingham in a letter dated 16 April, how it grieved him 'to see your youths in England, how clean they be marred and spoiled for ever being able to serve her Majesty and the realm. I am ashamed to think, much more to speak, of the young men that have come over. Believe me, you will all repent the cockney [pampered] kind of bringing up at this day of young men.'[31]

Unfortunately things were exacerbated by a split in the camp. Leicester did not get on with Sir John Norreys, and totally ignored the fact that he was a very able soldier, who had already fought for William of Orange. Leicester wrote to Walsingham of him on 10 June 1586: '. . . he will so dissemble, so crouch, so cunningly carry his doings, as no man living would imagine there were half the malice or vindictive mind that doth plainly his deeds prove to be.'[32] When told, however, that the Queen held Norreys in high regard, Leicester simply retorted: 'I will not write any more of Mr John Norreys' backwardness. He hath too good friends, and so hath all that like me not.'[33] This somewhat paranoic attitude was certainly not helped by the fact that he felt keenly the Queen's public disclaiming of his action in accepting the title of Supreme Governor, but unfortunately it coloured his relations with the States themselves. Again it was Walsingham who, in a letter dated 18 June, received his complaints: 'I have been fain of late . . . to handle some of my masters somewhat plainly and roughly, too, for they thought I would droop, but I will rather be overthrown by her Majesty's doings, than overboarded by these churls and tinkers.'[34]

Churls and tinkers perhaps, but the fact that they looked to Leicester as their source of salvation was something he ought to have borne in mind when he spoke of them in this way. At least two eulogistic works on his activities in the Low Countries were published in 1586 and dedicated to him, as well as Geoffrey Whitney's *A Choice of Emblems*, which was printed in Leyden at the house of Plantin.

Parma captured Grave in June, but in July Philip Sidney took Axel, by swimming the moat at night with forty men, scaling the walls and opening the gates for the rest of his force. This brought with it four nearby cities, and many felt that if the English would only take an offensive role they would soon put the Spaniards to rout. However, this was not what the Queen wanted. As Walsingham informed Leicester on 9 July:

> She gathereth upon the view of your lordship's letter, that the only salve to cure this sore is to [make] herself proprietory [of] that country and to put [in] such an army into the [same] as may be able to make head to the enemy's. The[se] two things being so contrary to her Majesty's disposition, the one, for that it breedeth a doubt of a perpetual war, the other, for that it requireth an increase of charges, doth marvellously distract her, and make her repent that she ever entered into the action.[35]

Money was indeed one of the most worrying aspects of the whole affair as far as the Queen was concerned, and it was a pity, to say the least, that Leicester would not, or could not, set his house in order. It is much to the Queen's credit that she did not tax him with this, despite his letter of 27 June, but wrote to him in one of her tenderest veins: 'Rob: I am afraid you will suppose by my wandering writings that a midsummer moon hath taken large possession of my brains this month, but you must needs take things as they come in my head, though order be left behind me.' She did not want Norreys and such men to be discouraged, but at the same time, if they cheated the troops, then he had to let her know, and she would deal with it, for:

> It frets me not a little that the poor soldiers that hourly venture life, should want their due, that well deserve rather reward: and look in whom the fault may duly be proved, let them smart therefor . . . though you know my old wont, that love not to discharge from office without desert, God forbid . . . Now will I end, that do imagine I talk still with you, and therefore lothly say farewell, ⊕⊕ , though ever I pray God bless you from all harm and save you from all foes, with my million and legion of thanks for all your pains and cares. As you know, ever the same, ER.[36]

This summer saw the discovery of the Babington Plot, which finally proved what many people had long suspected, namely that Mary Queen of Scots had been involved in, or certainly a party to, virtually every threatened invasion or assassination plot since she arrived in England in 1568. Even after the discovery of the plot Walsingham waited until he had all the evidence he required before arresting those involved. However, true to her nature, Elizabeth was not going to be rushed into a swift conclusion of the affair as far as Mary herself was concerned. For all the trouble she had caused Elizabeth, she was still a queen, and whatever was meted out to Mary might prove to be a very unfortunate precedent. So the matter dragged on.

Meanwhile, in the Low Countries, September 1586 saw what was probably the most disastrous event of the whole campaign. The English had captured Doesburg, seen by them as a preliminary to the capture of the much more important Zutphen, the key to Guelderland. The siege of the latter city began on 13 September, but on the 22nd Philip Sidney was wounded by a musket ball in the thigh. Leicester sent him in his own barge to his headquarters at Arnhem, and Sidney's wife, who was six months' pregnant, went there from Flushing to look after him. At first it seemed as if there was no danger of blood poisoning, since the wound was not very serious. On 2 October Leicester was able to write to Walsingham: 'He amends as well as is possible in this time . . . he sleeps and rests well, and hath a good stomach to eat.'[37]

Perhaps Sidney knew better himself what was really going to happen, for on 30 September he made his will, and on 8 October he knew that gangrene had set in, and that there was no hope. It took a further nine days to kill him, however, and it was a further eight days after that before Leicester could bring himself to write to Walsingham, Sidney's father-in-law:

Sir, the grief I have taken for the loss of my dear son and yours would not suffer me to write sooner of those ill news unto you . . . For mine own part, I have lost, beside the comfort of my life, a most principal stay and help in my service here . . . Your sorrowful daughter and mine is here with me in Utrecht, till she may recover some strength, for she is wonderfully overthrown, through her long care since the beginning of her husband's hurt, and I am the more careful she should be in some strength ere she take her journey into England, for that she is with child, which I pray God send to be a son, if it be His will; but, whether son or daughter, they shall be my children too.[38]

There was, however, a more important matter to take away some of the grief of Philip Sidney's death. Once Mary Queen of Scots had been tried and found guilty, Elizabeth — so Walsingham informed Leicester — refused to have the death sentence passed on her. Although Leicester, in common with several others, had thought it advisable to keep on some sort of footing with Mary whilst the possibility remained that she might one day be Queen of England, now that she had been found guilty he saw no reason for delaying what he saw as inevitable. On 25 October he maintained to Walsingham, in the same letter as above: 'My heart cannot rest for fear since I heard that your matters are deferred.' In fact, he went on, if he had been at the Council he would have ordered the execution himself, rather than allow 'this dreadful mischief to be prolonged for her [Elizabeth's] destruction'. Camden even maintained that Leicester sent a cleric to Walsingham, in secret, to advise poisoning Mary, and to convince him that it was lawful to do so, but Walsingham declined. If there is any truth in the story at all, it showed how little Leicester appreciated Elizabeth's whole position vis à vis Mary. It was bad enough that things had come to this pass at all, but if anything had to be done, then it had to be done in the full view of the rest of the world.

The new session of Parliament was due to begin, and the summons for it was issued on 29 October. Leicester determined to be there, and told the States so. Burghley wrote to Sir Edward Stafford: '. . . the Earl of Leicester is like to be revoked with a pretence to give counsel to her Majesty'.[39] Stafford's reply showed that he had lost none of his animosity towards Leicester:

If I might be bold to tell you what I think . . . if I had as much credit as your lordship hath, and he [Leicester] born to do me no more good than he is, I would keep him where he is and he should drink that which he hath brewed . . . I would keep him there to undo himself and sure enough from coming home to undo others.[40]

In fact Leicester missed the opening of Parliament, which the Queen did not carry out in person, though a combined deputation of Lords and Commons waited on her at Richmond on 12 November to make plain what was uppermost in their thoughts. Towards the end of November Drake was sent over to the Low Countries to bring Leicester home. He had not resigned his title, nor had he promised that he would return. He reached Court at ten o'clock at night and, in his own words, 'Never since I was born did I receive a more gracious welcome.'[41] He soon made his presence felt. As we learn from Archibald Douglas, one of those sent by King James to ask Elizabeth to spare his mother's life, early in December:

> I drove back from Court with my Lord of Leicester, who represented to me that it was to your Majesty's interest that your mother should suffer justice. I assured him your Majesty could receive that persuasion in no good part. He made many protestations of service to your Majesty, for which I thanked him heartily, for he doth govern this Court at this time at his pleasure.[42]

So impressed was Douglas that he arranged to see Leicester on 6 December: 'to discuss your Majesty's affairs at greater length. It would be well to thank him in your next letter for his good offices.'

Meanwhile, Philip Sidney's widow had returned to England, and not surprisingly, in view of her ordeal, had given birth to a dead child. As the year drew to its close, Leicester had the sad duty of writing yet another letter of condolence to Walsingham. On 22 December he wrote: 'I am heartily sorry for any further visitation to come to that house, for I must every way be partaker thereof.'[43] The next day he sent another letter from Greenwich: 'I cannot be quiet till I may know how my daughter doth amend, wishing her even as to my own child, which, God willing, I shall always esteem her to be.'[44] He went on to tell Walsingham of a letter from Mary Queen of Scots which had made Elizabeth weep. Well might she weep, for despite all her procrastination, the time was coming when she would be forced to put her signature to the fateful document, and although she avoided the issue over Christmas and the New Year, by the end of January the game was up. On 8 February execution was carried out, and the poor Davison, who had come in for so much of Leicester's ill-temper the year before, now felt the more terrifying wrath of the Queen directly.

218

Early in February Leicester had written to Burghley from Wanstead, and it is evident from the letter that in spite of having her Sweet Robin back with her, and in spite of all the anxiety over the Queen of Scots, Elizabeth had not forgotten about Leicester's finances in the Low Countries. Leicester took the line with Burghley that it was an injury that he was being called to account. It was the work of a clerk or auditor, not someone in his position. Burghley's reply on 7 February was patient and tactful: 'I never did say nor mean to say that your lordship ought to be blamed for [the auditors'] imperfections in their accounts. For I did say and do still say that their accounts are obscure, confused and without credit . . .' He went on to stress that, far from being hostile to Leicester, he had earned himself the Queen's anger. She had taxed him 'very sharply, that in not applauding to her censures, I do commonly flatter and . . . hold opinions to please your lordship and others.' In fact he was heartily sick of 'these ungrateful burdens of office'.[45] That might be so, but there was worse to come; as a result of the execution of Mary Queen of Scots, Burghley was estranged from the royal presence for four months.

On 16 February, some three months after his embalmed body had been brought back to England, Sir Philip Sidney was finally laid to rest in St Paul's Cathedral with a state funeral. It had been so delayed because, despite his care over his will, it was found to be 'imperfect' when Walsingham had taken legal advice, and Sidney's plan to sell land to pay his debts was not therefore carried out. Walsingham had to find £6,000 for creditors before the funeral could take place. Leicester, too, was hard put to find ready money at that time, but he was unwilling to sell any of his land in order to help the family he made such protestations of loving as his own. More than that, when Walsingham asked the Queen for help, Leicester refused to support his application. Of course Leicester was still in a rather difficult situation as far as the Queen and finance were concerned, so it is perhaps not surprising that he chose to keep quiet. In the end it was Burghley who obtained a grant of land for Walsingham and in June 1587 the Chancellorship of the Duchy of Lancaster, an office for which Leicester had his own nominee.

Sidney's funeral was at last able to take place on 16 February 1587, with great magnificence, and some seven hundred people took part in the procession. Leicester and Huntingdon, Pembroke and Warwick, Lords Willoughby and North rode in pairs, and there were representatives from the Low Countries also. Even the Queen herself might have attended, had it not been for the proximity of the execution of the

Queen of Scots. It was the first State funeral, apart from that of a sovereign, and one that looked forward by a long time to Nelson, Wellington and Churchill.

In April 1587, in the operation known as the singeing of the King of Spain's beard, Drake made a lightning attack on Cadiz, where the supply ships for the Armada were, and when he had taken what provisions he wanted, he set fire to them and cut their cables. He then set sail for the mouth of the Tagus, intending to go to Lisbon and do as much harm as he could where the warships were being built. However, he was overtaken by a pinnace with a message from the Queen before he could get there, and had to abandon the idea. As a kind of consolation prize, on the way home he captured the *San Felipe*, which constituted the largest Spanish treasure ship ever taken by the English.

Meanwhile the absence of a single authority in the Low Countries was proving a grave problem, and despite the fact that Leicester's tenure of office had not been a success, it was nevertheless felt by the Dutch that they would be better off with him back. Burghley and Walsingham tended to agree with them, but from a different standpoint. Though Leicester had been neither a good general nor a good governor, and what was worse had created divisions in his own ranks, he still had such a strong influence with the Queen that Burghley and Walsingham felt that, back in the Low Countries, Leicester was their best guarantee that Elizabeth would not pull out of the war altogether. The medal struck by the Dutch this year, which shows the Queen crowned, seated on a throne, and holding orb and sceptre, with the arms of the five provinces brought to her feet by putti, has an element more of hope than assurance, since on the reverse it shows rays issuing from the divine name in Hebrew, and the papal party put to rout in a jumble of pope, bishop, cardinal and monks, monstrance, chalice and hosts.

Whilst Leicester was in England, Elizabeth had sent over Thomas Sackville, Lord Buckhurst, to weigh up the situation, and he was of the opinion that the command in the Low Countries 'had been better bestowed upon a meaner man of more skill'.[46] In a letter to Walsingham in July he maintained that Leicester 'doth abuse her Majesty', and used her name to cover 'his intolerable errors'.[47] Not surprisingly Leicester saw this merely as scheming on Buckhurst's part to get the command for himself, and wanted Elizabeth to have him arrested. But even Buckhurst had conceded that Leicester ought to go back, and that he ought to have with him sufficient money to pay the arrears of the English army. Leicester said that he was prepared to go, but that he would need

£10,000, and this the Queen was not prepared to give. She had been such a careful accountant herself that this spending of vast sums of money over which she had no control appalled her. This must be remembered throughout the haggling over expenditure in the Low Countries. It was not that she wanted to withhold money when it was due, once she had decided to spend it, but she needed to know that it was being spent wisely, and that the expense was justified.

Leicester then decided to go to Bath to take the waters, and whilst he was there Elizabeth agreed to lend him the money, but only on condition that he paid it back within a year. Leicester's initial reaction to this, in a letter to Walsingham dated 16 April 1587, was that it was impossible, especially if he were to maintain the state suitable to his position.[48] On 17 April Walsingham told him in a letter that matters were becoming so critical in the Low Countries that he had asked the Queen to allow him to call Leicester home, but she was unwilling to do so because, according to Walsingham, 'after the use of the bath, it would be dangerous for your lordship to take any extraordinary travail. There is some doubt that Ostend will be presently besieged.'[49] But April gave way to May, and still the Earl of Leicester had not left.

Early in June news reached him that Christopher Blount, his Master of the Horse, had been injured, and on 7 June he wrote to him:

> I am sorry Mr Kit for your hurt, and yet glad you have 'scaped so well, considering at whose direction you were, and whereof I was greatly afraid when I heard he had taken you with him [a reflection on Sir John Norreys, perhaps?]. Well I trust now to be with [you] very speedily, and I pray you let me find a fair band at my coming. I bring 200 fair liveries with me for them. Let all my friends understand of my coming, within fifteen days I trust to be in Flushing. My Lord Willoughby will be there by Tuesday next or Wednesday at furthest, so will the Lord Marshal also. There doth come with me 4,000 men which is the cause of my longer stay, but, they are almost ready to come higher.
>
> My Lord of Buckhurst hath almost marred all if it be true is advertised that he hath gone far with the States in the matter of peace, and in other sort doth it seem than ever her Majesty gave him authority . . .
>
> Commend me to my old servant Mrs Madleyn and bid her see all things handsome for me at the Hague against I come and if she be in any want I pray you let her have twenty nobles or £10 till I come.[50]

What had finally precipitated Elizabeth and the Council in general into sending off Leicester with the 4,000 men and £30,000 from the royal coffers was the fact that Sluys appeared likely to fall into Spanish hands, and although it was not of very much importance to the Dutch — who were in any case very reluctant to waste men and ships on it — it was of great strategic importance for the Spanish vis à vis England. In a letter to Burghley dated 30 September 1587, Leicester mentioned 5,000 men, and it would appear from a letter from Walsingham to Buckhurst dated 15 June previous that the Queen had actually intended 6,000, originally. [51] At all events, Leicester left London on 4 July, embarked at Margate, and as he sailed into Flushing past Sluys, heard the sound of the bombardment. [52] Once more complications over lines of command, in this case between Leicester and Prince Maurice of Nassau, delayed decisive action at a crucial moment, and on 29 July Sluys fell. Parma was so impressed with the way in which Sir Roger Williams had defended the port that he offered him service with the Spaniards, not against England, but against the Turks. He refused the offer, but all that Leicester could see was a lack of due deference to himself as commander. As he wrote to Walsingham on 6 August: 'I cannot, for many respects, how well soever I think of Sir Roger Williams' valour and the other captains', give them countenance, or access to me, before they do give some good reason for the delivery of the town without sending to me first.'[53] Walsingham had already pointed out on 2 August: 'The ill success of Sluys though your lordship hath done your uttermost . . . hath wrought some alteration in her Majesty's favour towards you . . . I find there is some dealing underhand against your lordship which proceedeth from the young sort of courtiers that take upon themselves to censure the greatest causes.'[54]

This was probably only too true, but there was one young person who was different, and who seemed to be looking after his interests in his absence, and that was his stepson, the Earl of Essex. As his father had gained the affection of Edward VI, so Leicester had gained the affection of Philip Sidney, Robert Devereux, Earl of Essex, and Christopher Blount. Nor was it a mere coincidence that Sidney bequeathed his best sword to Essex. In July 1587 the latter was with the royal party then staying with the Burghleys at Theobalds. As he wrote to his stepfather:

> She [Elizabeth] hath been long since with her Council. What is decreed I know not . . . I desired her . . . if they laid any matter to your charge, that she would suspend her judgement till she heard

yourself speak. I will watch with the best diligence I can, that your enemies may not take advantage of your absence . . . Your son, most ready to do you service, Essex.[55]

It is highly significant that although Leicester had refused to give up the office of Master of the Horse in 1585 when Elizabeth offered him the post of Lord Steward of the Household, on 18 June this year— 1587 — he now relinquished it, after almost nineteen years, to Essex.[56] Certainly Essex continued to work on the Queen all through the summer, and at the beginning of September was able to write to Leicester:

May it please your lordship, I have divers times since the receipt of your letters, but most earnestly this afternoon, dealt with the Queen for your lordship's return. After she had heard me awhile and the reasons I could allege, she said that there was not a lady in the land that should more desire news of your return than herself . . . many good words she gave of you, expressing her desire to have you here. I doubt not but within short time I shall so labour her mind that I will effect this to your lordship's contentment. Oatlands, this first of September, 1587. Your son, most ready to do you service. R. Essex.[57]

It was at this point that Leicester made his second will. There is a certified copy of it in the Pepys Collection, on which it is dated 1 August 1587.[58] This agrees with Collins, though at the end of it Collins gave the date 5 July. At all events, there is a codicil dated 30 September, and probate was eventually granted on 6 September 1588. A copy dated 11 September 1588 is also in the Pepys Collection. After a long religious preamble, Leicester went on:

Thus being in perfect health and memory, and having set down my faith as a true Christian, and being uncertain of the hour of death, I think it my part to settle my wordly matters in as good estate as I can, specially being hastily and suddenly sent over, and likewise having very little leisure, since my arrival, to get any time for my private business.

For his burial he wanted:

. . . as little pomp or vain expenses of the world, as may be, being persuaded that there is no more vain expenses than that is a convenient tomb or monument I wish there should be. And, for the place where my body should lie, it is hard to appoint, and I know not how

223

> convenient it is to desire it; but I have always wished, as my dear wife
> doth know, and some of my friends, that it might be at Warwick,
> where sundry of my ancestors do lie, either so, or else where the
> Queen's Majesty shall command, for as it was when it had life, a most
> faithful, true, loving servant unto her, so living, and so dead, let the
> body be at her gracious determination, if it shall so please her.

As to the state of his finances, that is made clear with disarming
frankness:

> Touching my bequests, they cannot be great, by reason my ability
> and power is little, for I have not dissembled with the world my
> estate, but have lived always above any living I had (for which I am
> heartily sorry) least that, thro' my many debts, from time to time,
> some men have taken loss by me . . . And first of all, before and
> above all persons, it is my duty to remember my most dear, and most
> gracious sovereign, whose creature under God I have been . . .

Elizabeth was to see to that when the time came. In any case she stood to
gain handsomely from the will. Specifically mentioned was 'the jewel
with three great emeralds with a fair large table diamond in the midst,
without a foil, and set about with many diamonds without foil, and a
rope of fair white pearl[s], to the number six hundred, to hang the said
jewel at'. Apparently this magnificent piece had been intended as a gift
to Elizabeth the next time she came to Wanstead, and in the will
Leicester enjoined his wife to make sure that it was disposed as intended.

As for Lettice herself, there is a slight hint that their marriage was less
than successful in the injunction — or hope: 'I trust this will of mine
shall find her no less mindful of me being gone, than I was always of her
being alive'. Denbigh and Chirk were mortgaged to the tune of
£16,000, and by his own admission Leicester was 'I know not how many
thousand, above twenty in debt'. But this still left more than enough —
Kenilworth to Ambrose, for him 'to build out the gallery which I once
intended', and his stepson Essex got Leicester House, amongst other
things. Christopher Hatton and Howard, Lord Admiral, also benefited,
but it was for Ambrose that perhaps the most touching words were
intended:

> To my dear and noble brother I leave to him, first, as dear an affection
> as ever brother bare to other. And, for a remembrance, I send him a
> cup of gold, which my old friend my Lord of Pembroke gave me, and
> a George, which hath the French order and the English in one, with a

plain gold chain at it. This token he must keep in remembrance, that his brother was of both the orders, and not only so, but also almost the oldest of both the orders in both the realms. But what is this but vanity, and too much vanity for me now to remember them?

It is hard not to respond with sympathy to such a testimony, and feel that the person who wrote it was by no means a total monster, but a human being like any other. There is inevitably an air of *Götterdämmerung*, and out of the ashes we see the phoenix Essex ready to rise — but the future did not lie in that direction.

Essex might well have been looking after Leicester's interests back in England, but there was still the rankling question of the accounts. As the Queen persisted in a memorial in Burghley's hand: 'Though it be continually alleged that great sums are due, yet why such sums are due, or to whom they are due, and who are paid, and who not paid . . . is never certified.'[59] At the other end of the scale, there was a band of ragged, starving soldiers roaming round London, and thirty of them presented themselves at the gates of Greenwich. Burghley did not want the Queen to be troubled, and opened a fund to provide the means for returning them to their homes. Nevertheless the Queen got to hear of them, and ordered that two of them appear before the Privy Council. When Leicester was informed of what they had reported, he said that their captains had been paid everything they had been owed — in other words there was no fault on high, it was lower down that the system failed. As a responsible leader, however, he ought to have made it his business to see that the men at the bottom of the ladder were fairly treated, despite the enormity of the task, for had he done so, his memory would have needed no apologia.

On 16 December 1587 the Council sent a directive to the lord-lieutenants of the counties to the effect that they would take care of any arrears owed to men who had served in the Low Countries. They were to send to Court 'all such soldiers as upon the last levies were sent and served in the Low Countries . . . if they could duly claim and show manifest proof for any wages behind and unpaid for their service . . . they should upon their repair to Court be fully satisfied thereof.'[60] By this time, however, Leicester was pulling out. At the end of November Mendoza, who was in Paris, heard that Leicester was expected in England just as soon as there was a favourable wind, and at the beginning of December he was at Flushing ready to embark.[61] The States sent no leave-taking party, which annoyed him considerably, and he wrote very tetchily on 4 December to his secretary Atey, who was following him: 'God send me shortly a wind to blow me from them all!'[62] He landed at Margate on 19 December. As Stow recorded it:

> And as he sat in his chamber, he clapped his hands upon his legs, saying, '(if God give me leave) these legs of mine shall never go again into Holland. Let the States get other to serve their mercenary turn if they will make themselves rich, for me that shall not have.' After that the States made choice of Grave Maurice [second son of the late Prince of Orange].[63]

This may well have been said in private, but in public Leicester was putting a very different complexion on things. He had medals cast which he gave to his friends, on the reverse of which he was depicted as a dog who unwillingly leaves his flock, with the legends: *Invitus desero* (I quit unwillingly), and *Non gregem sed ingratos* (not the flock, but the ungrateful). Camden described them: 'Tokens made in gold, on the one side whereof was his picture, and on the other . . . some straying sheep, and a dog, ready to go away looking back.'[64] The States, however, saw things in a very different light, and had issued their own medals, to which Leicester's may well have been a riposte, on which they were represented on one side as a man who, having attempted to avoid Spanish smoke, has fallen into Leicester's fire, and on the other side as an ape squeezing its offspring to death out of extreme affection — as they had strangled their liberties in their excessive fondness.

From the official English point of view things were little better. The venture into the Low Countries had been a costly and apparently unproductive mistake. Certainly it was felt that Leicester's personal record needed some investigation at Privy Council level. It was the custom that persons summoned in this way should appear and kneel before the Council until told to rise. Certainly Leicester's father had made use of this form of humiliation when in power, and that was what had been intended for Cecil, no doubt. Leicester could not entertain such a thought, and when the possibility of this kind of investigation was mentioned to him he went to the Queen, threw himself at her feet, and said that he was content to prostrate himself there, but asked her not to let him be degraded in that way before the Council. She agreed, and when the Council met he took his place among his peers. According to Camden, when pressed to give an account of himself, Leicester said that he had acted on secret instructions from the Queen, which he could not disclose to them.[65] It says a great deal for the depth of her affection for him that Elizabeth allowed Leicester to trade upon her personal credit and stature in this way. But in the face of the struggle that was about to come with Spain, it was possible to forgive, if not to forget.

Unfortunately Leicester had created so much ill will for himself, however, that many people were simply not prepared to do either, and the bitterness lingered on, and found its way into many of the accounts, both contemporary and the later ones that perpetuated them. As Speed put it:

> The care of preventing further mischiefs [in the Low Countries], moved her Majesty hereupon to recall the Earl of Leicester into England, well knowing that the kingdom divided could not long stand; who on his return, she commanded to resign his government of the Netherlands in the hands of the General Estates, which was performed by act, signed under his hand, and sent unto them: which resignation received, was presently proclaimed through all the Provinces, to the end that every man might know himself discharged of his oath to the Earl of Leicester.[66]

As we know from other information, this was not quite how it came about, but one detects the satisfaction with which someone wrote those final words. Leicester was, however, to live to fight another day — or if not to fight, then at least to preside over events when the Armada finally launched itself upon England the following year.

10

The Pageant Fades

Here lies the noble warrior that never blunted sword,
Here lies the noble courtier that never kept his word,
Here lies his Excellency that governed all the state,
Here lies the Lord of Leicester that all the world did hate.

Attributed to Sir Walter Raleigh[1]

When Leicester left the Low Countries he committed his general authority to a Council of State and left Lord Willoughby in charge of the forces. In December 1587 he decided to resign, however, but his resignation was not put before the States until March of the following year. Killigrew wrote to Burghley on 18 April that year:

> Since my Lord of Leicester's resignation (which being sent to me enclosed in a letter from your lordship and Mr Secretary dated 22 February I received at Dordrecht the 14th of March, and at my return from thence delivered it to the States General the 21st of the same, not without great suspicion and speech bruited abroad that I had retained the said resignation a long time in my hands, by reason the date thereof was so many months ago [December]) but since the delivery of the same a great change and alteration is fallen out, and good hope of reconcilement.[2]

228

After his resignation it would seem that Leicester lost interest completely in the progress of affairs in the Low Countries, for there is only one letter to Lord Willoughby, for example, that survives.[3] And indeed the official English line was to seek peace, and the commissioners sent over in January 1588 to this end were only recalled when the Armada was actually in the English Channel. Walsingham seems to have used his good offices to make peace between Leicester and Sir Roger Williams and the Norreys family, though there was to be a renewal of friction at the height of the Armada crisis. This was nothing to compare with the deterioration in relations in the Low Countries by any means, however. Through the winter of 1587/8 Walsingham and Leicester worked together in an attempt to induce the Queen, who was procrastinating as usual, to make the necessary preparations for facing the Spanish Armada which they knew must come at some time in the near future, and sooner rather than later.

In February 1588 Hatton, Leicester, Walsingham and Burghley held a meeting to discuss defence, for which the latter put forward a memorandum,[4] and there was a similar meeting of a small committee of the Council to consider naval problems on 18 March,[5] of which Leicester was a member. Indeed, he attended full Council meetings regularly throughout this period. The Armada set sail towards the end of May, but had to seek harbour because of storms and a variety of mishaps, and a certain amount of refitting was necessary, so that it was not until the third week in July that the great fleet finally arrived off the English coast. From 20 July to the 30th the Council met daily at Richmond, and thereafter daily at St James's until 10 August. On 23 July Leicester was made Lieutenant and Captain General of all the Queen's forces 'in the south parts of this our realm, to stay the invasion of our realm by any foreign forces'. The letters patent, dated at Richmond, are still at Longleat.[6] Leicester was to be in charge of the main army at Tilbury, and a second army to guard the Queen's person was based on St James's in London. Even at this point, however, there were logistic problems, and on 5 August Leicester was ordered by the Privy Council to discharge one third of his infantry, choosing those from neighbouring counties so that they could easily be recalled if need be.[7]

At such a crucial moment Elizabeth longed to see for herself what was happening, and expressed the wish to visit the coast, but Leicester forbade it. This may well, however, have suggested to him the master stroke for which, if almost for nothing else, he merits a place in the nation's history. It was decided that she would visit his camp at Tilbury, and accordingly he took for her the Rich house at Little Leighs. On 8 August she went down by barge, but when it came to inspecting the men she donned a steel corselet and mounted on horseback. Being so small, it ensured that she would be seen by as many of the troops as possible. To one observer she was 'like some Amazonian empress'. It was supreme stage-management on Leicester's part, and there was more to come. The next day she returned to make one of her most famous speeches. If she did in fact deliver it on the spot, then not many can have heard her, even with her high, rather penetrating voice. Doubtless it was written down also, and was communicated by the officers to the men. Certainly a version was recorded by one of her chaplains, Dr Lionel Sharp. Either way, the text is the most important thing:

> My loving people, we have been persuaded by some that are careful of our safety, to take heed how we commit ourselves to armed multitudes, for fear of treachery; but I assure you, I do not desire to live in distrust of my faithful and loving people. Let tyrants fear. I have always so behaved myself that under God, I have placed my chiefest strength and good will in the loyal hearts and good will of my subjects; and therefore I am come amongst you, as you see, at this time, not for my recreation and disport, but being resolved, in the midst and heat of battle, to live or die amongst you all; to lay down for God, my kingdom, and for my people, my honour and my blood, even in the dust. I know I have but the body of a weak and feeble woman; but I have the heart and stomach of a king, and a king of England too, and think it foul scorn that Parma or Spain or any prince of Europe, should dare to invade the borders of my realm . . .

As Leicester himself put it in a letter to Lord Shrewsbury, these words 'so inflamed the hearts of her poor subjects as I think the weakest person among them is able to match the proudest Spaniard that dares now land in England.'[8] Fortunately that was never required to be put to the test. The Queen remained there for a week, but danger was averted, and first one, and then the other, returned to London. Leicester's entry, it was noted, was little short of regal also, even if the populace did not greet him with corresponding warmth.

As we shall see later, it seems that Elizabeth had some idea of making Leicester a kind of viceroy, according to Camden, rather on the lines of what she had proposed during her smallpox crisis of 1562, but it was said that Burghley and Hatton so vociferously opposed it that she dropped the plan. Certainly the Queen was not well at this time, and she may have felt, in the aftermath of events, that she needed, or wanted, the sort of working relationship with Leicester that they had enjoyed in that week together at Tilbury when the nation's fate hung so in the balance. Reports had made things seem worse than they were, and at one moment, for example, Parma was said to be embarking. In such moments of crisis people tend to live on a different plane, and try as much as they will afterwards, it is never possible to recapture that spirit merely by exercise of the will. In the celebrations immediately after the defeat of the Armada, Leicester and Elizabeth were almost constantly together, but both were unwell, and Leicester decided to go away for a spell to recuperate. It may have been that his stay on the marshy land by the Thames had brought on an attack of his malaria, but at all events he decided to go to Buxton. One of the last occasions that they shared in public was the Earl of Essex's review in the Tiltyard at Whitehall.

Towards the end of August, then, Leicester set out with Lettice from London. Elizabeth felt the lack of him keenly, almost at once, for hardly had he left than his stepson the Earl of Essex wrote to him from York House on 28 August: 'Since your lordship's departure her Majesty hath been earnest with me to lie in the Court, and this morning she sent to me that I might lie in your lordship's lodging, which I will forbear till I know your lordship's pleasure, except the Queen force me to it . . .'[9] It was almost as if Elizabeth had to fill the void at any cost, and in Essex she saw a rejuvenated Leicester, the Robert of her own youth reincarnate. It was almost as if, with fatal instinct, Elizabeth knew that she would never see Leicester again, and that she had already replaced him.

When Leicester and his wife arrived at Rycote, Lady Norreys gave the earl the room normally reserved for the Queen, and it was from here that he wrote what was to be his last letter to Elizabeth:

I most humbly beseech your Majesty to pardon your old servant to be thus bold in sending to know how my gracious lady doth, and what ease of her pain she finds, being the chiefest thing in the world I do pray for, for her to have good health and long life. For my own poor cause I continue still your medicine and it amends much better than any other thing that hath been given me. Thus hoping to find perfect cure at the bath, with the continuance of my wonted prayer for your Majesty's most happy preservation, I humbly kiss your foot, from your old lodging at Rycote, this Thursday morning, ready to take on my journey, by your Majesty's most faithful, obedient servant, R. Leycester.

There was a postscript: 'Even as I had writ, thus much I received your Majesty's token by young Tracey.'[10] The Queen had sent a gift of some sort for him, or even some more medicine, perhaps, but it was of no avail. Leicester went on to Cornbury, to the Ranger's Lodge, and there he died on 4 September 1588, 'of a continual burning fever', Camden tells us.[11]

On receipt of the news of his death, according to a Spanish agent in London, 'she shut up herself in her chamber alone and refused to speak to anyone, until the Treasurer and other councillors had the doors broken open and entered to see her.'[12] In her own hand she wrote on the docket of the letter she had received 'His last letter', and kept it in the casket by her bed. Early in November a Spanish agent wrote: 'The Queen is much aged and spent and very melancholy. Her intimates say this is caused by the death of the Earl of Leicester', though he ventured that it was rather 'the fear she underwent and the burden she has on her'.[13] Either way, when she went to St Paul's for a service of thanksgiving on 24 November, there was no Leicester by her side. Did it matter, one cannot help but ask, to anyone but herself, and his family?

The climate quickly altered. As early as 16 September Thomas Fowler, Leicester's steward, complained of his inability to collect the duties on sweet wines, since those who owed money were 'slacker to pay now than when he lived'.[14] Indeed, now that his estate was being wound up, as it were, why should they bother? On the contrary, the creditors were closing in, and one of the most interested of these was the Queen herself. One may well imagine that her love of Robert was outweighed by her hatred for Lettice, and the extensive inventories at Longleat dated 28 October 1588 of Leicester House, Wanstead, Kenilworth and Grafton may well have been prepared in connection with the sale of contents.[15] Even so, Lettice was richly left, and though her new young husband ran through her money at an alarming rate, she seemed quite happy to let him do so. In fact the speed with which she married Christopher Blount after Leicester's death shows to what extent she was infatuated. Rumours of the way in which the money was being spent must have prompted the letter at Longleat from Elizabeth Sutton to Lettice, dated 29 December, probably of that year, in which she requests the latter to pay the 'great charge I was at when you, with the young lord [Denbigh?] and other your honour's friends and company, lay with me'.[16] The total cost had been £393 6s 8d, and although Leicester had promised faithfully that she would be reimbursed, nothing had been forthcoming after all this time, which must have been more than four years if it was indeed Lord Denbigh. But then Lettice had no compunction in such matters, and a similar problem prompted the Master of the Leycester Hospital in Warwick, Thomas Cartwright, to write to Burghley two years after Leicester's death, to try and get Lettice to hand over the £200 left the hospital in his will. On a much humbler, but more pathetic note, there is a letter at Longleat from one T. Domhale to Edward Barker, dated 4 July 1589, requesting Lettice to pay him his due. He had served Leicester for three years, 'and never left him alive or dead until I performed my last service unto him, helping to lay his noble corpse in the earth'.[17] In such a way is duty and devotion rewarded.

Not surprisingly, Leicester's son by Douglas Sheffield, Robert Dudley, had great difficulty in his dealings with Lettice and Christopher Blount. When Ambrose, Earl of Warwick died in 1590, Kenilworth passed to young Robert, but before he could take possession, Blount had entered by force and occupied it, and it required the Privy Council to make an order before he could be removed. Blount was executed in the aftermath of Essex's rebellion in 1601, and after the death of the Queen, Robert Dudley began, in May 1603, to attempt to prove that his mother and father had been legally married. This spurred Lettice into action, and in February of the next year she took him to the Star Chamber, which decided ultimately for her, though the issue at stake on that occasion was not the legality of the marriage, but the way in which Robert Dudley had attempted to prove it. His subsequent and highly varied career unfortunately lies beyond the scope of this book. Lettice, however, lived to the age of ninety-two, and raised the vast monument to her husband and herself in the Beauchamp Chapel at Warwick.

The tomb is remarkable by any standards, though in heavy competition with that of Bess of Hardwick in Derby Cathedral, and yet it conveys little of the glory that Robert Dudley actually enjoyed during his lifetime as Elizabeth's favourite. His memory faded with remarkable speed, and only Spenser, commenting on this very lack of public recognition, has left anything at all by way of a lasting tribute:

> He now is dead and all his glories gone
> And all his greatness vapourèd to naught
> That as a glass upon the water shone
> Which vanished quite, as soon as it was sought.
> His name is worn already out of thought
> Ne any poet seeks him to revive
> Yet many poets honoured him alive.[18]

There were, of course, plenty to recall the less worthy deeds, to retail the scandalous gossip, and to add something in the telling, so that the image that has come down to us is still largely coloured in this way.

Camden's appraisal is worth quoting at some length, since it gives us an insight into the prevalent attitude of that time:

> Neither was the public joy [at the defeat of the Armada] anything abated by Leicester's death (though the Queen took it much to heart), who about this time, namely on the 4th day of September, died of a continual fever upon the way as he went towards Kenilworth . . . and now, in the very period of his life, began to entertain new hope of honour and power, by being put into the high authority of lieutenancy under the Queen in the government of England and Ireland. Which indeed he had obtained, the letters patent being drawn, had not Burghley and Hatton prevented it, and the Queen in time foreseen the danger of trusting too great a power in one man's hand. He was esteemed a most accomplished courtier, spruce and neat, free and bountiful to soldiers and students, a cunning time server and respecter of his own advantages, of a disposition ready and apt to please, crafty and subtle towards his adversaries, much given formerly to women, and in his latter days doting extremely upon marriage. But whilst he preferred power and greatness, which is subject to be envied, before solid virtue, his detracting emulators found large matter to speak reproachfully of him, and even when he was in his most flourishing condition spared not disgracefully to defame him by libels, not without mixture of some untruths. In a word, people talked openly in his commendation, but privately he was ill spoken of by the greater part. But whereas he was in the Queen's debt, his goods were sold at a public outcry: for the Queen, though in other things she were favourable enough, yet seldom or never did she remit the debts owing to her treasury.[19]

Most of the 'untruths' found their way into *Leicester's Commonwealth*, and Camden almost takes the same phrase 'crafty and subtle to deceive', suggesting that he was no stranger to that work, perhaps. As the *Commonwealth* continues:

> For as for valour, he [Leicester] hath as much as hath a mouse: his magnanimity, is base sordidity: his liberality, rapine: his friendship, plain fraud, holding only for his gain, and no otherwise, though it were bound with a thousand oaths; of which he maketh great account, as hens do of cackling, but only for his commodity; using

them specially, and in greatest number, when most he meaneth to deceive.[20]

Plainly this was sheer malice, though there were plenty of people ready to voice such views at his death. Sir Robert Naunton, for example, could quite calmly write: 'I may fear he was too well seen in the aphorisms and principles of Nicholas the Florentine [Machiavelli], and in the reaches of Caesar Borgia.'[21] One could multiply the examples, from Dugdale, Stow and Speed, and at best one senses indifference, where there is not actually adverse comment. Strype alone says something positively favourable: '. . . he was a good soldier, a gallant courtier, and a favourer of learning',[22] and it is this which encourages one to look further.

There is a rather illuminating passage written by Francis Bacon, after the death of the Queen, and in relation to the Earl of Essex, but which nevertheless seems to put Leicester's career into perspective:

> Madam, I know not the particulars of estate, and I know this, that princes' actions must have no abrupt periods or conclusions, but otherwise I would think if you had my Lord of Essex here with a white staff in his hand, as my Lord of Leicester had, and continued with him still about you for society to yourself, and for an honour and ornament to your attendance and Court in the eyes of your people, and in the eyes of foreign ambassadors, then were he in his right element . . .[23]

In other words, Essex would have been better off playing the same role that Leicester played at the end of his life, and by implication, had Leicester stuck to that role, his story would have been a happier one.

Elizabeth certainly seems to have had a blind faith in Leicester. Camden was unable to accept that this was simply the attraction that such a handsome, athletic man held for the Queen. Of course to a certain extent any such deep attraction, in Elizabethan terms, was seen as the influence of some sort of spell, and so in this particular instance had to be explained otherwise. Camden suggested some quality which the Queen appreciated but which was, apparently, invisible to anyone else, some 'virtue of his, whereof he gave some shadowed tokens'.[24] He went on to suggest that it could also have been the fact that they shared their 'common condition of imprisonment under Queen Mary', and also the proximity of their births, mentioned at the outset. But it was at best a puzzling thing, whatever theory Camden advanced, and has remained an enigma ever since. It seems hard to accept, for example, that such a remarkable woman should have been so blind in the case of Leicester. True, his influence seemed to fade when she did not see him for any length of time, and then revived when they were together, but to those who find the relationship difficult to accept, or rather explain, the simplest motivation is overlooked or rejected. Which is why the Francis Bacon analysis is so fascinating, especially coming from him. He saw that Elizabeth needed a man for company, and 'an honour and ornament' for herself and her Court. It would have been an extremely difficult role for anyone with any spirit to have carried out, and given the Dudley temperament, one cannot really imagine that Leicester would have been content to play that role and no other. Nevertheless when he did play it, and when the Queen kept him in check, then he did it supremely well. He was probably the nearest person in the land to the ideal of the complete man of the Renaissance, and he could offer Elizabeth under one roof, as it were, all the qualities she liked to find in men, but which those around her only possessed as individual attributes or in small proportion when compared with Leicester.

It is hardly surprising, then, that he was an object of jealousy and envy, and that his failings should be so criticised. Only a person with charisma could have carried it off, and charisma was something which, by all accounts, Leicester patently did not have. But in any case, at the Court of Elizabeth only one person might have charisma, and that was the Queen herself. Was it Leicester's fault that he was not, and by the very nature of things could not have been, on a par with Elizabeth? Could there ever have been room for such a man, and had he existed, would the history of England have been the same?

SOURCE NOTES

CHAPTER ONE

1 See, for example, the Dictionary of National Biography (hereafter referred to as DNB), though with reservations

2 Aerary of St George's Chapel, Windsor Castle X, 4 23

3 I am indebted to Miss M. M. Condon of the Public Record Office for this information

4 Polydore Vergil, *Anglicae historiae libri XXVI* (1555). See also D. M. Brodie 'Edmund Dudley, minister of Henry VII', in *Transactions of the Royal Historical Society*, 4th series, XV (1932), 131–61

5 *Historical Manuscripts Commission* (hereafter referred to as HMC) Middleton, 126

6 'The petition of Edmund Dudley'; see *English Historical Review* LXXXVII (1972), 82–99

7 British Museum (hereafter referred to as BM) Lansdowne MS 127, 9 Sep. 1504– 28 May 1508

8 *The Tree of Commonwealth* has been published in a modern edition by D. M. Brodie (1948)

9 DNB — but see above

10 Calendar of State Papers Domestic (hereafter referred to as Cal. S. P. Dom.) 21 Mar. 1540, and Strype, J., *Ecclesiastical Memorials*, London (1721), 504

11 Camden, W., *The History of . . . Elizabeth*, London (1675), 419

12 Adlard, G., *Amy Robsart and the Earl of Leicester*, London (1870), 16

13 De la Forêt, *Dépêches*, 6 Aug. 1566 (St Germain vol.739), quoted in Von Raumer, *Elizabeth and Mary Stuart*, London (1836), 40

14 Ascham, R., *Works*, ed. J. A. Giles, London (1864–5), II 101–4

15 After Edmund Dudley's execution, his widow married a second time, in 1515, Sir Arthur Plan-

tagenet, a natural son of Edward IV by Lady Elizabeth Lucy. Plantagenet became Viscount Lisle in the right of his wife in 1523, on the death of her brother John, with whom she had been co-heir. The patent is in HMC 621; U1475; F30/1 in the Sidney-De Lisle papers in the Kent Archives Office — see catalogue p 75. There were three daughters of this second marriage (Bridget, the eldest, marrying Sir William Camden). It was thus, on Plantagenet's death in 1542, that the title came to John Dudley.

16 Cal. S.P. Dom. 24 Mar. 1547
17 Cal. S.P. Dom. 10 Aug. 1549
18 BM Harleian MS 353, 130
19 Cal. S.P. Spanish (hereafter referred to as Cal. S.P. Span.) 14 Jan. 1550
20 BM Cotton Nero CX — this has been published in a modern edition by W. K. Jordan, London (1966). See p.33
21 Acts of the Privy Council (hereafter referred to as APC) 27 Apr. 1550
22 HMC Hatfield I 337
23 Strype, *op. cit.*, I 493 and 459
24 DNB
25 Strype, *op. cit.*, II 393
26 His mother Mary was the eldest daughter of the Duke of Northumberland, and married Sir Henry Sidney. The settlement is HMC 613A; U1475; T327/2 in the Kent Archives catalogue p 68. Had Sir Philip lived, he was Robert Dudley's heir, and would have inherited the title of Earl of Leicester. As it was his brother Robert succeeded
27 HMC 1225; U1475/23 — an eighteenth-century copy. See also *Complete Works of Sir Philip*

Sidney, ed. A. Feuillerat, Cambridge (1922–6) III 66–70
28 APC 3 Oct. 1551 and 24 Jan. 1552
29 Strype, *op. cit.*, III 14. See also BM Cotton Vitellius 5
30 Cal. S.P. Span. 1558-67
31 HMC Pepys II 543
32 Kent Archives catalogue p.355
33 BM Cotton Nero CX 8 Nov. 1551. Jordan, *op. cit.*, 94–5
34 *Leicester's Commonwealth*, ed. F. J. Burgoyne, London (1904), p 204
35 HMC Pepys II 729
36 BM Cotton Galba C IX 113
37 Strype, *op. cit.*, II 501
38 Cal. S.P. Dom. 2 Jun. 1552
39 This probably accounts for the strange footnote in Jordan, *op. cit.*, p 124, that Northumberland's wife and his son Ambrose had just died, which is patently wrong, since they both outlived him. This was Ambrose's first wife, Anne Whorwood
40 Cal. S.P. Dom. 28 Oct. 1552
41 *ibid.*, 7 Dec. 1552
42 *ibid.*, 14 Jan. 1553
43 Strype, *op. cit.*, 520
44 *ibid., loc. cit.*
45 Nichols, J. (ed.), *Literary Remains of Edward VI*, London (1857–8), ccxiv *et seqq*
46 Strype, *op. cit.*, 425. There was also a match envisaged for the youngest sister, Mary Grey, but since she was barely in her teens, and a hunchback, she escaped matrimony at this juncture. Also, Andrew Dudley, John's brother, was to marry Margaret Clifford, daughter of the Earl of Cumberland and Eleanor Brandon, sister to Frances, and therefore daughter to Mary Tudor, sister of Henry VIII
47 *ibid., loc. cit.*

48 Longleat Dudley MSS Box II 2
49 Strype, *op. cit.*, 237
50 Nichols, J. G. (ed.), *Chronicle of Queen Jane*, London (1850), 5. BM Harleian 194
51 Stow, J., *Annals . . .*, London (1631), 611
52 *Chronicle of Queen Jane*, 17
53 Tytler, P., *England under the Reigns of Edward VI and Mary*, London (1839), II 228–9
54 Rowse, A., *The English Spirit*, London (1944), 136 — quoted without reference
55 Aerary of St George's Chapel, Windsor Castle, F 3
56 *Chronicle of Queen Jane*, 25
57 APC 10 Sep. 1553
58 *Chronicle of Queen Jane*, 35
59 APC 5 Jun. 1554
60 Collins, A., *Sidney Papers*, London (1746), I 31
61 Strype, *op. cit.*, III 202
62 Stow, *op. cit.*, 648. Collins (*op. cit.*, I 33) says that Ambrose was pardoned for life, though not restored in blood, on 6 Jun. 1 & 2 Ph. & Mar., then on p 36 restored in blood, along with the others, 4 & 5 Ph. & Mar., by act of parliament. In a document in the Sidney-De Lisle papers (T1, Kent Archives catalogue p 453), dated 4 Mar. 1556, he is still referred to as Sir Ambrose Dudley. Robert was pardoned by letters patent dated 22 Jan. 1555, the day his mother died (Longleat Dudley MSS Box 1 a)
63 Strype, *op. cit.* III, 209
64 Longleat Dudley MSS Box I a
65 Cal. S.P. Venetian (hereafter referred to as Cal. S.P. Ven.) 13 May 1557
66 Cal. S.P. Foreign (hereafter referred to as Cal. S.P. For.) 6 Aug. 1562
67 Strype, *op. cit.*, III 314
68 HMC Pepys I 29
69 BM Harleian 4712
70 *ibid*
71 Longleat Dudley MSS III 192
72 *ibid.*, III 27b-28
73 *ibid.*, XIV, 20 Dec. 1558–20 Dec. 1559
74 *ibid.*, XIV 32
75 Nichols, J., *Progresses of Queen Elizabeth*, London (1788), II 613

CHAPTER TWO

1 Cal. S.P. Span. 25 Oct. 1562 — Simancas, BM Add. MS 26056a
2 Strype, J., *Annals*, London (1709) 10
3 Dee, J., *Diary*, quoted in E. Jenkins, *Elizabeth and Leicester*, London (1972) 51
4 Strype, *op. cit.*, 188–9
5 *ibid.*, 190
6 *ibid.*, 192–3, but Stow's *Annals*, London (1631), 640 B23, says that Robert Dudley went as far as Harwich
7 Longleat Dudley MSS I 14
8 *ibid.*, 52
9 *ibid.*, 146
10 Cal. S.P. Span. 18 Apr. 1559
11 Cal. S.P. Ven. 4 May 1559
12 Cal. S.P. Span. 19 Jun. 1559
13 *ibid.*, 30 May 1559
14 Murray, J., *English Dramatic Companies*, Boston (1910) II 119
15 Cal. S.P. Span. 12 Jul. 1559
16 *ibid.*, 7 Sep. 1559
17 *ibid.*, *loc. cit.*
18 *ibid.*, 13 Nov. 1559
19 *ibid.*, 18 Nov. 1559
20 Longleat Dudley MSS Box II 6
21 *ibid.*, 4
22 Cal. S.P. Span. 7 Mar. 1560
23 *ibid.*, 28 Mar. 1560
24 Cal. S.P. Dom. 13 Aug. 1560

25 Cal. S.P. Span. 11 Sep. 1560
26 *ibid., loc. cit.*
27 HMC Pepys II 705.
28 *ibid., loc. cit.*
29 *ibid.*, II 703
30 *ibid.*, II 711
31 Aird, I., 'The Death of Amy Robsart', *English Historical Review*, Jan 1956
32 HMC Pepys II 707
33 HMC Hatfield I 252
34 Longleat Dudley MSS IV 23
35 HMC Hatfield I 251
36 Waugh, E., *Edmund Campion*, London (1935) 9 & 11
37 HMC Hatfield I 252
38 *ibid., loc. cit.*
39 *ibid.*, 253. See also 255 (items 810 and 811)
40 BM Add. MSS 35834–6, 35841, I 121–3
41 *ibid.*, 163–5
42 *ibid.*, 167
43 *ibid.*, 168
44 Cal. S.P. Span. 22 Jan. 1561
45 HMC Hatfield I 257
46 Longleat Dudley MSS I 183
47 Bruce Williamson, J., *The History of the Temple*, London (1924) 170 *et seqq.*, and Inderwick, F., *A Calendar of the Inner Temple records*, London (1896) I lxii–lxiv 215–9
48 Cal. S.P. Span. 30 Jun. 1561
49 Cardinal Granvella, *Memoirs*
50 Strype, J., *Life of Matthew Parker*, London (1711), I 212–4
51 Nichols, J., *Progresses* London (1788 ed.) 62 — year 1561 (this earlier edition is not paginated consecutively throughout)
52 BM Harleian 6286
53 HMC Pepys I 45
54 *ibid.*, 71
55 *ibid.*, 251
56 *ibid.*, 61
57 *ibid.*, II 667
58 Longleat Dudley MSS Box V 146–51
59 HMC Pepys I 31 and Dudley-De Lisle papers HMC 857; U1415; FO 30/2 (Kent Archives catalogue p 75)
60 *cf.*, Chapter one *n*.60
61 Talbot papers P 409
62 Lloyd, D., *State Worthies*, London (1670 ed.) 519
63 Longleat Dudley MSS Box II 8; and 7 is Sir Francis Englefield's surrender of same. Item 9 is the assignment, dated 26 Feb. 1562, of the Constableship of Warwick Castle and the Stewardship of Warwick from Sir Robert Throckmorton to Robert Dudley
64 Cal. S.P. For. 8 May 1562
65 HMC XII vii (Ancaster MSS, Grimsthorpe) 258
66 HMC Beverley 182
67 Rye, W., *The Murder of Amy Robsart*, London (1886) 79–80. Sir Andrew Dudley's will is at Longleat (Dudley MSS Box II 3). There is a letter from Montague to Robert Dudley about poundage at HMC Pepys I 399, and an assignment for woollen cloths at Longleat Dudley MSS Box II 10
68 Cal. S.P. Span. 20 Jun. 1562
69 Holinshed, R. (et al.), *Chronicles*, London (1577) IV 133
70 Cal. S.P. For. 27 Jul. 1562
71 *ibid.*, 15 Oct. 1562
72 Cal. S.P. Span. 25 Oct. 1562
73 Carew, R., *Memoirs*, 1628, see Halliday, F., in *History Today*, Aug. 1955
74 Quoted in Jenkins, *Elizabeth the Great*, London (1958), 108
75 Conway MSS, quoted by J. A. Froude in his *History of England* (1863) VII 384
76 BM Cotton Titus F 1 61–4
77 Cal. S.P. For. 23 Jan. 1563
78 HMC Hatfield I 295
79 Cal. S.P. Span. 28 Mar. 1563
80 Jenkins, E., *Elizabeth and Leices-*

ter, 110–111

81 Cal. S.P. Scottish (hereafter referred to as Cal. S.P. Scot.) Oct. 1565 (233)

82 *Archaeologia* XIII 201 (1800)

83 Forbes, P., *Public Transactions in the Reign of Elizabeth*, London (1740–41) II 486–7

84 *ibid., loc. cit.*

85 Strype, J., *Life of Matthew Parker*, London (1711) I 235

86 Cal. S.P. Span. 1 Sep. 1563

87 Longleat Dudley MSS Box II 12

88 Rye, *op. cit.*, 80

89 Longleat Dudley MSS Box II 11 and Box I D

CHAPTER THREE

All the references in this chapter are from HMC Pepys I & II, unless there are indications to the contrary.

1 I 87

2 I 91

3 I 95

4 HMC Hatfield I 290–91

5 *ibid.*, 301–2

6 *ibid*, 336–7

7 I 101

8 I 109

9 I 117

10 I 121

11 I 129

12 Bell, H., *The Huntingdon Peerage*, London (1820) 64–5

13 HMC Hatfield I 296

14 I 193

15 Cal. S.P. For. 15 Jun. 1564

16 *ibid.*, 14 Jun. 1564

17 I 131

18 I 125

19 I 167

20 I 171

21 I 175

22 I 183

23 I 179

24 II 663

25 I 187

26 Longleat Dudley MSS Box V 147

27 Cal. S.P. Span. 27 Jun. 1564

28 *ibid.*, 6 Aug. 1564

29 II 525

30 Longleat Dudley MSS Box IV 99

31 Nichols, J., *Progresses*, I 154

32 *ibid.*

33 *ibid.*

34 Cal. S.P. Span. 23 Sep. 1564

35 Haynes, S. (ed.), *Burghley State Papers*, London (1740), 420

36 Cal. S.P. Span. 23 Sep. 1564

37 Melville, J., *Memoirs*, Edinburgh (1827 ed.), 119

38 Stow, *op. cit.*, 657–8 B58

39 Melville, *op. cit.*, 120

40 Strype, J., *Annals*, 412

41 I 217, *cf.* Cal. S.P. For. 30 Sep. 1564

42 I 223

43 Cal. S.P. Span. 9 Oct. 1564

44 I 223

45 I 283, *cf.* Cal. S.P. For. 14 Dec. 1564

46 I 353

47 I 351

48 Wright, T., *Queen Elizabeth and her Times*, London (1838), I 181

49 Cal. S.P. Span. 2 Jan. 1565

50 *ibid.*

51 Longleat Dudley MSS Box II 14

52 II 677

53 Strype, *op. cit.*, 432

54 I 315

55 I 339

56 BM Add. MS 32091 172

57 I 361

58 II 701

59 Strype, *op. cit.*, 235

60 I 227

61 Strype, J., *Life of Matthew Parker*, II (appendix) 76–84

62 I 363

63 Cal. S.P. Span. 2 Jan. 1565

64 I 373, *cf.* Cal. S.P. For. 28 Mar. 1565
65 I 323
66 I 157
67 I 199
68 I 207
69 I 255
70 *ibid.*
71 I 357, *cf.* Cal. S.P. For. 12 Feb. 1565

72 II 749 and I 379
73 I 501
74 I 509
75 *ibid.*
76 Egmont went to Spain at the beginning of February, *cf.* Cal. S.P. For. 1564/5
77 I 545

CHAPTER FOUR

1 BM Lansdowne 102 59
2 Cal. S.P. Scot. 5 Feb: 1565
3 *ibid.*, 1 May 1565
4 HMC Pepys II 749 and I 379
5 *ibid.*, I 403
6 *ibid.*, I 383
7 *ibid.*, I 395
8 Cal. S.P. Span. 6 Jun. 1565
9 HMC Pepys I 377
10 *ibid.*, I 405
11 Cal. S.P. Span. 2 Jul. 1565
12 *ibid.*, 23 Jul. 1565
13 Wright, *op. cit.*, I 206–7
14 Murdin, W. (ed.), *Burghley State Papers*, London (1759), 760
15 Longleat Dudley MSS Box II 15
16 Cal. S.P. Span. 6 Aug. 1565
17 Strype, J., *Annals*, 477
18 HMC Pepys I 419
19 Wright, *op. cit.*, I 207–8
20 Cal. S.P. Span. 3 Sep. 1565
21 HMC Pepys II 593
22 *ibid.*, I 387
23 Cal. S.P. Span. 17 Sep. 1565
24 Leland, J., *Collectanea*, II
25 HMC Pepys I 443
26 *ibid.*, I 461, *cf.* Cal. S.P. For. of same date
27 *ibid.*, I 443
28 *ibid.*, I, 429, 451, 453, dated 5, 17 and 18 Oct. 1565
29 *ibid.*, I 435, dated 7 Oct. 1565
30 *ibid.*, I 457
31 Stow, J., *Chronicle*, 659 B4

32 *Notes and Queries*, 6th series, iii (1881), 283–4
33 HMC Pepys I 469
34 *ibid.*, I 477
35 Raumer, F. von, *Elizabeth and Mary Stuart*, London (1836), 37
36 *ibid.*, 39
37 *ibid.*, *loc. cit.*
38 HMC Pepys I 489
39 *ibid.*, I 497
40 *ibid.*, I 517
41 Von Raumer, *op. cit.*, 39
42 Swinburne, H., *A Treatise of Spousals*, London (1686), 219–20
43 Perkins, W., *Of Christian Economy* IV, in *Works* (1617 ed.), III 673
44 HMC Pepys I 505
45 Cal. S.P. Span. 4 Feb. 1566
46 *ibid.*, 11 Feb. 1566
47 HMC Pepys I 521
48 *ibid.*, I 525
49 Cal. S.P. Scot. 25 Feb. 1566
50 HMC Pepys I 533
51 *ibid.*, I 549, *cf.* Cal. S.P. For. of same date
52 *ibid.*, I 533
53 *ibid.*, I 247
54 Von Raumer, *op. cit.*, 39
55 HMC Pepys I 573
56 *ibid.*, I 681
57 *ibid.*, I 577, *cf.* Cal. S.P. Dom. Add. 1566–79, 31 Mar. 1566

and 3 & 4 Apr. 1566

58 Bradford, C., *Helena Marchioness of Northampton*, London (1936), 179
59 HMC Pepys I 605
60 *ibid.*, I 609
61 *ibid.*, I 613
62 *ibid.*, I 631
63 *ibid.*, I 617
64 *ibid.*, I 625
65 *ibid.*, I 627
66 *ibid.*, I 633
67 *ibid.*, I 99
68 Melville, *op. cit.*, 131
69 Rye, *op. cit.*, 80–81
70 Longleat Dudley MSS vol. XVII
71 *ibid.*, Box II, 16
72 *ibid.*, Box V 146–151, 215, 237
73 De la Forêt, *Dépêches*, quoted in Von Raumer, *op. cit.*, 40
74 Cal. S.P. Span. 30 Aug. 1566
75 Nichols, *op. cit.*, 3, under year 1566
76 Cal. S.P. Dom. 3 Sep. 1566
77 HMC Pepys I 639
78 Cal. S.P. Span. 4 Nov. 1566
79 HMC Pepys I 651
80 *ibid.*, I 659, 655, *cf.* Cal. S.P.

For. 19 Dec. 1566

81 *ibid.*, I 559
82 Cal. S.P. For. 5 Nov. 1566
83 HMC Pepys I 689, *cf.* Cal. S.P. For. of same date, and I 713
84 *ibid.*, II 756, 761
85 Cal. S.P. Span. 25 Jan. 1567
86 HMC Pepys I 585
87 *ibid.*, I 685
88 *ibid.*, I 701
89 Cal. S.P. Span. 17 Feb. 1567
90 HMC Pepys I 665
91 *ibid.*, I 693
92 *ibid.*, I 709, *cf.* Cal. S.P. For. 1 Mar. 1567, and I 717 and II 623
93 *ibid.*, I 697
94 *ibid.*, I 721
95 *ibid.*, I 569
96 *ibid.*, I 725
97 *ibid.*, I 733
98 Cal. S.P. Dom. Add. 4 May 1567
99 HMC Pepys I 737
100 *ibid.*, *loc. cit.*
101 *ibid.*, II 717, *cf.* HMC Hatfield I 350, items 1151–5 inclusive
102 Longleat Thynne MSS III 164
103 HMC Pepys I 799

CHAPTER FIVE

All the references in this chapter are from HMC Pepys I & II, unless there are indications to the contrary.

1 I 767
2 Cal. S.P. For. 24 Jul. 1567
3 *ibid.*, 26 Jul. 1567
4 *ibid.*, 6 Aug. 1567
5 *ibid.*, 14 Aug. 1567
6 Cal. S.P. Dom. 15 Nov. 1567
7 HMC Bath II 17 & 19, *cf.* Cal. S.P. Dom. 15 Nov. 1567
8 Longleat Dudley MSS Box II 17
9 *ibid.*, Box V 258, 261
10 II 213, *cf.* Cal. S.P. For. 29 Jan. 1568

11 I 771, *cf.* Cal. S.P. For. 30 Mar. 1568; and I 783, *cf.* Cal. S.P. For. 8 Apr. 1568
12 I 787
13 I 775
14 I 791
15 II 23
16 Rye, *op. cit.*, 81
17 There are some 15 letters in HMC Pepys between 14 Jul. and 30 Sep. 1568
18 I 803, *cf.* Cal. S.P. For. 29 Jun. 1568

19 II 65
20 I 15, cover at III 902c
21 II 29
22 II 33 & 41
23 II 61
24 II 67
25 II 71, *cf*. Cal. S.P. For. of same date
26 II 85
27 II 95
28 II 73 & 75
29 II 91
30 II 115 & 123
31 II 153
32 II 161
33 II 125, *cf*. Cal. S.P. For. 8 Dec. 1568
34 II 133
35 II 169
36 II 129
37 II 137
38 II 145 & 149
39 II 157
40 II 143
41 II 103
42 Peck, F., *Desiderata Curiosa*, London (1732) I 15–16
43 De la Mothe Fénelon, *Correspondence*, Paris (1838–40) I 233 ff
44 Cal. S.P. Span. 15 Jun. 1569
45 II 173
46 II 203
47 II 223
48 II 187
49 II 239
50 II 175

51 II 273
52 II 307
53 Collins, *op. cit.*, I 61
54 II 185
55 II 269
56 II 359, *cf*. Cal. S.P. For. 11 & 15 Jan. 1569
57 II 227, 257, 263, *cf*. Cal. S.P. For. 6 Apr. 1569, 279, 281, 293
58 II 301
59 II 569
60 II 365
61 Cal. S.P. Span. 1 Jul. 1569
62 II 315
63 Peck, *op. cit.*, VIII 47a
64 *Confession of the Duke of Norfolk*, quoted by Froude, *op. cit.*, IX 474
65 II 331
66 Froude, *op. cit.*, *loc. cit.*
67 II 349
68 II 651
69 II 357
70 II 341
71 II 345
72 Cal. S.P. Dom. Add. 1566–79
73 *ibid.*, *loc. cit.*
74 Cal. S.P. Span. 30 Jan. 1570
75 Cal. S.P. Dom. Add. 1566–79
76 Harleian miscellany
77 Cal. S.P. Span. 5 Aug. 1570
78 II 371
79 II 375
80 II 633
81 II 383

CHAPTER SIX

1 Cal. S.P. Span. 9 Jan. 1571
2 De la Mothe Fénelon, *Correspondence*, II 141–2
3 Digges, D., *Compleat Ambassador*, London (1655 ed.), 28–30
4 Longleat Dudley MSS Vol. I item 72 f.214
5 Digges, *op. cit.*, 47
6 Cal. S.P. Dom. Add. 1566–79

7 HMC Hatfield I 474
8 HMC Pepys I 235
9 D'Ewes, S., *The Journals of all the Parliaments during the Reign of Queen Elizabeth*, London (1682 ed.) 147, 229; Collins, *op. cit.*, I 45–6
10 Cal. S.P. Span. 10 May 1571
11 Cal. S.P. Ven. 7 Jun. 1571

12 Jenkins, E., *Elizabeth and Leicester*, 203
13 Cal. S.P. Ven. 28 Sep. 1571
14 HMC Hatfield I 1348, 1366, 1375
15 Cal. S.P. For. 8 Oct. 1571
16 Cal. S.P. Dom. Add. 1566–79
17 Dugdale, W., *Antiquities of Warwick and Warwick Castle*, Warwick (1786) 131–2; see also Sidney-De Lisle papers, Kent Archives catalogue 443, Z41
18 *ibid.*, 154
19 Cal. S.P. For. 8 Jan. 1572
20 Digges, *op. cit.*, 164, 166
21 HMC Pepys II 647
22 *ibid.*, II 389
23 Longleat Dudley MSS Box IV 77
24 Pennant, T., *A Tour in Wales*, London (1819 ed.), II 170
25 BM Cotton Vespasian F VI 77
26 Nichols, *Progresses*
27 Longleat Dudley MSS Box II 34
28 DNB, under Berkeley
29 Digges, *op. cit.*, 264–5, 270, 345
30 Stow, *Chronicle*, 673 B18
31 Digges, *op. cit.*, 274
32 *ibid.*, *loc. cit.*
33 *ibid.*, 288
34 BM Cotton Caligula C III 408
35 Murdin, *op. cit.*, (1754 ed.), 231
36 HMC XIII pt.vii
37 HMC XII pt.ix 469
38 HMC XIII pt.vii
39 Longleat Dudley MSS Vol. III 125
40 Feuillerat, A., *Accounts of the Office of Revels*, London (1908)
41 Lodge, *op. cit.*, (1838 ed.) II 17
42 Holles, G., *Memorials of the Holles Family*, London (1937) 70
43 *Leicester's Commonwealth*, 37
44 Dugdale, W., *Baronage*, London (1675-6 ed.) II 222 *et seqq.*
45 Longleat Dudley MSS boxes VI to VIII inclusive
46 Dugdale, *Antiquities*, 166b/167a
47 Read, C., 'A letter from Robert Earl of Leicester to a lady' in *Huntington Library Bulletin*, April 1936 15–26
48 Dugdale, *Antiquities*, 167a
49 Longleat Dudley MSS Box III 36
50 *ibid.*, 37
51 Rye, *op. cit.*
52 Longleat Dudley MSS Vol. XII
53 Blundeville, T., *The True Order . . .*, dedication
54 Collins, *op. cit.*, 168 (of letters section, and misplaced at this point)
55 Dee, J., *Compendious Rehearsal*
56 Nichols, J., *The History and Antiquities of the County of Leicestershire*, London (1795–1815), I 536

CHAPTER SEVEN

1 HMC Pepys II 607
2 *ibid.*, II 609
3 *ibid.*, II 517
4 Dugdale, *Antiquities*, 165b–166a
5 Longleat Dudley MSS Box III 38
6 Dugdale, *op. cit.*, 230a
7 Laneham, R., *Entertainment at Kenilworth*, London (1821) 55
8 BM Harleian MS 6395, para. 221 (a book of *Merry Passages and Jeasts*, collected by Sir Nicholas L'Estrange of Hunstanton, Bart., died 1669)
9 Shakespeare, W., *A Midsummer Night's Dream* II i 148 *et seqq.*
10 Halpin, N., *Oberon's Vision*, London (1843), 44
11 Camden, *Annals*, 1583
12 Dugdale, *op. cit.*, 681a
13 Laneham, *op. cit.*, 45
14 Halpin, *op. cit.*, 27, and

Nichols, *Progresses*
15 Cal. S.P. Span. 5 Dec. 1575
16 Longleat Dudley MSS Box III 39 and 40
17 *ibid.*, *loc. cit.*, 41
18 Gorhambury MSS B VIII 143 ff. 2v–3v (Ambrose Wood's commonplace book, deposited in the Hertfordshire Record Office, Hertford)
19 *ibid.*, ff. 24r–24v
20 Collinson, P., 'Letters of Thomas Wood, Puritan, 1566–1577' in *Bulletin of the Institute of Historical Research*, special supplement no.5, Nov. 1960, xxxi
21 Camden, *op. cit.*, 288
22 *ibid.*, 167a–b
23 Jenkins, E., *Elizabeth and Leicester*, 254

24 Longleat Dudley MSS Vol. II 51 f. 173
25 HMC Hatfield II 154
26 Talbot papers P 819
27 Cal. S.P. For. 16 Aug. 1577
28 *ibid.*, *loc. cit.*
29 *ibid.*, 28 Sep. 1577
30 *ibid.*, 3 Oct. 1577
31 *ibid.*, *loc. cit.*
32 Odberg, F., *Om Princessan Cecilia Wasa*, Stockholm (1896)
33 Cal. S.P. For. 9 Mar. 1578
34 BM Harleian Roll b35 I–XI
35 Cal. S.P. Span. 3 Jun. 1578
36 Longleat Dudley MSS Vol. II 178 & 181
37 Cal. S.P. For. 24 Jun. 1578
38 BM Add. MS 15891 53
39 Rye, *op. cit.*, 82
40 Cal. S.P. For. 7 Aug. 1578
41 Nichols, *Progresses* II 219

CHAPTER EIGHT

1 Collins, A. *Peerage*, London (1812 ed.), IV 461–2
2 Longleat Dudley MSS Vol. III 19 f.61 and Box IV 84
3 Cal. S.P. Dom. 27 Sep. 1578
4 Nichols, *Progresses* II 249–52
5 De Mauvissière, *Correspondence*
6 Cal. S.P. For. 28 Feb. 1579
7 Nichols, J. *Leicestershire* I 536
8 Cal. S.P. Span. 18 Feb. 1579
9 Cal. S.P. For. 27 Mar. 1579
10 Cal. S.P. Dom. Add. 1566–79 25 Apr. 1579
11 Camden, *History* II 95
12 Cal. S.P. For. 9 May 1579
13 Lodge, *Illustrations of British History* II 212, London (1791)
14 Cal. S.P. Span. 14 May 1579
15 Camden, *Annals* (1635 ed.) 205 (In 1578 Alençon took the title of Anjou vacated by his brother when he became king in 1574)
16 Greville, F., *Life of Sir Philip Sidney*, Oxford (1907 ed.) 60
17 BM Add. MS 15891 54b
18 BM Harleian MS 6992 57
19 Rye *op. cit.*, 83
20 Longleat Dudley MSS Vol. II 202
21 Cal. S.P. Span. 22 Aug. 1579
22 *ibid.*, 25 Aug. 1579
23 *ibid.*, 5 Sep. 1579
24 *ibid.*, 25 Aug. 1579
25 Sidney, P., *Works* (ed. A. Feuillerat) Cambridge (1912–26) III 51–60
26 Murdin, *Burghley State Papers*, 322-36
27 Longleat Dudley MSS Box III 54
28 *ibid.*, Vol. V 10–11v & 11-12r
29 Sidney-De Lisle papers, HMC F10 / V1475 / C6 / 9 and HMC B18/II 92/ C6/10 (Kent Archives Catalogue 84)
30 BM Cotton Titus B VII 90
31 Klarwill, V. von, *Queen Elizabeth*

and Some Foreigners, London (1928)
32 Cal. S.P. Span. 6 Apr. 1581
33 *ibid.*, 5 Jun. 1581
34 Hume, M., *Courtships of Queen Elizabeth*, London (1904)
35 Dee, J., *Diary* (Camden Soc. ed.) London (1842) 11–12
36 Read, C., *Lord Burghley and Queen Elizabeth*, London (1960) 565, *n*.57
37 Longleat Dudley MSS Vol. XVIII
38 *ibid.*, Box III 55
39 Cal. S.P. Span. 24 Nov. 1581
40 Longleat Dudley MSS Box III 56
41 Cal. S.P. Dom. Add. 1580-1625 27 Jan. 1581
42 Cal. S.P. Span.
43 Jenkins, E., *Elizabeth and Leicester*, 313
44 BM Add. MS 15891 58b
45 Cal. S.P. Span. 17 Mar. 1583
46 BM Add. MS 15891
47 Naunton, R., *Fragmenta Regalia*, London (1870) 49
48 Camden *op. cit.*, 286
49 Longleat Dudley MSS Vol. VI
50 Sidney-De Lisle papers HMC 646/E92 (Kent Archives Catalogue 359)
51 Von Raumer, *op. cit.*, 257
52 *ibid.*, 258–9
53 Cal. S.P. Dom. Add. 1580-1625 Oct. 1583

54 Von Raumer, *op. cit.*, 257
55 *ibid.*, 269–70
56 BM Harleian 1582 370
57 Longleat Dudley MSS Box III 59
58 Cal. S.P. For. 1 May 1584
59 Tomkys, J., *A Sermon Preached . . . before . . . the Earl of Leicester*, pub. 1586 (STC 24110)
60 Nichols, *Leicestershire* I 403
61 Cal. S.P. Dom. 31 Jul. 1584
62 Cal. S.P. Dom. Add. 1580-1625
63 Sidney-De Lisle papers, HMC A116/U1475–253/29; Collins I 297–8 (Kent Archive Catalogue 446)
64 Longleat Dudley MSS Vol. VII
65 *Leicester's Commonwealth* 50
66 BM Add. MS 15891 128
67 Cal. S.P. Scot. 2 Aug. 1584
68 BM Cotton Titus B VII 10
69 e.g. HMC XIII pt.iv 332
70 Murdin, *Burghley State Papers*, 436–7
71 Cal. S.P. For. 30 Mar. 1585
72 Longleat Dudley MSS Vol. VIII 4
73 Cal. S.P. Dom. Add. 1580-1625 2 Apr. 1585
74 Cal. S.P. Span. 12 May 1585
75 *ibid.*, 1 Jun. 1585
76 Warrender papers (ed. Cameron, Scottish Historical Society, 1931 ed.) CXV I 187

CHAPTER NINE

1 Motley, J., *History of the United Netherlands*, London (1867) I 307
2 Strype, J., *Life and Acts of John Whitgift, DD*, I iii 434
3 Cal. S.P. Dom. 14 Aug. 1585
4 BM Lansdowne 102 122
5 *ibid.*, 45 34
6 Longleat Talbot MSS I 107
7 HMC Hatfield II 108 item 192

8 BM Cotton Galba C VIII 134
9 Cal. For. 5 Sep. 1585
10 Cal. S.P. Dom. 21 Sep. 1585
11 BM Harleian MS 285 135
12 *ibid.*, 146
13 *ibid.*, 133
14 BM Harleian MS 6993 119
15 BM Harleian MS 6845 26
16 Motley, *op. cit.*, I 353
17 BM Harleian MS 285 171

18 STC 7288
19 BM Cotton Galba C VIII 29
20 *ibid.*, C IX 79
21 BM Harleian MS 287 1
22 *See* Chapter one *n*.36
23 BM Harleian MS 285 230, see also Cal. S.P. For. 9 Mar. 1585
24 BM Cotton Galba C VIII 46
25 BM Harleian MS 6994 art.2
26 BM Cotton Galba C IX 167
27 *ibid.*
28 Stow, J. *Annals* 717 A45
29 BM Cotton Galba C IX 179
30 Cal. S.P. For. 23 May 1586
31 Ouvry MS 5b
32 *ibid.*, 25b
33 *ibid.*, 45
34 *ibid.*, 30
35 BM Cotton Galba C IX 292
36 Cal. S.P. For. 19 Jul. 1586
37 BM Harleian MS 285 253
38 Ouvry MS 62
39 HMC Hatfield III 179, item 366
40 Cal. S.P. For. 6 Nov. 1586
41 Motley, *op. cit.*, II 179
42 Warrender papers CXLIII Vol. I 242
43 BM Harleian MS 285 266

44 *ibid.*, 268
45 BM Cotton Galba C XI 227
46 Cal. S.P. For. 22 Jun. 1587
47 BM Cotton Galba D I 93
48 Motley, *op. cit.*, II 202
49 BM Cotton Galba C XI 327
50 HMC Pepys II 725
51 Cal. S.P. For. 15 Jun. 1587
52 Motley, *op. cit.*, II 254
53 *ibid.*, II 262
54 BM Cotton Galba D I 234
55 Jenkins, E., *Elizabeth and Leicester*, 391
56 Stow, *Annals* 743 A32
57 BM Cotton Galba D II 139
58 HMC Pepys II 406, *cf.* Collins, *Sidney Papers* I 70
59 Cal. S.P. For. Oct. 1587
60 APC 16 Dec. 1587
61 Cal. S.P. Span. 28 Nov. & 4 Dec. 1587
62 Motley, *op. cit.*, II 327
63 *ibid.*, *loc. cit.*, see also Stow, *op. cit.*, 713 A60 (though misplaced there)
64 Camden, *Annals* (1635 ed.) 355
65 *ibid.*, 356
66 Speed, *History*, 883

CHAPTER TEN

1 *Notes and Queries* 3rd series V (1864) 109
2 Cal. S.P. For. 10 & 18 Apr. 1588
3 *ibid.*, 482
4 BM Cotton Vespasian C VIII 12 *et seqq.*
5 Cal. S.P. Dom. 18 Mar. 1588
6 Longleat Dudley MSS Box III 62
7 APC 5 Aug. 1588
8 Lodge *op. cit.*, II 345
9 Longleat Dudley MSS Vol. II 265
10 PRO S.P. XII 215 65
11 Camden, *Annuals* 419-20
12 Cal. S.P. Span. 17 Sep. 1588
13 Stow, *op. cit.*, 751
14 Longleat Dudley MSS Vol. II 275

15 *ibid.*, Vol. X & XI
16 *ibid.*, Vol. IV, ii 33
17 *ibid.*, *loc. cit.*, 212
18 Spenser, E., *The Ruines of Time, Complaints*, London (1591) ll. 218–224
19 Camden, *Annals*, 419–20
20 *Leicester's Commonwealth*, 238
21 Naunton, *Fragmenta Regalia* (1641) 15
22 Strype, *Annals*, 478
23 Speeding-James, *The Life and Letters of Francis Bacon*, London (1861–72), and Bacon, F., *An Apologia* (ed. A. Millar, 1765)
24 Camden, *Annals*, 44–45

INDEX

249